D1527794

Routledge Philosophy

Aristotle and the *Poetics*

Aristotle's *Poetics* is the first philosophical account of an art form, and the foundational text in the history of aesthetics. It is one of the most widely read of Aristotle's works. The meaning of its key ideas – especially the concept of catharsis – has been hotly disputed, having had enormous influence and lasting significance.

The *Routledge Philosophy Guidebook to Aristotle and the Poetics* is an accessible guide to this often dense and cryptic work. Angela Curran introduces and assesses:

- Aristotle's life and writings
- grounding principles and concepts
- the definition of tragedy
- philosophy, poetry and knowledge
- comedy and epic
- the *Poetics* and contemporary aesthetics.

Through the use of examples from ancient Greek drama, modern literature and contemporary films, this guidebook explores key concepts in Aristotle's theory such as mimesis, catharsis, *hamartia*, preferred plot patterns, and the pleasure in tragedy.

Providing a clear and engaging overview of the philosophical arguments in the *Poetics*, as well as a chapter-by-chapter analysis, this is an essential introduction for all students of philosophy, literature, art theory, classics and media studies approaching Aristotle's work for the first time.

Angela Curran is a Faculty Fellow in Philosophy at Colby College, USA.

ROUTLEDGE PHILOSOPHY GUIDEBOOKS

Edited by Tim Crane and Jonathan Wolff

University of Cambridge and *University College London*

Plato and the *Trial of Socrates* Thomas C. Brickhouse and Nicholas D. Smith
Aristotle and the *Metaphysics* Vasilis Politis
Rousseau and the *Social Contract* Christopher Bertram
Plato and the *Republic,* Second edition Nickolas Pappas
Husserl and the *Cartesian Meditations* A.D. Smith
Kierkegaard and *Fear and Trembling* John Lippitt
Descartes and the *Meditations* Gary Hatfield
Hegel and the *Philosophy of Right* Dudley Knowles
Hegel and the *Phenomenology of Spirit* Robert Stern
Berkeley and the *Principles of Human Knowledge* Robert Fogelin
Aristotle on Ethics Gerard Hughes
Hume on Religion David O'Connor
Leibniz and the *Monadology* Anthony Savile
The Later Heidegger George Pattison
Hegel on History Joseph McCarney
Hume on Morality James Baillie
Hume on Knowledge Harold Noonan
Kant and the *Critique of Pure Reason* Sebastian Gardner
Mill on Liberty Jonathan Riley
Mill on Utilitarianism Roger Crisp
Spinoza and the *Ethics* Genevieve Lloyd
Heidegger on *Being and Time,* Second Edition Stephen Mulhall
Locke on Government D.A. Lloyd Thomas
Locke on *Human Understanding* E.J. Lowe
Derrida on Deconstruction Barry Stocker
Kant on Judgement Robert Wicks
Nietzsche on Art Aaron Ridley
Rorty and the *Mirror of Nature* James Tartaglia
Hobbes and *Leviathan* Glen Newey

Routledge Philosophy Guidebook to

Aristotle and the *Poetics*

Angela
Curran

Routledge
Taylor & Francis Group
LONDON AND NEW YORK

First published 2016
by Routledge
2 Park Square, Milton Park, Abingdon, Oxon OX14 4RN

Simultaneously published in the USA and Canada
by Routledge
711 Third Avenue, New York, NY 10017

Routledge is an imprint of the Taylor & Francis Group, an informa business

© 2016 Angela Curran

British Library Cataloguing in Publication Data
A catalogue record for this book is available from the British Library

Library of Congress Cataloging in Publication Data
Curran, Angela, author.
Routledge Philosophy Guidebook to Aristotle and the Poetics / Angela
Curran.
pages cm. — (Routledge philosophy guidebooks)
Includes bibliographical references and index.
1. Aristotle. Poetics. 2. Poetics—History—To 1500. I. Title. II. Title: Aristotle
and the Poetics.
PN1040.A53C87 2016
808.2—dc23
2015012124

ISBN: 9780415780087 (hbk)
ISBN: 9780415780094 (pbk)
ISBN: 9781315771991 (ebk)

Typeset in Times New Roman
by Swales & Willis Ltd, Exeter, Devon, UK

For my parents, Lucille and John

CONTENTS

ACKNOWLEDGMENTS

It is my pleasure to thank friends, family, colleagues, teachers, and students for the special role they have played in supporting my work on the book.

I am grateful to have had wonderful and inspiring professors, both as an undergraduate and graduate student. I especially would like to thank three graduate school professors, Cynthia Freeland, Gareth Matthews, and Fred Feldman. It was in Cynthia's classes that I found myself becoming increasingly fascinated with ancient philosophy. Her work on aesthetics and philosophy of film has also been a great inspiration to me. Gary was a wonderful dissertation director and mentor, and his classes and work inspired in me a deep and enduring interest in Aristotle's philosophy. I miss him greatly. Fred Feldman was instrumental in helping me to improve in the craft of philosophical writing and argumentation and his work continues to be a model of clarity to which I continue to aspire.

Friends, family, and colleagues helped me get this project going, keep it on track, and finish it. I especially thank my cousins Maureen, Brian, Peter, and Patsy for their encouragement and friendship. I am grateful to Gina Black, Alice Chang, Horst Lange, Judy Robey, Marc Schneier, Barbara Simerka, Steve Smith, and Tom Wartenberg for always checking in with words of encouragement. At Carleton College, I thank Bill North and Clara Hardy for discussions on the *Poetics* that helped me to think of the text in a new way, my fellow cinemaphile, Carol Donelan, for many interesting and fun discussions, and philosophers Jason Decker, Daniel Groll, and Anna Moltchanova for being great colleagues. I am grateful to Dana Strand, Steve Strand, Paula Lackie, and Mija Van der Wege for providing help just when it was needed. I thank my St. Mary's College colleagues Sybol Anderson, Betül Basaran, Barrett Emerick, Brad Park, Chad Peveateaux, Chuck Stein and Michael Taber for valuable feedback on the ideas in Chapter 11 in a faculty work-in-progress group. I am grateful to Dr Robert Davidson for the special role he has played in my life and the life of my family over the course of many years. I honor my cat, Bebe, my constant companion, for (mostly) understanding about all the times I had to work and could not play. I especially thank my sister Felicia Curran, a fellow philosophy major and a valuable sounding board for all things, philosophical and not, for many helpful discussions pertaining to the content of the book. I am also grateful to the wonderful musicians at Playing for Change (https://playingforchange.com) for music that inspired, energized or relaxed me after a long stretch of writing.

Some of the material in the book was presented in lectures and discussions in my classes, and I am grateful to my students for valuable input. Above all, my students' intelligent and apt responses showed me that it is essential not to dumb down material, but instead aim things so that students can engage fully with the text as well as the debates around the meaning of the *Poetics*. In particular, I thank Marika Christofides, Pat

Doty, Lina Feuerstein, Danny Forman, Max Henkel, Rebekah Frumkin, Martha Perez, and Dan Schillinger for their outstanding contributions in classes on Aristotle and aesthetics.

The expert team at Swales and Willis did an excellent job of preparing the manuscript for production. I especially thank my copy-editor, Kate Reeves, and I thank Colin Morgan, Elizabeth Kent and Caroline Watson for their great work proofreading and organizing the typesetting. I save my greatest debts for last. I thank the commissioning editor at Routledge, Tony Bruce, for sharing my sense that there is a need for this introduction to the *Poetics*. My greatest debt is to my editor, Adam Johnson, at Routledge. This book took longer than planned, and Adam was always the epitome of kindness and professionalism as he encouraged me to press on. Thank you, Adam!

Adam also had the wisdom to select two reviewers for the manuscript who were the best that any author could hope for. The draft they read had some factual and scribal errors (Empedocles wrote in verse not prose!), and their comments helped me to correct them. I thank the first reviewer, who remains anonymous, for his or her very helpful insights, suggestions, and corrections. This reviewer's ideas for additions to the comedy chapter were especially valuable. I am very grateful to the second reviewer, Malcolm Heath, in so many ways. He provided detailed comments on each chapter and he also followed up in email correspondence with many helpful suggestions. His comments, and those of the first referee, have made the book much better and I am grateful for their time, dedication, and expertise. Of course the only person who is responsible for remaining errors is myself.

This book is dedicated to my parents, Lucille and John Curran, for all the years of love, laughter, and support.

PREFACE

Aristotle's *Poetics* is the first philosophical account of an art form ever written. The *Poetics* is one of the most widely read and living of Aristotle's works, and it has attracted the interest of a wide range of philosophical and literary commentators. The meaning of its key ideas—especially the concept of *catharsis*—has been hotly disputed. The *Poetics* has also had enormous influence. Authors and screenwriters have followed Aristotle's recommendations for how to construct narrative drama and critics have used his ideas for how to assess these same forms of dramatic art.

But the *Poetics* can be cryptic, disjointed, and hard to understand. Students who have little or no previous exposure either to philosophy or to Aristotle can especially find the *Poetics* a challenge to read. This book aims to follow the style and format of the Routledge Philosophy Guidebook series to introduce students in philosophy classes, as well as in literature, classics, art theory, cinema and media studies, and theater to the philosophical meaning, significance, and lasting influence of Aristotle's work.

I have benefitted enormously from the tremendous scholarship on the *Poetics* and this Guidebook aims to introduce students to some of the lively debates in the literature around significant concepts such as *mimēsis* and *catharsis*. I have tried to steer a middle ground between overwhelming the reader with too much detail on these scholarly debates and not mentioning them at all or just in the footnotes. My understanding of the *Poetics* is indebted to a variety of scholars, but I would like to acknowledge the help I have received, in particular, from the works of Elizabeth Belfiore, Pierre Destrée, Gerald Else, Dorothea Frede, Richard Janko, Stephen Halliwell, Malcolm Heath, Jonathan Lear, Deborah Roberts, Amélie Rorty, and Paul Woodruff. It is a testament to the richness of these scholars' work that, even when these authors disagree with the line of interpretation of the *Poetics* that I tend to favor, I have found something very valuable to use in each author's ideas.

Most discussions of the *Poetics* assume that Aristotle was replying to the criticism leveled against poetry made by Aristotle's teacher, Plato, in his dialogues the *Ion* and in Books 2, 3, and 10 of the *Republic*. Aristotle's arguments in the *Poetics* are often presented as direct lines of reply to Plato's criticisms. When I first began to work on this project, I thought that this is the way that I, also, would proceed. But as my work went on I found that trying to shape Aristotle's arguments so that they responded to Plato's concerns impeded rather than promoted an accurate understanding of them.

Instead I have found it more fruitful to situate the ideas in the *Poetics* within the larger context of Aristotle's writings. I hope this can also be a way that a student of the *Poetics* can come to understand that the work is not tangentially related to Aristotle's writings in other areas, such as philosophical psychology, ethics, metaphysics, and epistemology. Instead these other areas of Aristotle's thought are crucial to understanding their meaning. References to Aristotle's works can be found in the index under "Aristotle's writings."

The student who is interested in learning how Aristotle's views in the *Poetics* compare with Plato's will find several comparisons between the ideas of the two philosophers in places throughout the text (see also entries in the index under Plato and Socrates). The final chapter is a consideration of how the lines of argument in the *Poetics* could be thought to reply to Plato's criticisms of the arts, without assuming that this is in fact how Aristotle did reply. Plato is never mentioned by name in the *Poetics*, so it would be misleading and confusing, from my point of view, to present these as Aristotle's defense of poetry in response to Plato's criticisms.

Finally, I end with a word of encouragement to the reader. While this book aims to help you understand the main lines of argument in the *Poetics*, this work is no substitute for a direct and sustained engagement with the text. Do not shy away from the tasks of wrestling and coming to terms with Aristotle's meaning, and do respond to and challenge the interpretations offered in this book of the *Poetics*. Your effort and diligence will truly be repaid in spades.

1

ARISTOTLE'S LIFE AND WRITINGS

ARISTOTLE'S THOUGHT AND HIS CHARACTER

One of the most memorable descriptions of Aristotle comes from the medieval poet Dante, in his *Inferno*, the first part of his epic poem, *Divine Comedy*. The *Inferno* tells the story of Dante as he journeys with his guide, the poet, Virgil, through hell in search of his beloved Beatrice. In the first ring of hell, Dante meets poets, next, heroic warriors, and finally a group of philosophers. Foremost among this group is Aristotle, who is deemed so renowned that he is one whom other prominent philosophers, including his teacher, Plato (427–347 BCE) and Socrates (470–399 BCE), the teacher of Plato, look upon with veneration. Aristotle's reputation as one of the world's most influential philosophers had been well established by the time Dante writes his poem in the fourteenth century.

This recognition was a long time coming. Aristotle died in 322 BCE. Many of his works were lost, including dialogues similar in nature to those of Plato, of which only fragments have survived.[1] Most of the writings that did survive were likely not written for a broad public: they are not polished works, and in places they are written in an obscure and abbreviated manner that is not easy to follow. It was not until the first century BCE that the ancient collection of Aristotle's existing writings was put together. It took two more centuries of commentary on the works for philosophers to grasp the philosophical brilliance of Aristotle's ideas. Finally, by the Middle Ages, Aristotle was so well known that Dante does not see a need to name him: he simply is referred to by the title: "The Master of Those Who Know" (*Inferno* 4.131).

If an ancient legend is to be believed, it is somewhat of a fortunate accident that we have come to know of Aristotle and his writings at all. When Aristotle died, he left his library, which included his writings, to his friend and colleague, Theophrastus, whom he had named as the successor of his school. When Theophrastus died, he passed Aristotle's writings to his non-philosopher ancestors, who in the first part of the second century BCE buried the writings in a damp, underground tunnel in Asia Minor, leaving them to suffer mildew and worms. Luckily, the story continues, Aristotle's library was sold to a bibliophile and edited in Rome during the early first century BCE. From this was established a canon of legitimately Aristotelian works.[2] However colorful, there is a scholarly debate as to whether this ancient story of how Aristotle's works came to us is true, for the legend relies on sources that are difficult for us to verify.[3]

There is much else that we do not know about Aristotle. A major source about his life comes from Diogenes Laertius' third-century *Lives of Eminent Philosophers*, a work that cites some two hundred sources to give biographies of ancient philosophers ranging from the fifth to the third centuries BCE. This work is helpful because it is one of the few ancient biographies that have come down to us. Still, Diogenes' biography is not critical historiography; it was written some five centuries after Aristotle's death and in a style of literature whose aim was to entertain with ancient anecdote and gossip.[4] So, for example, regarding Aristotle's appearance, Diogenes reports, "he spoke with a lisp . . . further, his calves were slender (so they say), his eyes small, and he was conspicuous by his attire, his rings, and the cut of his hair" (Book V, Chapter One).[5] One bust of Aristotle that has come down to us, on the other hand (likely a copy of an original that was commissioned by Aristotle's pupil, Alexander the Great), depicts a dignified figure bearing the wise and bearded look of a philosopher, rather than the ostentatious personality as described by Diogenes. Unfortunately, we lack reliable and independent sources that would help us decide if either of these representations is true or if they were taken from two different periods in Aristotle's life.

When it comes to Aristotle's character, conflicting accounts in the ancient biographical tradition have also passed down to us. One has it that Aristotle was an arrogant self-promoter, someone who regarded himself as a self-styled genius, and that he was ungrateful for all he learned at Plato's school the Academy. On the other hand, another tradition speaks of Aristotle as a kind and generous friend and family man, and a grateful pupil who was devoted to teaching and research.[6] Most scholars think that we have no reliable direct reports to which we can appeal to determine what sort of person he was.

Nevertheless, we do have Aristotle's writings, although only about one-fifth of his prodigious output has survived. They give us some indirect evidence about what sort of thinker he was and also what sort of activities and pursuits he valued.

What picture of Aristotle as a thinker and a person emerges, from his writings? Aristotle was a philosopher and polymath with a wide range of interests. He invented many of the major areas in philosophy today, including ethics, logic, metaphysics, aesthetics, history of philosophy, philosophy of mind, philosophical psychology, and philosophy of science. He was an empirically minded philosopher who whenever possible strove to make use of the observations of science in his philosophy. Aristotle's *Nicomachean Ethics* shows the great value he placed on friendship in the good life of a human being. Aristotle was an appreciative student who believed he owed his teacher, Plato, a debt of gratitude that was impossible fully to repay.

From his writings we also get some insights into Aristotle's philosophical temperament. Some philosophers think the task of philosophy is *descriptive*: philosophers should clarify and systematize pre-existing beliefs and concepts, such as *justice*, *knowledge*, *God*, as they are expressed in everyday language. Philosophers of this stripe do not seek to challenge everyday opinion; rather, the goal is to explain and shed light on our everyday beliefs and concepts, which are sometimes vague, incoherent, or poorly articulated. Other types of philosophers can be described as more radical in their approach. These philosophers are *revisionists* who want to correct and challenge our commonplace views, to show where these views have gone wrong. Philosophers are also divided by their views on how we obtain knowledge. *Rationalists* hold that reason, and not sense experience, is the source of all our knowledge. *Empiricists* maintain that all knowledge comes from sense experience.

Plato, Aristotle's teacher, is often categorized as a revisionist, for he takes views—such as that the ultimate reality is immaterial objects, Forms, such as Beauty-Itself or Justice-Itself, and not sensible particulars, such as beautiful flowers or just actions—that fly in the face of common sense beliefs. He is also a rationalist, for like another famous rationalist, René Descartes, the seventeenth-century philosopher and mathematician, Plato insists that the senses cannot be trusted, and instead human reason is the source of all knowledge.

Aristotle, on the other hand, is often thought to be a descriptivist and an empiricist. It is thought he is a descriptivist for he advocates a philosophical method that seeks to preserve as many of the widely accepted beliefs, or *endoxa*, as possible. Aristotle also has the leanings of a philosophical empiricist. He gives extended discussions in *Metaphysics* and *Posterior Analytics* on how knowledge is acquired, and he is clear that sense perception is the basis of scientific knowledge (*epistēmē*):

> All men by nature desire to know. An indication of this is the delight we take in our senses; for even apart from their usefulness they are loved for themselves; and above all others the sense of sight. For not only with a view to action, but even when we are not going to do anything, we prefer sight to almost everything else. The reason is that this, most of all the senses, makes us know and brings to light many differences between things.
>
> (*Metaphysics* 1.1.980a22–27)

As this passage makes clear, Aristotle has solid empiricist credentials; but his method of inquiry does not make exclusive use of direct sense experience, as latter day empirically minded philosophers often do. The phenomena that Aristotle consults when he inquires are drawn from a wide range of sources. There are: direct observations of the facts; the reports and testimonies of skilled practitioners, such as hunters, fisherman, and those involved in the care of animals; the reputable opinions held by his philosophical and scientific predecessors; and the widely held opinions of everyone or most people.

Aristotle's use of widely held opinions in his philosophical method has given Aristotle a reputation as a common sense philosopher who commits himself to the view that philosophy should seek to support our everyday beliefs rather than offer philosophical theories that revise or possibly shake up those beliefs. However, Aristotle's way of doing philosophy does not fit easily into either the descriptive or the revisionist views of philosophy.[7]

It is true that Aristotle holds the view that we can count on people's ability, in the right circumstances and over a period of time, to arrive at the truth. "It may also be noted that men have a sufficient natural instinct for what is true, and usually do arrive at the truth" (*Rhetoric* 1.1.1355a15–16).[8] He goes on to say that anyone who inquires on the basis of that which is generally accredited (*ta endoxa*) advances on the basis of what is likely to be true (1.1.1355a16–18). These comments support the view that Aristotle thinks the commonly accepted beliefs have epistemic weight or evidentiary value, meaning that they should be taken into consideration in an inquiry into the truth of some matter.

That said, Aristotle does not equate the views that have proven true over time and are supported by all or the majority with the opinions of the "many" that he sometimes ends up rejecting. So, for example, in *Nicomachean Ethics* 1.4.1095a20–25, Aristotle ends up disagreeing with "the many" who say that pleasure, wealth, or honor are happiness (*eudaimonia*). In contrast, opinions that reflect a consensus of many or all people concerning the same question over a significant period of time are a valuable source of experience that a philosopher should consider in her inquiries into a matter.

At the same time, Aristotle does not think that the widely accepted views must be shown to be true at all costs, and his writings present arguments that show that widely held beliefs are imprecise and are in need of refinement and clarification. One example occurs in *Nicomachean Ethics* 7.4, where Aristotle seeks to find a principle of moral psychology that accounts for the commonly accepted belief that *akrasia*, knowing what is best but not doing it, is possible (*NE* 1145b21–31). Aristotle ends up agreeing with Socrates that a certain sort of person, the person of practical wisdom (the *phronimos*) whose knowledge is always active and unified, cannot experience *akrasia* (1047b17). By revealing the various ways in which a person's knowledge of what is right to do may be deactivated by the passions, without altogether being expelled from the soul, Aristotle shows that there is something correct about the widely accepted view that doing wrong while knowing this is wrong, is possible. But the sense in which the weak person has knowledge needs to be refined and clarified.

Aristotle's writing, therefore, suggests that he is not a champion of common sense, nor does he think that the goal of philosophy should confine itself to the activities of describing and systematizing commonplace beliefs.

Certain parts of Aristotle's philosophy continue to be widely studied and accepted by a number of philosophers. His ethics, which give central importance to the role that virtue plays in a happy life, has been enormously influential in shaping the direction of philosophical ethics in the twentieth century to the present day.[9] Recently scholars have also been turning to ideas in Aristotle's metaphysics, or study of the fundamental structure of reality, to make arguments for the robust place that metaphysics should have in philosophy.[10] Aristotle's *Poetics* is also undergoing a renaissance of interest from philosophers of art who, as we will examine further, see in the work a forerunner of many ideas that are currently being debated, such as the autonomy of art, the role of the emotions in appreciating art, and the debate over whether it is part of art's value that we learn from it.

Other parts of Aristotle's philosophy have troubled philosophers and other readers. In the *Politics* Aristotle defends the idea that there are certain human beings, "natural slaves" that are by nature suited to serve as slaves.[11] In a number of passages Aristotle expresses the view that females are inferior to males. For example, Aristotle is notorious for his claim in the *Generation of Animals* that a female is "as it were" a deformed male (2.3.737a27–31), as well as for his remark in the *Politics* that in woman the character of her deliberative faculty is lacking in authority (1.13.1260a12).

It might be tempting to register our disagreement with Aristotle on these points and chalk these comments up to the deep-seated cultural biases of his time and place. Yet some of the most interesting recent work on Aristotle, while rejecting his conclusions, has engaged the questions of whether Aristotle offers well-considered reasons for his views and whether these ideas can be made to be consistent with other parts of Aristotle's philosophy, in particular his commitment to the view that sexual difference, being male or being female, is not a distinction that pertains to an animal's basic nature or essence.[12]

One of the most intriguing documents that Aristotle wrote was his will.[13] In it Aristotle does something surprising: he says that his slaves are to be freed.[14] Given Aristotle's view that the subjugation of people who are natural slaves is just (*Politics* 1.8.1253b23–26), this raises some intriguing but also unsettling questions. Did Aristotle think that his slaves were simply slaves by convention or custom (*nomos*), or by an unlucky accident of their birth or personal history? If so, why did he hold these individuals, when he thought it would be unjust to hold a person who became a slave as the spoils of war or for some other such reason? If these individuals were, in Aristotle's view, slaves by nature, then why did he think it right to release them, when his view was that such individuals are not capable of carrying out the basic deliberations necessary to live a good life? Unfortunately, we do not have the answers to these questions.

ARISTOTLE'S LIFE

Even as there is much we do not know about Aristotle, we do have a grasp on some of the main events in his life.[15] Here is a chronology of his life, keeping in mind that some of these dates are not known for certain.

Aristotle was born in 384 BCE in Stagira, a small city-state in the Chaldice peninsula, Northern Greece. In spite of living half his life in Athens, he never become a citizen, and his Macedonian roots and the connection he maintained with the region caused him to be looked at with suspicion by the Athenians later in his life. His father, Nicomachus, was a physician attached to the court of King Amyntas of Macedon. His mother, Phaestis, came from a family with good civic relations. His father descended from a line of physicians, the Asclepiads that were known for practicing physical observations and dissections, as well as

advancing theories about a wide range of biological phenomena; and, according to Galen (*On Anatomical Procedures* II 1),
the Asclepiad guild passed this tradition from father to son.

We cannot be sure, but it may be that Aristotle was introduced to the study of physiology early in childhood. Scholars
have also noted that with its proximity to the Aegean Sea, his
hometown of Stagira would have made an ideal place to develop
an interest in marine life. It may be that from these early influ-
ences Aristotle acquired a scientific orientation that carried with
him throughout his life.

In 367 BCE Aristotle moved to Athens at the age of seventeen
and studied at Plato's Academy, the most celebrated center for
learning in ancient Greece. One invented account, promoted by
his detractors, has it that philosophy was a second career choice
for Aristotle, and that he went to study philosophy at Plato's
Academy at the age of thirty, only after living an extravagant
lifestyle in which he squandered his inheritance and tried his
hand at a military career. Aristotle stayed for twenty years at
the Academy—most likely first as a student, then as a teacher
and researcher— until the death of Plato in 347 BCE. For reasons
that are not clear—whether it was to keep Plato's property in
the family, because there was a legal difficulty in turning over
the property to a non-citizen, or because of philosophical disagreements between Aristotle and Plato's other followers—the
headship of the Academy went to Speusippus, Plato's nephew.

Upon Plato's death, Aristotle left Athens and embarked upon
a period of travels and biological research. He and a colleague
from the Academy, Xenocrates, accepted the invitation of
Hermeias, a former fellow student at the Academy, to come to
Assos, on the northwest coast of Asia Minor, where Hermeias,
a eunuch and former slave, was tyrant. Here Aristotle married a
relation of Hermeias, Pythias, and had a daughter with her of the
same name. After three years in Assos, Aristotle moved to the
nearby island of Lesbos, where he worked with Theophrastus,
a former colleague from Aristotle's Academy days. Due to

references in Aristotle's biological works, it is likely that Aristotle and Theophrastus conducted extensive biological investigations along the northwest coast of Asia Minor and also in Macedonia, where he next traveled.

After two years in Lesbos, in 342, Aristotle went to Macedonia at the invitation of King Philip II to tutor Philip's thirteen-year-old son, Alexander. First under the direction of Philip, and then of Alexander, Macedonia went on to conquer cities in Greece, Egypt, and Asia Minor. We have little reliable evidence about the relationship between Alexander and Aristotle. Pliny the Elder, the Roman historian, reports that Alexander continued to support Aristotle after the tutorship ended by making available to him the services of thousands of hunters, fishermen, bird, bee, and insect keepers, and others engaged in the care of animals.[16] Stories have been told many times over that suggest that Aristotle might have influenced Alexander's desire for empire building.

For example, in the film *Alexander the Great* (Robert Rossen, 1956), Aristotle (Barry Jones) is shown lecturing to an eager group of young pupils that includes Alexander (Richard Burton), telling them about the superiority of the Greek way of life: "We Greeks are the chosen, the elect. Our culture is the best. Our civilization is the best. Our men, the best. All others are barbarians and it is our moral duty to conquer them, enslave them, and if necessary destroy them."

A more recent telling of the Aristotle–Alexander connection is found in *Alexander* (Oliver Stone, 2004). Here Aristotle (a very British-sounding Christopher Plummer) not only gives the young Alexander the idea it is wrong that an "inferior" race, the Persians, should rule four-fifths of the known world. He even points out to Alexander a route on a map that shows how an explorer could travel from Greece to the end of the world and back. These films suggest that Aristotle is in some way responsible for Alexander's campaign of colonizing much of the world that was known to the ancient Greeks.

Is this accurate? We can distinguish two sets of issues, historical and philosophical. From an historical viewpoint, there is no reliable evidence that shows that Aristotle influenced Alexander to extend his father's expansionist vision of Macedonian domination into Persia and India. Philosophically speaking, however, we might wonder how far apart were the worldviews of Alexander and Aristotle.

As we might expect, there are no easy answers to this question, as Aristotle's political and ethical views are multi-sided.[17] On the one hand, Aristotle writes that all Greeks are intellectually and morally superior to non-Greeks (*barbaroi*, a transliteration of the term for "non-Greeks," is the root of the English term "barbarians").[18] His evidence is that non-Greeks do not organize themselves according to the superior political arrangements found in Greece, and that they lack the combined traits of spirit and intelligence that are necessary for proper governance.[19] He also holds that non-Greeks belong to the class of human beings that are slaves by nature.[20] As noted earlier, Aristotle notoriously maintains that human beings are divided into those that, by nature, are suited to rule and those that, by nature, are suited to be slaves and ruled over.[21] Those who are slaves by nature lack the ability to deliberate.[22] While they are capable of understanding their master's instructions, they are not capable of deliberating, of making choices between different possible courses of action that accomplish a desired end.[23] It is this inability to deliberate, which Aristotle traces to aspects of the climate in which non-Greeks live, that is the source of their inferior political arrangements.

Aristotle, therefore, believed that the enslavement of non-Greeks by Greeks is naturally just.[24] Whether Aristotle reaches his conclusions about natural slavery owing to profound cultural and social biases against non-Greeks or on the basis of reasoning that is internally consistent and plausible, is open to debate.[25] But it could not be that he would think that the imposition of Greek culture on the non-Greek population resulted in their intellectual or cultural betterment, in the way that Rudyard Kipling talked about the burdens of the White colonialist to educate the Black Africans in his poem, "The White Man's Burden." For Aristotle doubted the capacity of non-Greeks to adopt the superior political arrangements and way of life of the Greeks.[26] There would be no "moral duty" for the Greeks to rule over the non-Greeks and make them better, for the latter would not be capable of this. Rather, the enslavement of non-Greeks by Greeks was just because it was thought fitting that the superior should rule the inferior.

On the other hand, if Alexander's motive in empire building was to attain wealth and power, his actions would not conform to the ideals about which Aristotle writes in his ethical works. For it is likely that Alexander and his father, Philip, were at least partly motivated by the desire to acquire personal and political power. If this was their motive, then their actions would come into conflict with what Aristotle says about the good life in his ethical writings. For Aristotle happiness (*eudaimonia*, sometimes translated as "flourishing") is the final end of human life and what makes for happiness in a life are virtuous actions that are in conformity with reason.[27] A moderate amount of political power may be necessary to perform the noble acts that constitute a happy life; if one is cut off from participating in civic life, for example, it is hard to help others. Acquiring or exercising political power is not the proper final goal or end of a happy life.[28] Further, virtue or human excellence (*aretē*) consists in a mean of feeling and action, meaning that the virtuous person is not excessive or deficient in her emotions and actions.[29] If Alexander engaged in war out of a desire to acquire unlimited political power and influence, then his actions were not virtuous, and he would fall short of the ethical norms for feeling and action that Aristotle lays out in his *Ethics*.

In 335, at the time of Philip's assassination, Aristotle returned to Athens. Rather than rejoining Plato's Academy, Aristotle set up his own school, the Lyceum, in a public gymnasium, named after the grounds dedicated to the god, Apollo Lykeios, and frequented by Socrates.[30] His school came to be called the Peripatetics, either because Aristotle and his students were in the habit of philosophizing while taking a walk about the grounds[31] (*peripatein*, in Greek, to walk around) or because of the existence of an ambulatory (*peripatos*), or covered walk on the grounds of the Lyceum.[32]

This second stay in Athens was a highly productive one for Aristotle. It is likely, though not certain, that during this period Aristotle completed or composed most of his philosophical treatises, including the philosophical works for which Aristotle is known today. At the Lyceum Aristotle engaged in extensive research with students and colleagues, such as Theophrastus, on a wide range of subjects, including cosmology, botany, music, astronomy, medicine, the arts, psychology, politics, mathematics, history of philosophy, and rhetoric.

Aristotle is reported to have collected hundreds of manuscripts and other teaching materials on these subjects, and the collection, held in his house, is said to have been the first great library in antiquity and the model for the great libraries in Alexandria and Pergamon.[33] During this time in Athens his wife, Pythias, died and Aristotle began a new relationship with Herpyllis, a woman originally from his hometown of Stagira, and with her had a son, Nicomachus.

In 323 Alexander succumbed to illness while on a campaign in Babylon and concurrently Aristotle decided to depart Athens. With Alexander's death, anti-Macedonian feelings were running high, as Macedonia had attempted to conquer many Greek city-states. The Athenians charged Aristotle with impiety, the grounds of the charge being that he had offered a hymn to his friend, Hermeias, the tyrant who had invited him to Assos, and that he had made a blasphemous inscription on Hermeias' statue at Delphi, comparing him to legendary Greek heroes.[34]

This indictment seems to have been fabricated, perhaps as a way to get rid of a philosopher that the Athenians regarded with suspicion because of his alien status and his Macedonian connections. We cannot be certain of Aristotle's reasons for leaving Athens. It is said that in a letter to Antipater, a Macedonia general and supporter of Philip II and Alexander, Aristotle says he is leaving because he did not want to see the Athenians "twice outrage philosophy,"[35] a reference to Socrates' death on the conviction of impiety, a charge that Socrates vigorously disputes in Plato's *Apology*. Aristotle departed Athens in 323, and went to his mother's hometown of Chalcis, where he died of natural causes the next year, in 322. Theophrastus succeeded Aristotle as the head of the Lyceum.

NOTES

1 See M.F. Burnyeat 1986.
2 For fascinating accounts of how Aristotle's works were transmitted from Aristotle's death to their present form, see Richard Shute 1888 and Myles Burnyeat 1986.
3 For this argument see Jonathan Barnes 1997.
4 See the Introduction to the work by R.D. Hicks in Diogenes Laertius 1925.
5 Translation refers to Diogenes 1925.
6 For an account of the two competing traditions in Aristotelian biography, see Düring 1957, especially 460–469. Christopher Shields (2013: 8–17) has an accessible discussion of the conflicting ancient traditions regarding Aristotle's character.
7 Recent years have seen a considerable amount of discussion and debate about the nature of Aristotle's method. For some divergent views, see John Ackrill 1981: 107–115; Jonathan Barnes 1980; Martha Nussbaum 1986: 240–263; Owen McLeod 1995.
8 Jonathan Barnes 1984. See also *Metaphysics* 2.1.993a26–993b2:

> The investigation of the truth is in one way hard, in another easy. An indication of this is found in the fact that no one is able to attain the truth adequately, while, on the other hand, no one fails entirely, but every one says something true about the nature of things, and while individually they contribute little or nothing to the truth, by the union of all a considerable amount is amassed.

> (in Barnes 1984)

9 For an overview of the issues in Aristotle's ethics, see Richard Kraut 2014.
10 Tuomas E. Tahko 2012.
11 *Politics* 1.3–6.
12 *Metaphysics* 9.10.1058a29ff. For distinct approaches to the *Generation of Animals* view, see Karen Nielsen 2008 and Devin Henry 2007. For articles that address whether Aristotle's reasoning concerning natural slavery is coherent see

Marguerite Deslauriers 2006; Malcolm Heath 2008; and Christopher Shields 2013: 432–436. See also Jean Roberts 2009: 41–51. Shields is perhaps the most critical of all, arguing that Aristotle's defense of natural slavery is "a desperate measure and in some ways simply bewildering."

13 See Jonathan Barnes 1984 Volume Two: 464–2465.

14 In his will Aristotle gives different provisions for each of his slaves. The ones that are underage are to be held until they come of age. One slave will only be freed when his daughter is married. Others are to be freed and then given money or slaves of their own!

15 Carlos Natali 2013 is thought to give the latest definitive biography of Aristotle's life and school.

16 Pliny the Elder, *Natural Histories*, VIII, 16 and 18.

17 For a contrasting view, see Jonathan Barnes 1995: "Philosophers will find nothing—or virtually nothing—in Aristotle's political writings which betray interest in the fortunes of the Macedonia empire" (5).

18 See for example, *Politics* 1.1.1252b9; *Politics* 3.14.1285a20; and *Politics* 7.7.1327b19–34, quoted below:

> Having spoken of the number of citizens, we will proceed to speak of what should be their character. This is a subject which can be easily understood by anyone who casts his eye on the more celebrated states of Greece, and generally on the distribution of races in the habitable world. Those who live in a cold climate and in Europe are full of spirit, but wanting in intelligence and skill; and therefore they retain comparative freedom, but have no political organization, and are incapable of ruling over others. Whereas the natives of Asia are intelligent and inventive, but they are wanting in spirit, and therefore they are always in a state of subjection and slavery. But the Hellenic race, which is situated between them, is likewise intermediate in character, being high-spirited and also intelligent. Hence it continues free, and is the best-governed of any nation, and, if it could be formed into one state, would be able to rule the world.
>
> (J. Barnes 1984)

19 As indicated in the passage quoted in note 18, the problem, from Aristotle's point of view, is that those who live in a cold climate and in Europe have "spirit" but lack intelligence, while those who live in Asia have intelligence, but lack spirit, as evidenced by the fact that they remain in a state of subjugation and servitude. See also *Politics* 1.1.1252b1–10.

20 See *Politics* 1.2.1252b5–9; 1.6.1255a28–b2; 3.14.1285a19–21.

21 *Politics* 1.2.

22 *Politics* 1.13.1260a9–14.

23 *Politics* 1.5.1254b20–23.

24 *Politics* 1.8.1253b23–26.

25 For the former interpretation, see Jean Roberts 2009: 118. For the latter view see Malcolm Heath 2008. Both scholars, however, reject Aristotle's conclusions as well as the assumptions upon which they are based.

26 See the text quoted in note 18.
27 *Nicomachean Ethics* 1.
28 *Nicomachean Ethics* 1.8.1099a32–b7.
29 *Nicomachean Ethics* 1109a20–29.
30 For a discussion of the institutional and internal aspects of Aristotle's Lyceum, see Carlos Natali 2013: 72–119.
31 Diogenes Laertius 1925 V 2.
32 Düring 1957: 404–405.
33 Düring 1957: 337–338.
34 Diogenes Laertius 1925: V 6.
35 Düring 1957: 342.

WORKS CITED

PRIMARY SOURCES

Barnes, Jonathan (ed.) 1984. *The Complete Works of Aristotle. The Revised Oxford Translation* Volumes One and Two. Princeton, NJ: Princeton University Press.

Diogenes Laertius 1925. *Lives of Eminent Philosophers*, translated by R. D. Hicks. London: Loeb.

Plato 1935. *Republic* Books 6–10, translated by Paul Shorey. Cambridge, MA: Harvard University Press.

SECONDARY SOURCES

Ackrill, John 1981. *Aristotle the Philosopher.* Oxford: Oxford University Press.

Barnes, Jonathan 1980. "Aristotle and the Method of Ethics." *Revue Internationale de Philosophie* 34: 490–511.

———— 1995. "Life and Work," in Jonathan Barnes (ed.), *The Cambridge Companion to Aristotle.* Cambridge: Cambridge University Press: 1–26.

———— 1997. "Roman Aristotle," in Jonathan Barnes and Miriam Griffin (eds.), *Philosophia Togata II. Plato and Aristotle at Rome.* New York: Oxford University Press: 24–44.

Burnyeat, M. F. 1986. "Good Repute." *London Review of Books* 8 (19): 11–12.

Deslauriers, Marguerite 2006. "The Argument of Aristotle's *Politics* 1." *Phoenix* 60 (1/2): 48–69.

Düring, Ingemar 1957. *Aristotle in the Ancient Biographical Tradition.* Stockholm: Almqvist & Wiksell in Komm.

Heath, Malcolm 2008. "Aristotle on Natural Slavery." *Phronesis* 53: 243–270.

Henry, Devin 2007. "How Sexist is Aristotle's Developmental Biology?" *Phronesis* 52: 1–19.

Kraut, Richard 2014. "Aristotle's Ethics," *The Stanford Encyclopedia of Philosophy* (Summer 2014 Edition), Edward N. Zalta (ed.), http://plato.stanford.edu/archives/sum2014/entries/aristotle-ethics/.

McLeod, Owen 1995. "Aristotle's Method." *History of Philosophical Quarterly* 12 (1): 1–18.

Natali, Carlos 2013. *Aristotle: His Life and School*, edited by D.S. Hutchinson. Princeton, NJ: Princeton University Press.

Nielsen, Karen 2008. "The Private Parts of Animals: Aristotle on the Teleology of Sexual Difference." *Phronesis* 53: 373–405.

Nussbaum, Martha 1986. *The Fragility of Goodness: Luck and Ethics in Ancient Greek Tragedy and Philosophy*. Cambridge: Cambridge University Press.

Roberts, Jean 2009. *The Routledge Philosophy Guidebook to Aristotle and the Politics*. London and New York: Routledge.

Shields, Christopher 2013. "Aristotle: Life and Work," in Christopher Shields, *Aristotle* Second Edition. London: Routledge: 8–42.

Shute, Richard 1888. *On the History of the Process by which the Aristotelian Writings Arrived at their Present Form: An Essay*. Oxford: Clarendon Press.

Tahko, Tuomas E. (ed.) 2012. *Contemporary Aristotelian Metaphysics*. Cambridge: Cambridge University Press.

INTERNET SOURCES

Christopher Shields, "Aristotle," *The Stanford Encyclopedia of Philosophy* (Spring 2014 Edition), Edward N. Zalta (ed.), http://plato.stanford.edu/archives/spr2014/entries/aristotle/.

2

GROUNDING PRINCIPLES AND CONCEPTS

PRELIMINARIES

The *Poetics* opens up with the claim that the work will discuss poetry but much of the *Poetics* focuses on a specific genre of poetry: ancient Greek tragedy, specifically Greek tragedy performed in the fifth and fourth century BCE.[1] The meanings of its key ideas, especially the key concepts of *mimēsis* and *catharsis*, have been hotly disputed. Aristotle's recommendations for how to construct narrative drama have been followed widely by playwrights as well as chastised by others for their rigid prescriptions for plots and characters. Whether adopted or criticized, Aristotle's analysis of the rules of effective poetic composition still hold sway today and they are often taken to have implications for other forms of narrative fiction, such as the novel or film.

Where does the *Poetics* fit into contemporary discussions in philosophical aesthetics? Originally "aesthetics" (from the

Greek term, "*aisthēsis*," meaning "sense perception") was a term coined by the philosopher Alexander Baumgarten in 1735 to refer to the study of the perception of beauty in art by means of the senses.[2] Aesthetics in the eighteenth century was a discipline that studied the apprehension of beauty in art and nature. As the area of aesthetics has evolved, its subject matter has broadened out to include a variety of topics in the philosophy of art, including not only the apprehension of beauty, but also the interpretation, experience and evaluation of art, the definition of art, and the nature of specific disciplines of art, such as music, literature, dance, and film. Philosophers have more recently become more interested in using the tools of analysis employed in other areas of philosophy, such as philosophical psychology, metaphysics, and ethics, to investigate these central questions in aesthetics. With the increased interest in aesthetics by philosophers, the *Poetics* is receiving renewed attention from philosophers. For in the *Poetics* Aristotle does not write as a literary critic. He writes as a philosopher and he draws on his extensive writings in metaphysics (the study of reality), epistemology (the theory of knowledge), philosophical psychology, and other areas, to give a philosophical account of the art of composing poetry.

Aristotle's writing style in the *Poetics* is often cryptic and difficult to follow, with many terms in need of clarification.[3] Even reading just a few paragraphs into *Poetics* 1 a reader can see that the text is especially challenging in this respect, likely owing to its poor state of preservation. Internal and external evidence (including Aristotle's *Politics* 8.7.1341b38–40) suggests that there was a lost second book of the *Poetics* that discussed comedy and the concept that is often supposed to be central to the work, *catharsis*.

What remains is the first book, and there is a great deal of scholarly disagreement, both at the level of details of the text and at the broader level of what overall arguments this book contains. This *Guidebook* will for the most part focus on the task of understanding Aristotle's arguments, rather than introducing the reader to debates over the status of the Greek text.[4] The goal here is not to summarize the meaning of each of the chapters, but to provide some clarification of key concepts and arguments so that the reader has a framework within which to work as she or he reads through the text.

The highlights of the *Poetics* are roughly as follows: (i) *Poetics* 1–3 analyze the grounding concept of *mimēsis*; (ii) *Poetics* 4 and 5 deal with the origins of poetry; (iii) *Poetics* 6 presents Aristotle's definition of tragedy, and Poetics 7–19 discuss tragedy's various component parts, especially the elements of the plot; (iv) *Poetics* 23–26 address epic poetry, the poet's use of wonder, surprise, and the impossible, and the difference between epic and tragedy.

ARISTOTLE'S METHOD: DETERMINING THE FIRST PRINCIPLES OF POETRY

The beginning of the *Poetics* is compressed and, unlike many of Aristotle's other works, he does not help orientate the reader by reviewing what has been said before on the topic.[5] At the same time, Aristotle makes his intentions in writing the work clear right at the start. He says in the opening paragraph that the treatise will discuss poetry and also explain the distinct capacities of its different genres (1447a7f.). It is understood that by "poetry" (*poiētikē*) he means "the art of poetry." This raises two questions: first, what does Aristotle mean by "art" (*technē*)? And what does he mean by "poetry"?

We have to appeal to Aristotle's discussion of the concept of "art" (*technē*) in other works to understand that idea (see discussion that follows). As to what he means by "poetry," he does not tell us immediately, but instead starts by listing examples of the forms of poetry that he will be discussing: epic poetry, tragedy, comedy, and dithyramb.[6] His project is to refine our understanding of the larger group to which all these examples belong by giving an account of poetry's fundamental nature or essence.

Aristotle's second sentence tells us his method of inquiry. He will proceed as he does in his other philosophical writings, by outlining the fundamental first principles that govern his subject matter (1.1447a12).[7] A thing's "first principle" (*archē*) is its origin or beginning, an account that explains why that thing originated. It should also help us understand why the features of that thing are as they are observed to be and also why these must be the way they are (*Metaphysics* 1.1.981a30). The first principles of poetry will, therefore, be an explanation that helps us to understand its causes and fundamental properties.

It follows that the *Poetics* is not a handbook for interpreting ancient Greek poetry. He is not trying to give his reader advice about how to interpret these plays and poems, and the work is not an empirical or descriptive study of ancient Greek poetry. Rather, Aristotle's task is what he would regard as properly philosophical: he wants to find a definition of poetry that will explain its distinctive features, its effects, and its goals. As such, the *Poetics* has implications for other forms of literary art that share these same features and ends. This explains the lasting influence and interest of the *Poetics* today.

The project in the *Poetics* is, therefore, no different than that of his other works in philosophy. Poetry gives rise to certain puzzles and questions; a philosophical account of poetry proceeds to try to address them through the formulation of "first principles" (*Poetics* 1.1447a12). Aristotle supposes that poetry is a certain sort or kind of thing, comprised of certain features that are essential to poetry being the sort of thing that it is. To understand the causes and properties of poetry, he aims to state the principles that regulate its production.

The norms that Aristotle establishes for poetry do not relate to the goals the playwrights and poets took themselves to be aiming for (see *Poetics* 8.1451a24; 14.1454a10); for poets need not have a theoretical grasp of their subject in order to practice it well. The norms that Aristotle establishes for poetry are instead based in his philosophical views about the proper form that poetry should take if it is to achieve the purpose for which it was created.

Aristotle's approach to his subject matter in the *Poetics* is, therefore, broadly teleological (from the Greek word, "*telos*," meaning end or goal). He assumes that poetry, like processes in nature, came into existence in order to serve a certain end or goal, and its development stopped when it had achieved its proper end (*Poetics* 4). What is that goal? Aristotle does not tell us directly in one place; rather, his answer unfolds in stages as his argument progresses. Because he thinks that the making and appreciation of poetry is a characteristic human activity, we can expect that Aristotle will try to connect the goal of poetry with our nature or essence as human beings.

As we work our way through the text, we will consider the most viable answers to this question of poetry's final end or goal and consider Aristotle's views on how the experience of poetry serves the realization of distinctively human capacities.

ART OR *TECHNĒ*

The *Poetics* concerns the art of poetry. The term "poetry" (*poiēsis*) has several meanings. It derives from a term meaning "to make" (*poiein*). In one sense it refers to a large class of activities that includes makings of all kinds, such as shipbuilding, carpentry, as well as the composing of poems and paintings. In a second more specific sense, it refers to what we would call the poetic arts, such as tragedy, comedy, and epic. When Aristotle says that we will discuss "the poetry in general, and the capacities of each of its species," he immediately goes on to list examples of specific poetic arts. Poetry is an example of the larger category of the productive arts: these concern the art (*technē*) of making something.

Aristotle's notion of "art" (*technē*) is much broader than the modern notion of art as in "the fine arts."[8] The ancient Greeks had no word that corresponded to the modern notion of "art."

The closest term is "*technē*," which refers to a broader category of activities: a skill that involves the production of something through the use of knowledge (or "know-how") on which the skill is based. "Arts" in this sense would refer to skilled practices such as carpentry and shipbuilding, what we would call "crafts," and so comprise a much broader category than what we think of as the "fine arts."

Aristotle contrasts art (*technē*) with two other disciplines, the theoretical sciences and the practical sciences:

SCIENCES		
Theoretical	*Practical*	*Productive*

• First philosophy or metaphysics
• Mathematics
• Physics
	• Ethics
	• Politics
	• Economics
		• Crafts
		  Shipbuilding
		  Medicine
		
		• Mimetic arts
		  Poetry
		  Music
		  Painting
		  Sculpture
		  Dance

First philosophy or metaphysics, mathematics, and physics belong to the branch of knowledge that Aristotle calls the theoretical sciences. These are rational activities that involve demonstration or arguments.[9] Theoretical sciences are distinguished on the basis of the nature of their objects: they concern that which cannot be otherwise and what is universally the case. These disciplines involve seeking out the first principles that govern reality simply for the sake of acquiring knowledge. The person who engages in theoretical sciences, then, engages in the virtue of contemplation (*theorein*) of the nature and causes of things in the universe, for its own sake.

Second, ethics, politics, and economics are disciplines that require the virtue of practical wisdom (*phronēsis*), or the ability to deliberate well about how to act.[10] The goal of these branches of knowledge is not theoretical knowledge, but the performance of an action (*praxis*). Thus, Aristotle calls them practical sciences.

Third, there is the branch of knowledge that Aristotle calls "the arts" (*technai*), sometimes also translated as "the productive arts." Here the goal is to not to contemplate or to do (*prattein*): the aim is making (*poiein*). Arts involve the virtue of making something well based on a true knowledge of it. This is the essence of an art (*technē*). Shipbuilding is an art as it involves the making of a good and functioning ship based on knowledge of shipbuilding. Medicine is also a productive art, because it produces healthy patients based on knowledge of the causes and treatment of diseases. Poetry, likewise, is an art because it involves the making of successful poems by means of the principles of poetic composition, for example, generalizations that pertain to how to construct an effective plot, what sorts of characters to use, how to compose the action, and so on.

The *Poetics* is, therefore, an investigation into the nature of the poetic art (*technē*). It follows that poetry has its own methodology of proceeding and its own body of knowledge that underwrites it. Having said this, Aristotle, is not, for the most part, very concerned in the *Poetics* to analyze the state of mind of the poet. This explains why, in *Poetics* 1, Aristotle immediately turns to the analysis of the means of making the various sorts of poetic arts, such as color and form, for the visual arts, and rhythm, language, and melody for different sorts of poetry, and so on (1.1447a17–22).

In *Poetics* 1 Aristotle engages with the question whether the practitioners of poetry worked according to art or some other way (1447a17f.). Some artists do work according to "art" (*technē*), while others work according to habit ("knack"). Later in the *Poetics* Aristotle remarks that Homer, a highly successful poet, works either according to "art or nature " (8.1451a23–24). In these comments, working by "art" (*technē*) has the sense it is given in *Metaphysics* 1.1, where it is said that the sign of some-one that has an "art" (*technē*) is that he is able to articulate and teach the principles that regulate and guide a productive prac-tice. The person who has experience only but lacks art (*technē*) knows, for example, *that* a certain medicine cures a patient who has certain symptoms, but does not know *why* this is so.

In these remarks about poets working not by "art" but by nature (*physis*) or knack, we see Aristotle marking out several different ways that poets work: (a) those who make success-ful poems through the appeal to explicit principles of poetic composition (and have an "art" (*technē*) in the precise sense of having a theoretical grasp on the principles that govern the craft of poetry), and others who work from (b) experience, trial or error; or (c) an instinctive understanding of what works and what does not.

Aristotle needs to make this distinction between several dis-tinct ways that poets work because he later argues in *Poetics* 4 that tragedy and comedy evolved to their mature, proper form through the trials and errors of earlier poets, starting with poets at Homer's time (4.1449a10–15). During the early part of this period, Aristotle says that poets experimented and "it was not art (*technē*) but chance that made the poets discover how to pro-duce such effects in their plots" (15.1454a10–13). These poets hit upon what families make the best tragic subjects by chance and not because they had an explicit understanding, articu-lated in the form of a general principle ("Characters of families from type x and y make the best subjects *because* of reasons a and b"), of a pattern that could be relied upon to produce the proper tragic outcome.

In another passage, already noted, Aristotle praises Homer as superior because unlike others before him he "evidently grasped well, whether by art or nature (*physis*)" (8.1451a23–24)[11] the right way to create a poem that is unified and coherent. This implies that it is possible that Homer succeeds due to innate talent or natural aptitude and not because he has a theoretical account that explains the reasons *why* his plots in the *Odyssey* and the *Iliad* succeed as they do.

On the one hand, Aristotle's view that a successful poet need not have an explicit grasp of the reasons *why* his poems work seems true to how poetic practice works. Poets do not need to have what we might call theoretical knowledge of what makes good poems good in order to succeed at their craft. In this sense poetry is no different from many other productive activities, such as cake making or shipbuilding, where we would say that someone knows *how* to bake a good cake even if she is not able to articulate the principles that underlie the art of pastry making.

Aristotle thinks, then, that as far as poetic practice goes it is not necessary to have knowledge, in the sense of an explicit articulation, of the theory or set of principles that constitute the craft of poetry. "With a view to action experience seems in no respect inferior to art, and we even see men of experience succeeding more than those who have theory without experience" (*Metaphysics* 1.1.981a13–15). Yet those who want to understand and appreciate in a deeper way what makes for good poems will want to study the principles that underlie the practice of effective poets.[12] This is Aristotle's task in the *Poetics*: to articulate the principles of poetic composition that explain what makes good poems good, and bad poems bad.

Still, there is a puzzle in reconciling Aristotle's comments that even highly successful poets might be working according to instinct and not from art (*technē*) with Aristotle's view that poetry is an art (*technē*). If such poets do not have a rational understanding of their craft, then it follows that they are not truly "artists," in the technical sense defined in *Metaphysics* 1.1 and *Nicomachean Ethics* 6.4, in that they lack the knowledge of the principles that govern the composition of poetry. If *all* the practitioners of poetry, even its most successful ones, lack a theoretical understanding of their craft, then it would seem to follow that poetry's status as an art (*technē*) is threatened. For, according to *Metaphysics* 1.1 and *Nicomachean Ethics* 6.4, poetry operates as a *technē* only when its practitioners grasp explicit principles that constitute knowledge of *why* poems work as they do. But the *Poetics* tells us that even highly successful poets such as Homer need not operate according to art (*technē*), but instead operate out of an instinctive grasp of what works and what does not.

There are different ways around this problem.[13] First, perhaps Aristotle might try to avail himself of the distinction that contemporary philosophers make between knowing how versus knowing that. Knowing *how* to make a cake or *how* to ride a bike is a kind of knowledge that is manifest in one's action, and need not be preceded by an implicit or explicit grasp of some principle that explains how to do the action. Knowing *that* this is the right way to make a cake involves knowledge of the principles that govern pastry making. The poet, such as Homer, who perhaps does not operate with a grasp of the rules of poetic composition, nevertheless knows *how* to make an effective poem. But Aristotle's view that *technē* involves working explicitly "with" (*meta*) reasoning (*NE* 6.4.1140a20–23) does not permit him to describe Homer as a practitioner who practices an art (*technē*). So this solution will not work.

Second, Malcolm Heath proposes an answer to the problem that has received wide support.[14] Heath suggests that *technē* in Aristotle's work has a dual aspect. Sometimes, as in *Metaphysics* 1.1 and *Nicomachean Ethics* 6.4, it refers to the state of mind of the practitioner òf an art (*technē*), specifically, a state that enables the practitioner to explicitly articulate and teach the principles of her art. In the context of the *Poetics*, "*technē*" in this first sense refers to the state of mind of the poet who operates with a theoretical understanding of what makes good poetry as she makes her poem. In this first sense poetry would not be an art if all of its practitioners lacked a theoretical understanding of the craft. Heath notes a second, and looser, sense of "*technē*" in which it refers to the principles of the poetic craft, as they are embodied in good poems. Here poetry will be a *technē* because one can look at the products of poetic practice and articulate the rationale behind successful poems, what works and what does not.

If Aristotle operates with several senses of "*technē*," one that refers to the state of mind of the poet-practitioner and the other to the knowledge that underwrites the successful *products* of poetic practice, then poetry's status as a *technē* will not be threatened by the fact that its most successful practitioners do not operate by articulating a theory of poetry of the sort outlined in the *Poetics*.

My worry is that Heath's proposal does not entirely resolve the puzzle. For the distinction between the two senses of *technē* is not as clearly marked out in Aristotle's writing as one would like. Indeed, Aristotle seems to make the status of the product, a house or health in a patient, dependent on the reasoning the producer operates with to make the product. So, for example, art (*technē*) is a beginning of a change in something.[15] Change involves the imposition of some form or structure on some suitable materials that have the potential to be made into a certain kind of thing. The form first exists in the mind of the producer, for example, the house builder, and then through the action of the artist on the matter, suitable materials are changed through taking on that form, for example, the wood takes on the structure of a house.

Aristotle says that the form exists, without the matter, in the soul of the artist and this is the essence of a *technē*. An artifact, the house, is created when the form in the soul of the artist is transferred and imposed on the matter, thereby creating something that is the embodiment of the form or structure that was in the soul of the artist. By the logic just described, if the structure of the artifact exists, prior to its creation, in the soul of the artist, then we can inspect the artifact for evidence that it was produced with a certain plan or structure in mind. In this sense, the art of carpentry is "in" the furniture that is produced, and by analogy,[16] the art of poetry is "in" the successfully produced poem.

The problem is, when Aristotle describes the process whereby the craftsperson transfers and imposes the form or structure on to some matter, he writes as if there is an explicit train of reasoning that the producer, e.g. a physician, goes through in order to produce her product, e.g. good health in a patient.[17] This makes the outcome, the healthy patient (in Heath's terms, the "product") dependent on the state of mind of the producer. If this is correct, the two senses of "*technē*" that Heath notes may not be independent of one another, and perhaps we are back to the problem of how poetry can be a *technē* in Aristotle's specific sense when its practitioners lack a theory, an explicit understanding, of what makes good poems good.

There is a different way to approach the problem, and it is the one I am inclined to put forth and favor. Perhaps Aristotle is quite clear eyed in thinking that the practitioners of poetry do not have *technē* at all as it is described in *Metaphysics* 1.1. There the ability to articulate and express the generalizations that give the *why* of the practice is a hallmark of *technē*. This requirement of being able to articulate is presented in the context of disciplines that proceed collectively and so depend on interpersonal communication. Poetry evolved and presumably achieved its proper nature without the explicit articulations of the principles of poetic composition, and well before Aristotle wrote the *Poetics*. This would mark out poetry as a different kind of enterprise, one that does not rely on the explicit articulation of the rules of the craft in order to advance.

Aristotle does think that Homer grasped the natural kind of poetry, because, among other reasons, he "saw" (*idein*) that poems should be composed around a unified action (8.1451a24). We can say that Homer grasped the kind, poetry, as evidenced by the fact that Homer consistently composes his poems in accordance with the principles that govern a coherent and unified plot. Aristotle comes along and explains the science behind what makes good poems, such as Homer's, good. While Homer did not need to articulate a theory of what he is doing or why he composes as he does, there is no reason to think that he was incapable of articulating the principles that underlie his poetic practice, if he needed to.

When Aristotle says that Homer "saw" that the effect of poetry depends upon a unified plot, perhaps he is saying that the principles of plot construction that Aristotle articulates are the very ones that Homer would articulate, if he were interested in doing so. Strictly speaking, then, it is Aristotle, and not Homer, who has the "art" (*technē*) of poetry, because he is the one who gives an explicit articulation of the principles that make good poems good. Still, Aristotle, perhaps, implicitly recognizes that good poetic practice, unlike the other productive sciences he discusses (such as shipbuilding or carpentry), does not need to advance through the explicit theorizing of its practitioners. In this sense, there is a science or art (*technē*) of poetry making, without poetry's practitioners needing to articulate the theory behind the practice.

The *Poetics'* account of poetry as an art (*technē*) can be usefully compared with the view that Socrates holds in Plato's dialogue, the *Ion*, in which the character after whom the work is named, is a rhapsode, a reciter of poetry at festivals. Socrates argues that artists were the passive receivers through which the Muses, the Greek goddesses of the arts, worked. Ion supports this view, claiming that he has no idea what comes over him when the words of Homer come out of his mouth to have a great impact on his listeners. Socrates argues further that the poet, such as Homer, who writes the works that the rhapsode recites, works by divine inspiration and is filled with emotion, not reason.[18]

This notion of the artist as working according to inspiration, not reason, persists through today, and in modern aesthetics receives support from the discussion of the "artistic genius" by Immanuel Kant in the eighteenth century, who maintains that a true artistic genius does not operate according to rules or general principles about how to make great art. Because of this, the creative genius cannot teach others nor can he articulate the thought process involved in making a great work of art. Instead great art emerges as a natural endowment or gift housed within the artist (Kant, *Critique of Pure Judgment*, Second Book, section 46).

Socrates concludes that poetry is not an art (*technē*) because he holds that artisans and craftspeople must possess knowledge, in the sense of explicit principles that explain what makes a good ship, building, or poem. The paradigms of an art (*technē*) he frequently refers to are shipbuilding, carpentry and medicine. These are examples of art because its practitioners can articulate the principles on which their art is based and teach others. The problem with poetry, according to Socrates, is that its practitioners cannot explain why their poems are effective. This inability in the practitioners of poetry to explain and teach the principles of poetry rules out poetry as an art (*technē*).

Aristotle would not disagree with Socrates that poets work by means of inspiration, nor would he challenge Kant's idea that the ability to make great poetry is a natural endowment. The *Poetics* does not have a lot to say about the creative process of the poet. Yet Aristotle seems to allow that poets may work according to inspiration, that making poetry requires a gifted person, and that an adaptable imagination is a feature of the poet. "Hence poetry is the work of a gifted person, or of a manic; of these types, the former have versatile imaginations, the latter get carried away" (*Poetics* 17.1455a34–35).

Without disagreeing or challenging Socrates' account of the state of mind of the poet, Aristotle seeks to demonstrate that there is a theory or base of knowledge behind a successful poet's practice. While the poet may not have taken it upon herself to explain the principles that regulate poetic composition, Aristotle is saying in effect, that is okay, for the poet does not need to know why her poems work in order for her to carry out her craft well. The job of articulating the principles of poetry is a task for the *Poetics*.

MIMĒSIS: SOME BACKGROUND

The *Poetics* asks: what is poetry? To answer this question Aristotle lists the species that are included in poetry, and then adds that these species of poetry differ among themselves by means, object, and manner of *mimēsis* (1.1447a13–15). Aristotle does not offer a definition of "*mimēsis*," so the task has been left to commentators to look at the work as a whole to grasp Aristotle's meaning.

"*Mimēsis*" in the *Poetics* is often translated as either "representation" or "imitation."[19] In this book I will in most contexts use "imitation" as a translation for "*mimēsis*." The term "imitation" carries considerable philosophical baggage, and it can also mean different things to different people. It is important to clear the decks by disentangling Aristotle's notion of "*mimēsis*" from its association with what has come to be known as the imitation theory of art: this is the widely influential view that paintings, poems, sculpture, and other works of art are made with the purpose of creating a likeness or imitation of some really existing thing. On this view, suggested by Socrates in *Republic* 10, painting and poetry are essentially a matter of making a copy of something in the world, in the way that a mirror copies the appearance of something.[20] Here the goal of the artist is to provide a likeness or verisimilitude of reality in the way that the ancient Greek painter, Zeuxis, was said to have drawn a picture of grapes that was so realistic that birds tried to eat it.

The imitation theory of art has been enormously influential: it was the dominant account of the nature and value of art that held sway into the nineteenth century, and it still captures something significant in how many people think of art. When we look at a painting or sculpture we try to ascertain what the work stands for and whether or not it is a good likeness. Should we go to a museum of contemporary art, we might be non-plussed upon finding a painting such as Mark Rothko's *Untitled (Black on Grey)*, 1970, a painting of a black rectangle adjacent to a grey rectangle. Some might even say that this painting is not really art because it does not imitate or look like anything in the world.

In spite of its impact, the mimetic theory of art is flawed as an account of art, as developments in visual, literary, and musical art in the late nineteenth and early twentieth centuries made clear. Romanticism in the nineteenth century emphasized the idea that art is a vehicle for the expression of the ideas and emotions of the artist. Modernism in the late nineteenth and early twentieth centuries found the conventions of the mimetic theory of art too restricting, and instead stressed form and abstraction. If Aristotle's view is that the nature and interest in poetry, painting, and other arts lies in its ability to faithfully copy something that already exists, then it would have historical interest as an influential theory of art, but it would not have much relevance for us today, given current developments in art. This would be even more so when we think of the importance the category of fiction, made-up people and events, plays today in art forms such as drama, the novel, and film.

Moreover, as practitioners of modernism and avant-garde art in the late nineteenth and early twentieth centuries recognized, the idea that artworks are copies of reality would imply that they are derivative or secondary with respect to the reality they imitate. The function of artworks, in other words, is to direct our attention outward towards the world they imitate or copy. The view assumes that the value of a work of art resides in its ability to imitate its subject realistically and accurately. The first popular paintings, for example, of the landscape in Yosemite Valley painted by Thomas Ayres in 1855, are valuable according to this theory to the extent that they succeed in reproducing the look of the waterfalls and mountains of Yosemite in the mid-nineteenth century, and for no other reason. The notion that art is an "imitation" of sensible reality is also often taken to mean that the work of art is made to be a substitute, artificial likeness, or counterfeit of some real thing.[21] Yet, if this is so it is hard to understand why artworks would interest us in the way that they evidently do.

There is a further problem in trying to understand how it is that the mimetic theory applies to poetry. Homer's epic poems, the *Iliad* and the *Odyssey*, focus on the Trojan War and its aftermath, but it is not based on real life characters. There is no real life Odysseus who, after fighting for years in the war, takes ten more years to reach his home in Ithaca. Although the themes of much Greek poetry were taken from myths from the Archaic past (800 BCE–480 BCE), the character developments and plots were inventions of the poets. The Athenian poet Solon (638–558 BCE) was reported to have said, "Poets tell many lies." While the poets in most cases drew from traditional myths, there was no presumption on the part of the audience that what the poet was saying was necessarily true or that the characters in poems or plays, such as Odysseus, Oedipus, and Antigone, were real life individuals. It is puzzling, then, on the imitation theory of *mimēsis* how poetry is an imitation of something that already exists.

MIMĒSIS AS IMITATION

This observation returns us to the *Poetics* and the question whether "imitation," in the sense of a copy, reproduction, or likeness of something, is the right concept to understand Aristotle's idea that poetry, along with other arts such as painting and dance, are forms of "*mimēsis*." We can break the question down of whether imitation is the right way to understand Aristotle's use of "*mimēsis*" into two further questions. First, does a *mimēsis* reproduce all or almost all of the features of the thing it imitates? That is, does *mimēsis* aim for an accuracy in its reproducing the features of the object that is imitated? This is one aspect of an imitation. Second, must the *mimēsis* be an imitation of something that actually exists? Perhaps the phrase "x is an imitation of y" suggests that y is some really existing thing.

Certainly some aspects of Aristotle's discussion of "*mimēsis*" in the *Poetics* favor the idea that *mimēsis* takes as its object something that exists. In *Poetics* 4, the genesis of *mimēsis* is the imitative behavior of children: here Aristotle may have in mind how children learn by taking adults as their models and imitating their speech and behavior. In that chapter Aristotle also gives an example in which the implication is that a viewer compares elements of a portrait with some subject familiar to her (4.1448b12–18). These examples might suggest that *mimēsis* depends upon a familiarity with its subject and that the point of *mimēsis* is to make a likeness of something that already exists.

In fact, there are other places in the *Poetics* that go against this idea. The subject matter of poetic *mimēsis* is either the actual (*Poetics* 9.1451b29–32) or what does not already exist, the possible (9.1451b5; 15.1454a16–b17), and Aristotle notes that the poet has the freedom to invent characters and events, as in Agathon's *Antheus* (9.1451b22). Aristotle also stresses that poetry should represent three kinds of things: (1) what was or is the case; (2) what people say and think; as well as (3) what *ought* to be the case (*Poetics* 25.1460b9–10). This third category suggests that *mimēsis* in poetry is in the service of some goal other than making a copy or imitation of something that already exists.

Poetics 4 speaks of the *mimēsis* of things that are repulsive in real life, such as vile looking animals or corpses, as a cause of pleasure when the images are precise or accurate (1448b11). It might be thought that this example points there being some selection in the mimēsis, otherwise it would not be possible to take pleasure in the image of something repulsive looking, such as a corpse or a vile looking animal.[22] For if the painter reproduces *all* the features and effects of the subject, the viewer will find the portrait as repugnant as the real life object.

Instead, we find in *Poetics* 4.1448b7–13 that Aristotle says that the most precise or accurate images of the forms of vile animals and corpses gives pleasure (1448b11), suggesting that the pleasure the viewer takes in the *mimēsis* does not depend on the artist subtracting or selecting *out* the unpleasant features.

Instead he goes on to suggest that the *mimēsis* is an occasion for the viewer to contemplate and understand something about the subject, and that it is this understanding that is the source of the pleasure, not the fact that certain unpleasant looking features of the subject have been selected out (4.11488b12-16).

Later in the *Poetics*, when Aristotle discusses the errors a poet can make, he says, "it is less serious not to know that a female deer has no horns than to depict one unconvincingly" (25.1460a30–31). This comment needs to be read in context to understand its full meaning.[23] It helps us understand that what is at stake in *mimēsis* is not a copying of all of the features of some model, but the idea that the *mimēsis* must be accurate or true to life, in some broader sense.

This suggests that "imitation" as a translation of "*mimēsis*" gets hold of something right in the concept, but in other ways is misleading. A *mimēsis* is like an imitation, in that it aims to be true to the subject, but it need not take as its object something that actually exists.

MIMĒSIS AS FICTION

Given that poetry can concern actual or possible characters and events, perhaps "fiction," in the sense of writing that relates to imagined characters and events, rather than ones that actually exist, is the right way to think about the notion of "*mimēsis*."[24] Fiction, whether in poetry, drama, or other art forms, allows the artist freedom from the constraint of having to make a work that directly resembles reality. In saying that *mimēsis* is fiction, we can stress an aspect of Aristotle's thinking about the mimetic arts that is central to the *Poetics*: this is the idea that poetry and other art forms engage the imaginations of their audience by evoking make-believe situations and characters. This aspect of art, the ability to engage the imagination, is something that is sorely missing in the idea that poetry or painting is an imitation or a faithful copy of reality.

While Aristotle thinks that *mimēsis* can take fictional events and characters as its object, he nonetheless thinks that the mimetic artist must render fictional events in a way that is true to life. There may not be an Oedipus, Odysseus, or Antigone, but granted that the characters are fictional, what happens to them must nevertheless progress according to what the viewer or reader expects is likely or probable to happen to these sorts of individuals in their particular circumstances (*Poetics* 9.1451b28–31).

A work that we call "fiction" need not be true to how things are in the world. It can widely diverge from how the audience might expect the action to unfold if it were to happen in real life. In this respect the idea of *mimēsis* as "imitation" captures that realistic aspect of "*mimēsis*" more accurately. Yet "imitation" can imply that what the artist strives to represent in her work is the literal truth, something that Aristotle thinks is not the goal of mimetic artists. While "imitation" and "fiction" each capture an important aspect of Aristotle's thinking, neither concept is a quite accurate way to understand *mimēsis* in the *Poetics*.

MIMĒSIS AS REPRESENTATION

We might understand "*mimēsis*" as "representation," which allows for the idea that the representation *stands for* or is *about* something that need not exist. Further, representation can be selective, with a focus placed on certain aspects of a subject while its idiosyncrasies can drop out. This goes well, in certain respects, with Aristotle's idea that the artist does not simply provide a copy of something: she gives shape and form to her subject, by showing the order and pattern in events that resemble what we could imagine observing in everyday life.

The exact nature of representation in art is highly disputed, however, so the translation of "*mimēsis*" as "representation" is bound not to settle the question of just what Aristotle means by "*mimēsis*." There is also an important point of difference between how Aristotle understands "*mimēsis*" and contemporary thinking around the concept of representation. This concerns the issue of whether a representation must resemble the thing it represents. Some philosophers of art argue that something, x, can be a representation or about something else, y, without x resembling y.[25]

Cartoons provide good examples of this point. As Peter Kivy notes, a cartoon picture of a dog in motion can be represented with motion lines behind her as a way of showing physical speed, but these lines bear no natural resemblance to what a dog actually looks like when she is in motion.[26] A reader understands what the cartoon is about by learning a set of conventions that enable her to interpret the motion lines "as" the dog running. Likewise, the inverted triangles that represent a cold front on a weather map also do not resemble an advancing mass of cold air, but the reader learns to see the triangles "as" a cold front. More generally, resemblance cannot be necessary for representation in art for the only thing that looks like or resembles a picture, for example, is another picture. Resemblance between x and y cannot be sufficient for representation either, otherwise my twin sister would be a representation of me, when she is not.

In contrast, Aristotle thinks that poems, plays, paintings, and other works of mimetic art are in some significant way like the subjects they represent, and he also maintains the ability to interpret a work of mimetic poetry or a painting comes naturally to the viewer (*Poetics* 4). A painting that is a *mimēsis* of a subject draws on the viewer's natural ability to see the painting as a likeness of the subject. Drama can be thought of as in some sense like its subject insofar as what happens on stage resembles or is like the kind of actions we are likely to see happen in real life. Further, when the viewer hears or reads the words in a play, she experiences certain thoughts and images that resemble those the viewer has or could have in response to the kind of events described in the play. The resemblance between mimetic art and reality need not, therefore, be direct.

Aristotle also thinks that the poetry and other arts draw on a natural instinct to engage in *mimēsis* (*Poetics* 4.1448b4–5).[27] This means that a work of mimetic art draws on the audience's life experiences as well as their natural ability to interpret what they see in the painting, poem, or play as like events and characters that are previously familiar to them. For these reasons, Aristotle is not thinking of *mimēsis* in quite the same way that contemporary philosophers of art talk of "representation."

MIMĒSIS AS "AS IF" EXPERIENCES

When discussing music in the *Politics*, Aristotle uses "likeness" (*homoioma*) as a synonym for "*mimēsis*."

> In rhythms and melodies there is the greatest likeness to the true natures of anger and gentleness, and also of courage and temperance, all of their opposites, and the other characters. This is obvious from the facts: we undergo a change in our souls when we listen to such things. Someone who is accustomed to feeling pain and pleasure in things that are likenesses is close to someone who reacts in the same manner to the true things.
>
> *(Politics* 8.5.1340a19–25; Kraut 1997)

In this passage Aristotle observes that listeners' characters and emotions can change as a result of listening to music (*Politics* 8.5.1340a2–3). Listening to music we might become enthusiastic, angry, mild, and even courageous or temperate. His explanation for this fact is that a likeness of emotion and character is in some sense *in* the sounds, rhythms, and melodies of music and that the listener experiences an emotion that is the same in kind as the emotion that is in the music (8.5.1340a12–14).

When Aristotle says that through rhythm and melodies music contains a "likeness" of character and emotion he is not thinking of the capacity of music to reproduce sounds that are like those found in nature, in the way, for example, found in Joseph Hayden's *The Seasons* or Beethoven's *Sixth Symphony*, both of which contain imitations of the sound of storms, frogs, birdcalls, and other natural phenomena. He also does not mean simply that music stands for or represents emotion and character. Although we can say that Aristotle thinks that the representations contained in music "express" emotions, this is not the only point Aristotle is making.[28] He is talking about the ability of music to deliver a distinctive kind of *experience*. Through rhythms and melody that are likenesses of emotions and character traits, music produces certain emotional effects on the listener that are close to those that are produced by witnessing human characters in action in real life. I will refer to these effects as "as if" experiences.

Paul Woodruff uses the points Aristotle makes about music to develop an interpretation of what Aristotle means by "*mimēsis*."[29] According to this account, Aristotle holds that a *mimēsis* is something that is capable of producing "as if" experiences.[30]

> Something, x, is a *mimēsis* of something, y, if and only if: (i) x is an artifact or behavior that reproduces some of the features of y; (ii) with the goal of eliciting a natural effect(s) that is of the sort that could be produced by experiencing y in real life.[31]

This account of Aristotelian *mimēsis* is especially useful in bringing out the idea that a poetic *mimēsis* is not simply a certain kind of artifact or behavior that is an imitation of something: it is designed to produce a certain kind of cognitive and emotional *experience* in the audience. It also incorporates Aristotle's view, articulated in the *Politics*, that likenesses are capable of producing the same emotional responses in viewers and listeners as the ones that would be called forth in real life: "Someone who is in the habit (*ethismos*) of feeling pain and pleasure in things that are likenesses is close to someone who reacts in the same manner to true things" (*Politics* 8.1340a23–25; Kraut 1997).

This, in broad outline, gets at an important strand in Aristotle's thinking on *mimēsis*.

Yet while the emotions and moral judgments the audience has are like those they would have to real life events, Aristotle also thinks that there are important *differences* between them. Humans have a natural capacity to feel pity and fear, for example, and Aristotle thinks these responses are the natural effects of witnessing certain situations. Normally these responses are elicited in real life, everyday events that call for them. If we were to witness someone in real life gouging out his eyes, as Oedipus does at the end of Sophocles' play, we would be horrified and pained. Yet there is something pleasurable about experiencing the tragic emotions in the context of tragedy and the theater.

This means that there is an important sense in which what one experiences watching a tragedy is *not* what one would feel in real life. As Aristotle says, "the poet should create the pleasure which comes from pity and fear through mimesis" (*Poetics* 14.1453b12–13). Aristotle's phrasing indicates that there is something about experiencing the tragic emotions in the context of a work of imitation that is pleasurable in the way that feeling them in real life is not.

THE COMPLETION ACCOUNT OF *MIMĒSIS*

Taken all together, the points above suggest that while:

1) The emotions and moral judgments we have in response to works of *mimēsis* are like those we would have in real life,

It is also the case that:

2) Poets and other mimetic artists are able to use the art of *mimēsis* to create an overall experience that is unique to the specific context of viewing art.

How should we understand or explain the notion of *mimēsis*, then, if the idea that a *mimēsis* produces certain natural effects is not quite accurate? Here is a tentative suggestion. Aristotle sometimes uses the notion of "completion" or "perfection" (*telos*) to refer to the specific pleasure that comes from the distinctive emotional experience of tragedy.[32] The idea seems to be that there is a certain potential to have a distinctive and pleasurable experience of the events that tragedy imitates, something that is not brought out in our everyday witnessing of such happenings. Normally, feeling pity and fear in response to a person's suffering is not pleasurable. While evoking pity and fear, tragedy is able to alter the overall character of the emotional experience, so that while feeling painful emotions, a distinctive pleasure is produced.

Perhaps we can use the notion of a complete or perfected emotional experience to understand the sense in which a *mimēsis* of something, x, both: (a) prompts an effect that is natural to have if one were to experience x in real life; but also: (b) alters the overall character of the experience of this effect, by adding something missing in our everyday lived experience of the emotions.

Following along with this idea, we might explain Aristotle's notion of *mimēsis* as follows:

> The completion account of mimēsis: Something, x, is a *mimēsis* of y if and only if: (1) x is an artifact or behavior that is made with the goal of reproducing some of the features of y; (2) x produces a natural effect(s) that is of the sort that could be produced by experiencing y in real life; (3) x completes or perfects this effect in a way that makes the overall experience pleasurable.

What is the point of having this distinctive experience? How can such an encounter with imitations in poetry be pleasurable when the emotions an imitation elicits are painful? What are the features of a work of mimetic art that make this pleasurable experience possible? In the chapters that follow we will investigate Aristotle's answer to these questions.

NOTES

1 Reading for this chapter is *Poetics* 1.
2 Baumgarten 1735 (= Baumgarten 1954).
3 In discussing Aristotle's writing, a distinction is sometimes made between exoteric and esoteric works. Exoteric works are those that Aristotle intended for the public; others (esoteric) were works that were intended for Aristotle's students and others familiar with philosophical jargon. There is not universal agreement as to whether the *Poetics* was an esoteric or exoteric work. What no one accepts is that the *Poetics* is a finished work of Aristotle's.
4 For the reader who is interested in this approach, see Gerald Else 1957, whose extensive commentary focuses on both formulating Aristotle's arguments as well as examining controversies surrounding the Greek manuscripts and translations. For a comprehensive discussion of the history of the transmission of the text of the *Poetics* also see Tarán and Gutas 2012.
5 Some scholars think that Aristotle's lost dialogue, *On Poets*, of which only a few fragments remain, contained a fuller discussion of the issues discussed in the *Poetics*. See Richard Janko 1987.
6 See the glossary at the end for the definitions of these forms of poetry.
7 See *Physics* 1.1.
8 What has come to be called "system of the fine arts" is a way of grouping the arts that was codified in the eighteenth century and it included painting, drama, music, dance, and sculpture, and now also includes movies and literature. See Charles Batteux 1746.
9 *Nicomachean Ethics* 7.5. However, elsewhere Aristotle distinguishes art (*technē*) from scientific knowledge (*epistēmē*). See *Nicomachean Ethics* 6.3–4.1139b14f.
10 Ethics is concerned with the knowledge of good action and good character, and is a part of politics, which deals with knowledge of the actions and happiness of the citizens of a *polis*, a relatively small and cohesive Greek city-state such as Athens. "Economics" in ancient Greek comes from two words, "*oikos*" and "*nomos*." The first term means "household," while the second one means "management" or "distribution." So "economics" in Aristotle's time was household management, not what we mean by economics today.
11 All translations and references to the Greek text of the *Poetics* are from Halliwell 1999 unless indicated otherwise.
12 This need not mean that Aristotle in the *Poetics* is advancing a "theory" of art in the way that modern art theorists attempt to do. The issue of whether the *Poetics* advances what we nowadays would call a theory of art is discussed in Butcher 1911; Bywater 1909; and Halliwell 1998: 42–43.
13 See Heath 2009: 58–62. Halliwell offers another approach by arguing that with respect to poetic *technē* Aristotle understood the art of poetry in more objective terms, which involved nature working through the poet to accomplish the ends for which poetry came into existence. See Halliwell 1998: 43–51, 56–61, 82–92. But both scholars come to the conclusion that Aristotle is operating with a sense of art (*technē*) where the evidence that a work is produced in accordance with art (*technē*) can be found in well-made poems.

14 Heath 2009: 58–62.
15 *Metaphysics* 12.3.1070a7f.
16 *Generation of Animals* 1.22.730b7–8.
17 See *Metaphysics* 7.7.1032b5–10.
18 See Plato *Ion* 533–534e.
19 Malcolm Heath 1997, Gerald Else 1957, and Francis Ferguson 1961 translate "*mimēsis*" in the *Poetics* as "imitation." Richard Janko 1987 and W. Hamilton Fyfe 1927 translate "*mimēsis*" as "representation." Stephen Halliwell 1999 leaves the term un-translated ("mimesis").
20 *Republic* 10.596d10.
21 See Plato's *Republic* 10.
22 For this suggestion see Christopher Shields 2013: 459. See also Paul Woodruff 1992: 92–93 and James Redfield 1994: 54, who both suggest that there is some aspect of selectivity in the features that an Aristotelian *mimēsis* produces.
23 See the discussion in Chapter 10 of *Poetics* 25.
24 For this suggestion see Halliwell 1998: 21–23 and Halliwell 2002: 166–168; and Redfield 1994: 55–67. Halliwell's interpretation has been a major influence in the understanding that *mimēsis* in the *Poetics* means not just (in Halliwell's words) "world copying" or "world reflecting" but "world-creating."
25 Goodman 1968 and Gombrich 1980.
26 Peter Kivy 1984: 9.
27 See Aristotle's discussion of this point in *Poetics* 4 and Chapter 4.
28 For an interpretation of Aristotle's views in *Politics* 8.5 on the representational and expressive aspects of *mimēsis* in music see Sörbom 1994.
29 Paul Woodruff 1992.
30 Note that the phrase "'as if' experience" is my terminology, not Woodruff's. Woodruff also offers a definition of the "art" (*technē*) of *mimēsis* where I am offering an explanation of the product of that art, an artifact, or human behavior.
31 This is an explanation of *mimēsis* in the context of human behavior and artifacts. Aristotle also uses the terms "*mimēsis*" in connection with natural resemblances.
32 See *Poetics* 26.1462a18–b1.

WORKS CITED

Barnes, Jonathan (ed.) 1984. *The Complete Works of Aristotle. The Revised Oxford Translation* Volume Two. Princeton, NJ: Princeton University Press.

Batteux, Charles 1746. *The Fine Arts Reduced to a Single Principle* (*Les beaux arts réduits à meme principe*). Paris: Durand.

Baumgarten, Alexander 1954. *Reflections on Poetry: Meditationes Philosophicae de Nonnulis ad Poema Pertinentibus*, translated by K. Aschenbrenner and W. B. Holther. Berkeley, CA: University of California Press.

Butcher, S. H. 1911. *Aristotle's Theory of Poetry and Fine Art with a Critical Text and Translation of the Poetics*. London: Macmillan and Co.

Bywater, I. 1909. *Aristotle on the Art of Poetry. A Revised Text with Critical Introduction, Translation, and Commentary*. Oxford: Oxford University Press.

Else, Gerald 1957. *Aristotle's Poetics: The Argument*. Cambridge, MA: Harvard University Press.

Fantl, Jeremy 2014. "Knowledge How," *The Stanford Encyclopedia of Philosophy* (Fall 2014 Edition), Edward N. Zalta (ed.), http://plato.stanford.edu/archives/fall2014/entries/knowledge-how/.

Ferguson, Francis 1961. *Aristotle's Poetics with an Introductory Essay*. New York: Hill and Wang.

Fyfe, W. Hamilton 1927. *Aristotle: The Poetics; "Longinus": On the Sublime; Demetrius: On Style*. Cambridge, MA: Harvard University Press.

Gombrich, E. H. 1980. "Meditations on a Hobby Horse," in Morris Philipson and Paul Gudel (eds.), *Aesthetics Today*. New York: Meridian Books: 172–186.

Goodman, Nelson 1968. *Languages of the Arts*. Indianapolis, IN: Bobbs-Merrill.

Halliwell, Stephen 1998. *Aristotle's Poetics: With a New Introduction by the Author*. Chicago: University of Chicago Press.

—— 1999. *Aristotle's Poetics Edited and Translated by Stephen Halliwell*. Cambridge, MA: Harvard University Press.

—— 2002. *The Aesthetics of Mimesis: Ancient Texts and Modern Problems*. Princeton, NJ and Oxford: Princeton University Press.

Heath, Malcolm 1996. *Aristotle: Poetics*, translated with Notes and an Introduction. New York and London: Penguin Press.

—— 2009. "Cognition in Aristotle's *Poetics*." *Mnemosyne* 62: 51–75.

Janko, Richard 1987. *Aristotle, Poetics: With the Tractatus Coislinianus, Reconstruction of Poetics II, and the Fragments of the On Poets*. Indianapolis, IN and Cambridge: Hackett Publishing Company.

Kivy, Peter 1984. *Sound and Semblance: Reflections on Musical Representation*. Ithaca, NY and London: Cornell University Press.

Kraut, Richard 1997. *Aristotle: Politics Books VII and VIII*. Translated with a Commentary by Richard Kraut. Oxford: Clarendon press.

Pratt, Louise H. 1993. *Lying and Poetry from Homer to Pindar: Falsehood and Deception in Archaic Greek Poetics*. Ann Arbor: University of Michigan Press.

Redfield, James 1994. *Nature and Culture in the Iliad*. Durham, NC and London: Duke University Press.

Shields, Christopher 2013. *Aristotle*, Second Edition. London: Routledge.

Sörbom, Göran 1994. "Aristotle on Music as Representation." *The Journal of Aesthetics and Art Criticism* 52 (1): 37–46.

Tarán, Leonardo and Dimitri Gutas 2012. *Aristotle Poetics. Editio Maior of the Greek Text with Historical Introductions and Philological Commentaries. Mnemosyne Supplements (Book 338)*. (Greek, English, and Arabic Edition). Leiden, The Netherlands: Brill Academic Publishing.

Woodruff, Paul 1992. "Aristotle on *Mimēsis*," in Amélie Oskenberg Rorty (ed.), *Essays on Aristotle's Poetics*. Princeton, NJ: Princeton University Press: 73–97.

3

DIFFERENTIATING THE IMITATIVE ARTS[1]

POETICS 1: THE MEDIA OF MIMĒSIS

Towards the goal of providing an adequate account of the art of poetry, Aristotle starts *Poetics* 1 by following the everyday practice of grouping various forms of poetry (tragedy, comedy, epic, dithyramb) together as forming one grouping along with other music arts such as music for aulos and lyre (*Poetics* 1.1447a12). In ancient Greece, there was a strong conceptual link between poetry and music. Ancient Greek poetry made use of meter, which is associated with rhythm. We can think of rhythm, which comes from a Greek word, *rhythmos*, meaning "measured motion," which in turn derives from a Greek verb meaning "to flow." Edward Hirsh explains that we can think of rhythm like waves in a sea.[2] Just as the waves come and go in a regular pattern that creates expectation of constancy and change, so also do the rhythmic patterns in poetry, music and dance. "Meter" derives from the ancient Greek term "*metron*," which means "measure," and is a way to measure the rhythmic flow in a line of poetry, music or a dance. We can think, for example, of the rhythmic structure of the waltz, "one, two, three, one, two, three . . . "

Using rhythm and meter, a poet can create a sense of movement, change, as well as constancy that can help convey the poetic meaning to the spectator. To illustrate, Hirsch explains that the three-beat structure in Theodore Roethke's poem, "My Papa's Waltz," creates a rhythmic form (with two sequences of three beats in each line) that helps convey the poem's meaning by imitating the steps of a boy dancing with his father:

> The whiskey on your breath
> Could make a small boy dizzy
> But I hung on like death:
> Such waltzing was not easy.[3]

The ancient Greek term "*mousikē*" referred to not only instrumental music, but also to all forms of art that used meter or measured speech.[4] Rhythm and musical accompaniment were an important aspect of many forms of poetry, and so it would have been natural in everyday speech to group instrumental music and poetry under one larger grouping as distinct from visual arts like painting and sculpture.[5]

From this starting point Aristotle goes on in the chapter to build on the ordinary way of grouping poetry together with musical arts by seeking a more adequate definition of it. A proper definition is an account that does not simply track how a term is used in ordinary language, but instead reveals a thing's essence. An adequate definition of poetry will settle, among other questions, the similarities and differences between poetry and music, the differences between the different kinds of poetry, and the connection between poetry and the visual arts.

In a modern setting, poetry is often associated with writing that is in verse, that is, writing that is organized with stressed and unstressed syllables that make for rhythmic patterns. For example, this is a section of the verse poem, "The Definition of Love" by Andrew Marvell:

And yet I quickly might arrive
Where my extended soul is fixt
But fate does iron wedges drive,
And always crowds it self betwixt.

In *Poetics* 1 Aristotle considers and rejects a closely related idea: this is the definition of the poet as a maker of meter. Gorgias offered this same account of poetry in his *Encomium of Helen*:

Speech is a powerful lord, who
    With the finest and most invisible body
        achieves the most divine works:
        it can stop fear and banish grief
        and create joy and nuture pity
I shall show how this is the case,
For I must offer proof to the opinions of my hearer.
I both deem and define all poetry as speech possessing metre.[6]

Aristotle says that the writings of Empedocles, a pre-Socratic philosopher-scientist who wrote in verse about the nature and origin of the universe, are not an example of poetry. "But Homer and Empedocles have nothing in common *except* their metre; so one should call the former a poet, the other a natural scientist" (1.1447b18–20).[7]

What is the problem with counting Empedocles' writing as poetry? It is that there is something wrong with the representational content of Empedocles' work: it is not a *mimēsis* or imitation of human life and action. Being speech or writing in meter is not, therefore, a *sufficient* condition for something being a work of poetry.

On the other hand Chaeremon's drama, *Centaur*, which is a "medley of meters" would still be poetry, Aristotle says, because it is a *mimēsis* (1.1447b20). Whether a piece of writing or speech is in meter or in a specific kind of meter, Aristotle says, is not the central defining feature that is common to the arts that employ language.

Here we have hit upon the genus, the kind under which all forms of poetry and music, as well as other arts such as dance and painting, fall. They are all forms of imitation (*mimēsis*) of humans in action (1.1447a12–15). In *Poetics* 1 Aristotle finds three different factors or differentiae that can be used to distinguish the different poetic arts from one another. Poetry can be distinguished on the basis of:

1) the *media* or means through which they imitate (*Poetics* 1);
2) the *objects* of imitation (*Poetics* 2);
3) the *mode* or manner of imitation (*Poetics* 3).

Although it is the interaction of these three factors that distinguishes the various poetic arts from one another (tragedy, for example, has its own medium, objects and mode of imitation), in *Poetics* 1–3 Aristotle discusses these three features as independent characteristics of each form of poetry.

Poetics 1 examines the media or means through which the poetic arts operate. The medium of an art form can be thought of as the different methods by which the art form delivers representational content from the work of art to the audience.[8] His point is that different art forms can in part be defined by the specific means at their disposal to achieve *mimēsis* or imitation. A painting of a scene from Homer's *Iliad*, such as David's *Andromache Mourning Hector* (1783) uses a distinct means, such as color and shape, to convey the scene in comparison to how the epic poet uses the features of language, such as the ability of words to stand for things, to represent Andromache mourning the loss of her husband.[9]

By artistic "medium" Aristotle does not appear to mean the specific physical materials that a practitioner of an art form uses.

He does not say, for example, that the medium of sculpture is clay or marble or that the medium of painting is dye or paint. The medium of a mimetic form of art is instead some way of using or organizing certain materials so that it can convey to the audience a believable experience of humans in action.[10]

Aristotle explains his concept of the medium of the poetic arts by first introducing how the notion of a medium applies to the visual arts and to the art that uses the medium of the voice (*phōnē*) (1.1447a17).[11] Visual artists use colors and drawings or carved shapes to reproduce the sensory appearance of some thing. Acting and recitation arts use the human voice as a medium to convey believable experiences through the use of a voice of an actor to transmit how a human subject sounds. In both cases the more tangible, sensory qualities of a thing are reproduced in a work of art. The way in which the poetic-musical arts imitate is less direct: they achieve *mimēsis* or imitation through exploiting the features of language that enable it to be a symbolic representation of humans, their emotions and character as revealed in action. The three basic media these arts use to produce *mimēsis* are: 1) rhythm; 2) language; and 3) melody (1.1447a22). On the one hand, there are arts that use just one or two of these media in the service of imitation:

1) instrumental music, which uses rhythm and melody (1.1447a23);
2) dance, which was part of the performance of dithyrambic poetry as well as tragedy, uses bodily rhythm alone (1.1447a25; 6.1449b23; 26.1462a7); and
3) imitation in writing without musical accompaniment, either in prose or meter (Aristotle calls this category of the imitative arts that "have no common name").

(1.1447b5)[12]

In the third category are included the mimes of Sophron and the early dialogues of Plato, in which Socrates figures as the central philosophical figure. One might think that a philosophical dialogue such as Plato's *Phaedo*, which contains a series of arguments for the immortality of the soul, has more in common with the scientific writings of Empedocles than Homer. For science, like philosophy, is interested in making direct truth claims about the nature of reality, something that a poet does not try to do. But the Socratic dialogues of Plato contain more than philosophical arguments. They also present Plato's understanding of the actions, times and thoughts of Socrates. The common denominator between the Socratic dialogues, mimes and the poems of Homer is, in other words, that they imitate human beings in action. Here Aristotle's focus on imitation as the most essential aspect of poetry enables him to move towards our modern concept of "literature," that is, loosely speaking, verse with no musical accompaniment.[13]

On the other hand, certain forms of poetry, such as dithyramb and nomes, tragedy and comedy, involve all three factors, rhythm, language and melody, either used altogether or separately (3.1448a28). Tragedy, for example, which is a mixture of song and spoken verse, uses rhythm, language and melody in the parts where the chorus or the characters sing, but uses rhythm and language alone in the parts where the chorus chants and in the scenes with just the characters' dialogue (6.1449b28–30). Dithyramb uses all three factors at once in that it has choral lyrics that are sung and accompanied by music and dance.

Aristotle omits mention of which media epic poetry uses, but we can understand why he does not place it along with the forms of poetry that use all three media of rhythm, language and melody. Tragedy and comedy made use of spoken verse, song and, lastly, verse that was chanted to a musical accompaniment. While not a lot is known about this "recitative" form, it made use of the distinctive forms of spoken verse, in contrast to the forms used in verse that is sung. The musical accompaniment would not have been melodic in the way that tragedy and comedy were. The recital of Homer's poems accompanied by music would be in this last category of "recitative" poetry, and so not sung, in the way in which the *Poetics* talks about song in tragedy and comedy. Thus, epic poetry makes use of rhythm and language without melody.

Aristotle's discussion of the various media used in the imitative arts can be summarized as follows:

The media used in the imitative arts							
	Instrumental[14] music	Dance	Epic	Tragedy	Comedy	Dithyramb and Nomes	The "nameless" art (prose without melody or rhythm)
Rhythm	X		X	X	X	X	
Language			X	X	X	X	X
Melody	X				X	X	X

POETICS 2: THE OBJECTS OF *MIMĒSIS*

A second way in which we can differentiate forms of poetry is by means of a classification of the *objects* of imitation. This highlights an important aspect of poetry that has been missing up until now: the relevance of the moral standing of the characters for achieving the proper response in the audience. The proper objects of imitation are not cats, dogs or places, but instead "humans in action" (*Poetics* 2.1447b30), where by "action" (*praxis*) Aristotle means behavior that is deliberately undertaken to accomplish some end (*telos*). The goal of life is happiness or flourishing (*eudaimonia*)[15] and as Aristotle notes in *Poetics* 6 people are made happy or not by their actions (6.1450a19). Aristotle does not think that poetry is driven by character development or that it is about using action to reveal the inner workings of the individual personalities of a character, in the way that, for example, Flaubert's *Madame Bovary* does.

Ancient Greek epic and tragedy, in particular, features larger than life characters or "men and women of action," that is, those who are doing things (2.1448a1). While they are capable of self-reflection and introspection, Aristotle does not think that that is what primarily makes them objects of our interest and attention. It is what happens to them, as well as what they choose to do, that is the focus of our fascination.

What these characters think or say about their predicaments is, then, less important than what they do. First, everyone strives for happiness (*eudaimonia*) and it is one's actions that determine if one is happy or not.[16] Second, our actions have consequences, which whether intended or not can lead to happiness or its opposite. Sophocles' character, King Oedipus, for example, kills his father and marries his mother without knowledge of what he is doing. These are nonetheless *his* actions and as a result of them Oedipus and the people of his kingdom suffer the consequence of the plague that comes down on the city.[17]

As with his discussion of the media of poetic arts, Aristotle first illustrates the different kinds of objects of imitation with examples from another art form, painting.[18] There are three main divisions in the persons that are imitated in painting:

1) admirable or elevated (*spoudaios*) characters (2.1448a2–5);
2) inferior (*phaulos*) characters;
3) average characters (2.1448a3–5).

Polygnotus paints individuals that are admirable or better than most, Pauson paints those that are inferior or worse than most, and Dionysius[19] paints characters that are realistic in the sense that their characters are like most people.

Here the terms "admirable" and "inferior" refer to moral excellence as well as social standing.[20] Tragic characters have a high social standing, such as King Oedipus and others "who enjoy great renown and prosperity" (*Poetics* 13.1453a10) and characters of lower social standing, such as slaves, do not figure as central characters in tragedy. Comedy typically features individuals who are morally inferior to most people and often from a less than aristocratic social class.

Aristotle says this three-fold distinction in the objects of imitation extends to all the mimetic arts (2.1448a8f.). In relation to poetry, we can represent the distinctions between the objects of imitation as follows:

The objects of poetic imitation				
	Homer— epic	Hegemon— comedy	Nicochares— comedy	Cleophon[21]— tragic or epic?
Better than most	X			
Worse than most		X	X	
The same as most				X

Other than Homer, not much is known about the poets that Aristotle discusses in this section, and what Aristotle says about these poets raises some questions. A major point that Aristotle makes in *Poetics* 2 is that the distinction between tragedy and comedy is drawn using this difference in the objects of imitation: tragedy imitates those better than most and comedy imitates those worse than the average (2.1448a15f.). This distinction between the objects of imitation is crucial for the differences that Aristotle sees between the two genres, and it figures significantly in his view that tragedy is the more serious and highly developed art form of the two (*Poetics* 4).

POETICS 3: THE MODE OF IMITATION, NARRATIVE OR DRAMATIC

Aristotle next introduces the third way of distinguishing imitations: what he calls the manner or mode of imitation:

Again, a third difference among these [kinds] is the manner in which one can represent each of these things. For one can use the same

media to imitate the very same things, sometimes by (a) narrating
(either (i) becoming another, as Homer does, or (ii) remaining the
same and not changing), or (b) by representing everyone as in action
and activity.

(Poetics 3.1448a18–22)²²

This chapter is, argumentatively, a bit puzzling as we would
expect it to apply to all the imitative arts he mentions in *Poetics*
1, including painting, music and dance; but the chapter only discusses the mode of imitation in relation to poetry. This raises
a question as to how, or even if, these distinctions apply to the
other forms of imitative art Aristotle mentions in *Poetics* 1.

In relation to poetry, the difference between the modes of
imitation pertains to how the imitation of action takes place,
either using narration or dramatic presentation. In the narrative mode the story is told. In the dramatic mode the story is
dramatized or shown through the actions and words of characters. Epic is the manner of imitation that is associated with
the narrative mode. Tragedy and comedy are forms of poetry
that employ the dramatic mode. Dramatic modes of poetry are
written to be acted out on the stage. If the poet writes, "Once
upon a time there was a dear little girl called Little Red Riding
Hood. She saw the wolf trying to eat her grandmother and
prevented this in the nick of time," she writes in the narrative mode. To write this scene in the dramatic mode, the poet
makes use of the words and actions of Little Red Riding Hood:
"Little Red Riding Hood jumps on the wolf and says, 'Not so
fast, stop eating my grandmother!'"²³

While the distinction between narrative and dramatic modes
is a two-fold difference in the manner of telling a story, what we
have in the text of *Poetics* 3 appears to be a three-part distinction:

> It is possible to imitate the same objects in the same medium some-
> times by narrating (either (a) using a different *persona*, as in Homer's
> poetry, or (b) as the same person without variation), or else (c) with all
> the imitators as agents and engaged in activity.²⁴

Many scholars think that in this text of *Poetics* 3, Aristotle is drawing on and revising a three-fold distinction that Socrates draws in *Republic* 3 (392d–4c). The sticking points and controversy are about how much of Socrates' view Aristotle retains.

First, Socrates says, there is simple narration. This is where the poet, on stage, tells the story by narrating the events, and "not attempting to suggest to us that anyone but himself is speaking" (393a). Second, the characters speaking in direct speech tell the story. Socrates describes this as a situation where the poet tells the story through an "imitation" (*mimēsis*) of the characters (393c). Here "imitation" (*mimēsis*) means "impersonation" as the poet tries to "make us feel that not Homer is the speaker," but instead that it is the character speaking. Third, there is poetry that uses both narration and impersonation to tell the story (394c).

To sort out Socrates' view and Aristotle's differences with it, we should clarify some terminology. The poet as *author* creates or makes a work of fiction. She or he is something external to the work, its cause or creator. So, for example, Conan Doyle is the author of the Sherlock Holmes stories or Homer (we shall assume) is the author of the *Iliad* and the *Odyssey*. The author also sometimes creates a *narrator*, an internal component of the work of fiction who is the fictional voice that recounts the happenings and situations that take place in the story. For example, in the Sherlock Holmes books, it is Sherlock's trusty sidekick, Doctor Watson that is the narrator of the stories. In Harper Lee's classic novel, *To Kill A Mockingbird* (1962), it is Jean-Louise (Scout) who tells the story, looking back on some incidents when she was a girl.

The narrator can be a character that participates in the action of the story. This is often what happens in movies today, as for example, in *American Beauty* (Sam Mendes, 1999) where Lester Burnham (Kevin Spacey) narrates the film and is also the protagonist of the story. Sometimes the narrator is not a part of the action of the story, though she or he is a character in the world of the fiction. This is the way Homer uses the narrator in the *Iliad* and the *Odyssey*. Within the first lines of each of these stories, Homer creates the fictional narrator of the Muse, who proceeds to tell the story. So, for example, the *Iliad* begins with the poet's request that the goddess tell the story of the rage of Achilles, and he directs her where to begin the narrative, with the clash between Achilles and Agamemnon. The *Odyssey* also opens with the poet's request to tell the story of the wanderings of Odysseus, but he does not say where she should begin: "Launch out on his story, Muse, daughter of Zeus / start from where you will" (1.11–12).[25]

Homer's use of the Muse to narrate the story fails to fit within Socrates' classification. For Homer has created a fictional voice, the Muse, to tell the story. The Muse, in turn, at various points throughout the story turns things over to the characters and has them speak for themselves, for example a few lines into the *Odyssey* where Zeus speaks at a meeting of the gods (1.40). The Muse does not appear, as do the other characters, in the actions that make up the story; rather, she is the omniscient third-person narrator who recounts these happenings in the story.

To return to the passage above in *Poetics* 3, we can see that Aristotle is revising Socrates' account on several points:

First, both narration and the direct speech and action of characters are forms of imitation or *mimēsis*, which is in the *Poetics* an inclusive category that applies to all forms of poetry, but also the visual arts and music (1.1447a13–19). The poet is not simply a poet when she tells the story by using the direct speech and actions of the characters. Both narrative and dramatic modes are capable of affecting the audience so that they imagine some possible situation that is consistent with human experience and behavior.

Second, there is no suggestion, as in Socrates' account, that when the poet tells a story through the use of characters that the poet is impersonating those characters or trying to get the audience to think that he *is* the character. Aristotle is instead referring to different ways one can tell a story, either by using narration or by having the characters engaged in activity.

Third, Aristotle is making a distinction between two means of narrating that is missing in Socrates' account. *Poetics* 3 draws a distinction between narration with and without the creation of a fictional character that tells the story. In the *Iliad* Homer tells the story by introducing the character of the Muse, who then sets the stage, and turns things over to the characters, which use their direct speech and actions to tell the story.

To account for Homer's use of the character of the Muse as narrator, we need to recognize *two* forms of narration, as well as the dramatic mode of storytelling in which the characters tell the story through their actions and speech.[26] So the distinctions Aristotle makes in *Poetics* 3 above break down as follows:

A. *Narration*: an imitation of the same character in the same medium is made through narration (*diēgēsis*), either where: (1) the artist creates a fictional character (such as the Muse) that tells the story; or (2) the artist is the narrator.

B. *Dramatic*: imitation of the same character in the same medium is effected through the actions of the characters, without the aid of a narrator (as in tragedy and comedy).

This means that when Aristotle speaks in *Poetics* 3 of Homer "using a different persona" or "becoming another" (*heteron ti gignomenon*) he is not talking about Homer's method of combining narration with the dramatic mode.[27] He is rather talking about the aspect of Homer's work noted above: that within a few lines he discharges the job of narration over to a fictional character, the Muse, who takes up the telling of the happenings and circumstances in the story. Thus, when Aristotle speaks of a poet narrating by "remaining the same and not changing" he is referring to a narration in which the author tells the story without the creation of a fictional character, such as the Muse.

If this is correct, then *Poetics* 3 is not echoing the three-part distinction between narrative, dramatic, and mixed mode.[28] Rather, he is making a two-part distinction between narration and dramatization and suggesting that narration occurs in two ways: either by the poet telling the story (where the poet "remains himself") or the use of a fictional character, as we find in Homer's work.[29]

While both narrative and dramatic modes are forms of imitation, there is some evidence that Aristotle thinks that the dramatic mode is a superior form of *mimēsis*. For later, in *Poetics* 24, Aristotle commends Homer for saying very little "in his own voice," and quickly bringing on characters into the story, while other poets perform themselves throughout the poem and either use "imitation" (*mimēsis*) seldom or not at all:

> Homer deserves praise for many other qualities, but especially for realizing, alone among epic poets, the place of the poet's own voice. For the poet should say as little as possible in his own voice, as it is not this that makes him a mimetic artist. The others participate in their own voice throughout, and engage in mimesis only briefly and occasionally, whereas Homer, after a brief introduction, at once "brings on stage" a man, woman or other figure (all of them rich in character).
>
> (24.1460a5–12)

In the text above Aristotle seems to confine the notion of "imitation" (*mimēsis*) to the storytelling that the characters do (it is not when the poet speaks "in his own voice" that he is a mimetic artist). As other commentators have noted, this text stands out as an anomaly in the *Poetics*. Everywhere else he operates with the inclusive sense of *mimēsis*, where not only narrative and dramatic modes are forms of *mimesis*, but so are works of visual art and music. Unless Aristotle is guilty of a flagrant contradiction (something that is not likely) we can suppose that he is making another point: while both narrative and dramatic modes are forms of *mimēsis*, the dramatic mode is the superior form for achieving the goal of conveying the sense that the action being imitated is taking place as if in front of the audience's eyes.

Indeed, the view that Aristotle valued dramatization over narration has influenced many generations of literary critics, who have re-invented the distinction between the narrative and dramatic modes of storytelling as a difference between presenting fictional events by "telling" or "showing." In the telling mode, the reader or audience gets the sense that they are being told about the events that someone else, the narrator, is privy to, while in the showing mode the reader or audience gets the sense that they are somehow witnessing the events happening before their eyes. As Percy Lubbock says, in a widely quoted sentence, "The art of fiction does not begin until the novelist thinks of his story as a matter to be *shown*, to be so exhibited that it will tell itself."[30]

The idea that Aristotle was associated with the dramatic mode of storytelling influenced Brecht, who called his theater "epic" theater (with narrative being the mode of storytelling associated with epic poetry) in contrast to what he called traditional Aristotelian "dramatic" theater.[31] Epic theater makes use of captions, projections, posters, songs and choruses, which interrupt and comment on the action. Brecht hoped to use these techniques to make the audience aware and critical of the social causes of the suffering featured in his plays.[32] His view is that the audience is best able to learn about these social causes when the action and speech of the characters is interrupted and juxtaposed with comments that bring incongruities in the dominant views about society to the fore.

Going back to *Poetics* 24, it might be said that Aristotle is not raising a problem with narration, as such, but is worried about the specific case of the poet inserting himself as a presence by being the narrator of the events. The worry here might be that the poet creates the fictional world of the story, but still belongs to the actual world to which the audience also belongs. When the poet inserts himself as a presence into the telling of the story, this draws the audience's attention back to the actual world, rather than placing their focus on the imaginary world of the fiction, where it belongs. Perhaps if the poet creates a fictional character, such as the Muse, who is part of the world of the fiction, there is not the same problem.

Yet *Poetics* 24 draws a distinction between the poet versus the dramatic agents (who are with character) telling the story.

While Odysseus, Hector or Chryses are presented with detailed characters, the Muse, as a narrator, is not. She is just a device Homer uses so that he can turn the telling of the story to a character that is internal to the fictional world Homer creates. This suggests that Aristotle is praising Homer for his tendency to let the (non-narrator) characters speak and act for themselves. That is, he is praising Homer, above the other epic poets, for making more use of the dramatic mode to tell the story.

Aristotle, then, holds that both narration and dramatization are forms of *mimēsis*. Yet his praise of Homer's introducing characters to speak for themselves suggests that he thinks that using the direct speech of the characters, as Homer did, most readily accomplishes the sense that an action is happening as if before the audience's eyes.[33] This is because the dramatic characters stand in a more direct relation to the action that is being imitated than a narrator, so having them speak for themselves more easily creates a vivid mental picture of the action in the imaginations of the audience.[34]

Before we end this section, an important clarification concerning Aristotle's comment that the poet should speak as little as possible "in his own voice" is needed. Aristotle does not accept the view of the artist that came to have influence later in the eighteenth century and was embraced by Romantic poets: that art is the expression of the innermost thoughts and feelings of a creative person.[35] This means that when the poet is "speaking in his own voice," this does not entail expressing his personal views on the characters or their predicaments. Instead, Aristotle thinks that the poet is telling a story through the creation of a fictional world. What the poet, as narrator, relates may have nothing to do with how the poet looks upon the events of the story or the characters that he has created.

This point brings out an important point of similarity between how Aristotle thinks of poetry and how we nowadays understand literary and cinematic fictions.[36] Aristotle thinks that even when the poet narrates "as himself" this does not mean that the narrator is expressing his personal point of view. Rather the poet writes a story so as to enable the audience to imagine the world that the poet creates.[37] In addition, the Socratic idea that the mimetic poet is an actor who tries to deceive the audience by trying to impersonate the characters has no place in Aristotle's thinking. Instead the poet is a creator of stories. *Mimēsis*, whether in the narrative or dramatic modes, is about prompting the audience to imagine the fictional world that the author creates.

THE BIGGER PICTURE: MEDIA, OBJECTS, AND MODES

The point of the argument of *Poetics* 1–3 is to show that while painting, epic, tragedy, comedy, dance, music, and so on are all forms of imitation, each genre makes use of differences in media, objects and modes to create distinct effects.

Aristotle says that when we use a method of comparison in terms of both the objects and the modes of imitation, similarities and differences emerge that might otherwise have escaped our notice. So, for example, both the epic poems of Homer and the tragedies of Sophocles are alike in their objects of imitation (better than most), while differing in their manner of imitation (mixed versus dramatic). On the other hand, while Sophocles' tragedies and Aristophanes' comedies diverge in the objects of *mimēsis* (superior versus inferior), they both employ the dramatic mode of imitation.

Modes and objects of imitation (mimēsis)			
	Homer—epic	Sophocles—tragedy	Aristophanes—comedy
Better than most	X	X	
Worse than most			X
Narrative			
Dramatic		X	X
Mixed	X		

Using the three-part distinction of media, objects and manner of imitation, Aristotle is able to mark out the features that explain how tragedy, epic and comedy differ from one another:

Differentia of tragic, epic and comedic imitations							
	Medium	Medium	Medium	Objects	Objects	Manner	Manner
	Rhythm	Language	Melody	Superior	Inferior	Dramatic	Mixed
Tragedy	X	X	X	X		X	
Epic	X	X		X			X
Comedy	X	X	X		X	X	

As the *Poetics* progresses, Aristotle goes on to expound a more complete definition of tragedy that builds on these distinctions, but also incorporates the importance of the proper tragic plot, as well as mentions tragedy's final end (*telos*) or goal: that tragedy brings about a "*catharsis*" of pity and fear.[38] Other differences between epic and tragedy are also examined, including the fact that epic is composed in one meter; ancient Greek tragedy, on the other hand, while mainly composed in iambic trimeters, makes use of many kinds of verses.[39]

POETICS 4: THE TWO CAUSES OF POETRY

While *Poetics* 1–3 discuss the differences among the imitative arts (media, objects and modes), *Poetics* 4 considers a common genesis of all of these arts. Aristotle explains that the natural causes of the birth of poetry are related to two distinctively human instincts:

> It can be seen that poetry was broadly engendered by a pair of causes, both natural. For it is an instinct of human beings, from childhood, to engage in mimesis (indeed this distinguishes them from other animals: man is the most mimetic of all, and it is through mimesis that he develops his earliest understanding): and equally natural that everyone enjoys mimetic objects.
>
> (*Poetics* 4.1448b4–8)

Unfortunately, *Poetics* 4 raises a difficult question of interpretation: what exactly is the "pair of causes" to which Aristotle refers at 1448b3? Some scholars say that the two causes of poetry are: (1) the human instinct to imitate (1448b5–8); and (2) the delight humans take in imitative objects (*mimēmata*) (1448b8–9). Others say that the two causes are (1) the human instinct to imitate; and (2) the human instinct for melody and rhythm. For a bit later in *Poetics* 4 Aristotle says, "Because mimesis comes naturally to us, as do melody and rhythm" (1448b19–20).

The debate arises because the reference to "the pair of causes" at 1448b3 is not clear. At the start of *Poetics* 4 Aristotle appears to give an explanation as to why not just poetry, but other forms of *mimēsis*, such as portraits as well as imitative behavior, came into existence (see 1448b8–10). Here his concern is to elaborate the pleasure taken in *mimēsis* or imitation more generally. There are two causes: (1) human beings have a natural instinct to imitate; and (2) humans naturally delight in well-executed imitations. A bit later in the chapter, Aristotle appears to add a third cause of why poetry came into existence: (3) the human instinct for melody and rhythm (1448b19–20). Hence, there is uncertainty as to which "pair of causes" of poetry Aristotle refers at the start of *Poetics* 4. Is it (1) and (2)? Or is it (1) and (3)?

My sense of the passage is that Aristotle first gives a more *general* explanation of why poetry came into being—the instinct for imitation and the natural appreciation of imitation (1448b3). These factors explain the origins not only of poetry, but other forms of imitative art, such as the making of images, as well as the imitative behavior of children. In the second half of *Poetics* 4, he then brings in an additional reason for the development, in particular, of poetry: the human instinct for rhythm and melody (1448b19–20). An analogy here might be a biologist who first offers an explanation of why there are animals *at all*, and then goes on to account for the existence of specific animals, for example elephants, dogs, bison and humans.

Indeed, in his writings on the scientific method, Aristotle says that explanations should proceed by first picking out the fundamental generic attributes, for example what is common to animals, because they point to the causes of the specific attributes, for example being rational, in the case of human beings.[40] This appears to be just how Aristotle is proceeding in his explanation of the origins of poetry. The "two causes" of poetry's origins to which Aristotle refers at 1448b3 are then, on my reading, the human instinct for imitation and the delight in mimetic objects. The appreciation of rhythm and melody is an additional third cause that accounts for the birth of poetry as a particular kind that exploits the features of language, rhythm and melody, in the service of the art of imitation.[41]

That said, Aristotle needs all three causes ((1)–(3) above) to account for the origin of the imitative arts as well as the development of poetry as a specific kind of mimetic practice. The first pair of causes he mentions (the instinct to imitate and the instinct to appreciate imitations) is needed to help him explain two different ways of engaging in imitation, creating versus viewing and appreciation. The third cause (rhythm and melody) is needed to explain the manner in which the poet imitates. Taken all together, factors (1)–(3) explain everything that Aristotle seeks to explain about the origin of the imitative arts, in general, and the origin of poetry, more specifically.

THE TWO STREAMS OF POETRY

In the second half of *Poetics* 4 and *Poetics* 5, Aristotle turns his attention to the development, in particular, of poetry as an imitative art. Poetry is said to be moving towards its end or goal (*telos*) and it ceased to evolve when it achieved its proper nature (*phusin*; 4.1449a15). Poetry is what we would call, in contemporary terms, a natural kind. While poetry is a social and cultural phenomenon, it evolved to serve certain natural outcomes and we can understand poetry's growth and development in terms of its progress toward fulfilling its goal.

Aristotle argues there are three phases of poetry's development.[42] First, poetry begins with the human instinct for imitation and the natural inclination for melody and rhythm. Second, poetry is brought into a form of art (*technē*) due to the improvisational talents of some individuals. Third, poetry further evolved and matured by several lines of influence for the development of poetry. One stream, a more serious form of poetry that included hymns (in praise of gods) and encomia (in praise of outstanding human beings), imitated the actions of noble characters (4.1448b25). A second stream, invectives or satires of individuals, imitated the actions of morally base and inferior characters (4.1448b27). Poets developed the serious or comic genre on the basis of their character, with the more serious poets imitating dignified and noble actions and the lighter and those with a less weighty character imitating the deeds of lesser individuals (4.1448b24–28).

According to Aristotle's genealogy, Homer figured significantly in each strand's development. On the more serious poetry side, Homer, first, focused on morally and socially admirable characters; second, he made extensive use of the dramatic mode of *mimēsis*, which allowed characters to speak for themselves (4.1448b35). Both innovations in content and style of storytelling influenced the development of ancient Greek tragedy. On the less serious side, Aristotle attributes the lost burlesque poem, the *Margites* (the "Madman") to Homer and credits him with two creative innovations that influenced the development of ancient Greek comedic poetry.[43] To begin, he shifted the form of comedy from the expression of verbal assaults on individuals to use of direct speech of the characters, which anticipated the dramatic mode of imitation used by comedy (4.1449a1); next, he imitated characters with humorously laughable faults (4.1448b38). This anticipated comedy's focus on characters whose faults are shameful, but not painful or destructive, prompting a response of laughter (*to geloion*) (*Poetics* 5.1449a31–38).

The influence of Homer on tragedy			
	Hymns	Homer's epic poems	Tragedy
Elevated and serious characters		X	X
Subjects—the gods and excellent humans	X		
Dramatic imitation		X	X
Improvised speeches	X		

The influence of Homer on comedy			
	Satires	Homer's Margites	Comedy
Laughable characters		X	X
Base characters	X		
Use of dramatic imitation		X	X
Improvised speech	X		

Aristotle traces a second line of influence on the development of tragedy and comedy in the sixth century: its development out of the dithyramb and phallic songs in honor of the god, Dionysius (4.1449a9–13). He is not explicit about just what form this development took, and scholars have debated the exact line of influence Aristotle has in mind.[44] There is the strong suggestion that dithyramb and the phallic song contributed to tragedy's and comedy's development. The dithyramb and phallic song both contained choral songs and dance. Both tragedy and comedy alternate parts where the chorus sing and dance with parts with character's dialogue and the dramatization of actions. In addition, prior to the development of tragedy and comedy, there was an earlier innovation in which the choral leader became the first actor (*hupocritēs*, the source for the English word "hypocrite"), a figure who engaged in discourse with the chorus, thus making dialogue possible (4.1449a1–19).

Tragedy and comedy may then have emerged out of dithyramb and phallic songs by retaining the chorus, but advancing the earlier innovation through Aeschylus' increase of actors from one to two (4.1449a18; 4.1449a24), followed by Sophocles' introduction of three actors and scene painting (4.1449a19). This introduction of a second and then third actor substantially reduced the role for the chorus.

Further developments followed, especially in tragedy, the use of the iambic trimeter, which is the speech of everyday conversation, presumably making possible dialogue that is more realistic sounding and true to everyday life (1449a25f.). Perhaps because comedy was a less serious form of poetry, the details of poetry's early development are lost (*Poetics* 5.1448a38–b2).

Dithyramb → Tragedy
Phallic Songs → Comedy

CONCLUSION

In the opening chapters of the *Poetics*, Aristotle examines quite a bit of ground in his attempt to define the essence of poetry. He ends up revising and correcting the ordinary way of thinking of poetry on a key point: he rejects the idea that poetry is writing or speech in meters. Instead, he argues that what the various forms of poetry have in common with each other is a feature they share with music, dance and the visual arts such as painting and sculpture: they are forms of *mimēsis* or imitation of human action. This assures that poetry has a content that is of human interest and is linked to Aristotle's view that the poetic arts must elicit a certain kind of emotional experience.

Of particular interest for modern readers is the way in which Aristotle addresses the imitative art that has no musical accompaniment (the art that "remains so far unnamed"). This, of course, is the way in which modern readers typically engage with the form of literature we call the novel. Given the close connection between the imitative arts and music at the time Aristotle was writing, it was a major conceptual breakthrough to introduce this kind of imitative art. When language separates from music, the words have to carry the meaning all by themselves. It is Aristotle's great insight that what is left is something even more important than rhythm or melody: it is a certain content, the imitation in language of something of great interest, human action, that is essential to achieving the desired effect.

NOTES

1 Reading for this chapter is *Poetics* 1–5.
2 Edward Hirsch 2014.
3 Quoted in an interview on June 20, 2014 on National Public Radio: http://www. npr.org/2014/06/20/323329319/how-rhythm-carries-a-poem-from-head-to-heart.
4 Gregory Nagy 2010.
5 Cf. Stephen Halliwell 2002, Chapter One for an argument that prior to Plato and Aristotle, there was a tradition of grouping together music arts, poetry and visual arts under the larger rubric of mimetic arts.
6 J. Dillon and T. Gergel 2003.
7 All citations to the *Poetics* are to Halliwell 1999 unless otherwise noted.
8 The idea that an art form can partially be defined by its medium is still alive in contemporary discussions in philosophy of art. See Richard Wollheim 1987: 22–23; David Davies 2003; and Berys Gaut 2010: 287–290.
9 *Rhetoric* 3.2.1404a21.
10 See the discussion of *mimēsis* in Chapter 2.
11 Here he is likely thinking of the arts of recitation and acting. In *Rhetoric* 3 Aristotle says regarding the human voice: "of all our organs can best represent other things" (1404a22).
12 This section in 1.1147a28–b29 presents some challenges of interpretation owing to some interpolations to the Greek text. Tarán and Gutas 2012: 226–230 argue that Aristotle is not proposing to extend the meaning of "poetry" to include the "anonymous art" of imitation in prose without musical accompaniment. Rather Aristotle is claiming that, included in the larger group of mimetic arts, there is a "nameless art" that includes imitations in prose and poetry (228). This category of the anonymous art is what we might call "literature" today.
13 The precise definition of "literature" is a rather philosophically vexed subject. For contrasting approaches to this subject, see Terry Eagleton 1996: 1–14; and Robert Stecker 1996.
14 The poetic arts that involve just instrumental music, or dance or poetry without music, are not given proper names. Music and dance occur in some literary arts, such as tragedy, comedy and dithyramb, and they share some of the same media

as these forms of poetry, as does the "nameless art" that uses language, either in prose or verse (*Poetics* 1.1447b1).

15 See Aristotle *Nicomachean Ethics* 1.

16 *Nicomachean Ethics* 2.

17 For the conditions of responsible action, see *Nicomachean Ethics* 3.

18 Aristotle expresses the view here in *Poetics* 2 (and *Poetics* 6.1450a27) that some painters are capable of imitating character, but elsewhere (*Politics* 8.5.1340a32–39) he says that the indications of moral character are there only to a "slight extent" in paintings. See also the mixed comments in *Problems* 19.919b27–920a7.

19 It is uncertain which painter Aristotle refers to here.

20 See also the discussion of admirable action in Chapter 5, the section "tragedy defined."

21 It is not certain whether Cleophon was a tragic or epic poet. Both epic and tragedy imitate the actions of those who are better than most, so if his imitations took as their objects realistic characters who were like most people, then it is unclear how Cleophon fits into Aristotle's classification.

22 Richard Janko 1987.

23 This does not mean that a tragedy will no longer be in the dramatic mode if it is read rather than performed. Reading is not the way that audiences took in tragedy and other forms of poetry at the time that Aristotle is writing. But the poet who works in the dramatic mode *writes* the play so that it can be performed or dramatized on the stage. This involves representing the action that is imitated in the story in a different way than if the story was told but not enacted.

24 Malcolm Heath *Aristotle Poetics* 1998: my addition of (a) and (b). I have followed Heath's translation because as Ayreh Kosman, among others, argues, the Greek grammar suggests that (a) and (b) make a single mode, which is contrasted with (c). See Ayreh Kosman 1992: 52–53.

25 Homer 1996.

26 See Paul Woodruff 1992: 79.

27 Some commentators (such as Gerald Else 1957: 95) think this language, which echoes Plato's *Republic* 3, was added in at a later date as a result of scribal error.

28 For an argument that Aristotle is echoing Socrates' three-part distinction, see Stephen Halliwell 1998: 132–137. For an argument that favors the two-part distinction see Paul Woodruff 1992: 78–80.

29 This schema can be thought of as bi-partite or tri-partite, depending on whether one stresses that the main distinction is between two modes of storytelling (narrative and dramatic) or between the dramatic mode and the narrative mode, which in turn breaks down into two forms. There is also no problem in thinking that Aristotle gets the distinction from *Republic* 3392d–4c: he clearly does. The important point is that Aristotle adapts the schema so that the two forms of *mimēsis* he is elaborating have nothing to do with the poet impersonating the characters. Cf. Woodruff 1992: 83–88 for the argument that the *Poetics* retains the idea that poetry involves a kind of deception.

30 P. Lubbock 1926/1957: 62.

31 See Bertolt Brecht 1964.

32 See A. Curran 2009.

33 See also *Poetics* 17.1455a21–25 and a parallel passage in *Rhetoric* 2.8.1386a33–1386b5 where Aristotle advises speakers to use dramatic touches such as tone of voice, gesture, and dress to place the action as if before their listener's eyes.

34 The notion that *mimēsis* involves directness is developed in Göran Rossholm 2012. This is an interesting analysis of the dramatic mode of imitation but if the relevant sense of "directness" excludes narration as a form of *mimēsis* it could not be an account of Aristotle's view. For a discussion of why Aristotle thinks that the use of lively, metaphorical language can impart a sense of direct action even in the narrative mode, see Deborah Roberts 1992: 143–144.

35 For the contrast between the Romantic view of the poet and Aristotle's, see Stephen Halliwell 1998: 50–51.

36 For a discussion, in particular of how narrative works in literature, see George Wilson 2003; and for a useful and accessible survey of the literature on cinematic narration, see Katherine Thomson-Jones 2009.

37 See Ayreh Kosman 1992: 62.

38 *Poetics* 6.1449b22f.

39 For a discussion of why certain meters are most suited to particular genres see *Poetics* 4.1449a20–22 and 24.1460a4–6.

40 See *Posterior Analytics* 2.14 and *Parts of Animals* 1.1.639a15–b7.

41 For the argument that the "two causes" referred to in the passage are the instinct to imitate and the instinct for rhythm and melody, see Malcolm Heath 2003: 9.

42 *Poetics* 4.1448b19–24.

43 If Aristotle believed that Homer is the author of the *Margites*, others in Antiquity did not. It is now thought that the poem was written later than Homer's supposed lifetime (between 750 and 650 BCE).

44 See Gerald Else 1957: 67.

WORKS CITED

Brecht, Bertolt 1964. "The Modern Theater is the Epic Theater," in John Willett (ed.), *Brecht on Theater: The Development of an Aesthetic*. New York: Hill and Wang.

Curran, Angela 2009. "Bertolt Brecht," in Paisley Livingston and Carl Plantinga (eds.), *The Routledge Companion to Philosophy and Film*. Abingdon, England: Routledge Press: 323–333.

Davies, David 2003. "Medium in Art," in *The Oxford Handbook of Aesthetics*. Jerrold Levinson, ed. Oxford: Oxford University Press: 181–191.

Dillon, J. and T. Gergel 2003. *The Greek Sophists*. London: Penguin Classics.

Eagleton, Terry 1996. *Literary Theory: An Introduction*, Revised Edition. London: Wiley-Blackwell.

Else, Gerald 1957. *Aristotle's Poetics: The Argument*. Cambridge, MA: Harvard University Press.

Gaut, Berys 2010. *A Philosophy of Cinematic Art*. Cambridge: Cambridge University Press.

Halliwell, Stephen 1998. *Aristotle's Poetics: With a New Introduction by the Author*. Chicago: University Of Chicago Press.

———— 1999. *Aristotle's Poetics Edited and Translated by Stephen Halliwell*. Cambridge, MA: Harvard University Press.

———— 2002. *The Aesthetics of Mimesis: Ancient Texts and Modern Problems*. Princeton, NJ: Princeton University Press.

Heath, Malcolm 1996. *Aristotle: Poetics*, translated with Notes and an Introduction. New York and London: Penguin Press.

———— 2003. "Aristotle and the Pleasures of Tragedy," in Øivind Andersen and Jon Haarberg (eds.), *Making Sense of Aristotle Essays in Poetics*. London: Duckworth: 7–24.

Hirsch, Edward 2014. *A Poet's Glossary*. Boston, MA: Houghton Mifflin.

Homer 1996. *The Odyssey*, translated by Robert Fagles. New York and London: Penguin Press.

Janko, Richard 1987. *Aristotle, Poetics: With the Tractatus Coislinianus, Reconstruction of Poetics II, and the Fragments of the On Poets*. Indianapolis and Cambridge: Hackett Publishing Company.

Kosman, Aryeh 1992. "Acting: Drama as the *Mimēsis* of *Praxis*," in Amélie Oskenberg Rorty (ed.), *Essays on Aristotle's Poetics*. Princeton, NJ: Princeton University Press: 51–72.

Lubbock, Percy 1926/1957. *The Art of Fiction*. London: Viking Press.

Nagy, Gregory 2010. "Language and Meter," in Egbert J. Baker (ed.), *A Companion to the Ancient Greek Language*. London: Wiley-Blackwell: 370–387.

Roberts, Deborah 1992. "Outside the Drama: The Limits of Tragedy in Aristotle's Poetics," in Amélie Oskenberg Rorty (ed.), *Essays on Aristotle's Poetics*. Princeton, NJ: Princeton University Press: 133–154.

Rossholm, Göran 2012. "Mimesis as Directness," in Gregory Currie, Petr Kot'átko, and Martin Pokorny (eds.), *Mimesis: Metaphysics, Cognition, Pragmatics*. London: College Publications: 14–39.

Stecker, Robert 1996. "What is Literature?" *Revue Internationale de Philosophie* 50 (198): 681–694.

Tarán, Leonardo and Dimitri Gutas 2012. *Aristotle Poetics. Editio Maior of the Greek Text with Historical Introductions and Philological Commentaries. Mnemosyne Supplements (Book 338)*. (Greek, English, and Arabic Edition). Leiden, The Netherlands: Brill Academic Publishing.

Thomson-Jones, Katherine 2009. "Cinematic Narrators." *Philosophy Compass* 4/2: 296–311.

Wilson, George M. 2003. "Narrative," in Jerrold Levinson (ed.), *The Oxford Handbook of Aesthetics*. Oxford: Oxford University Press: 392–407.

Wollheim, Richard 1987. *Painting As Art*. Princeton, NJ: Princeton University Press.

Woodruff, Paul 1992. "Aristotle on *Mimēsis*," in Amélie Oskenberg Rorty (ed.), *Essays on Aristotle's Poetics*. Princeton, NJ: Princeton University Press: 73–97.

4

THE PLEASURES IN IMITATIONS

THE ORIGINS OF IMITATION IN HUMAN NATURE

Why did poetry and other forms of art come into existence?[1] A dominant trend in the twentieth century was to regard these art forms as determined by and addressing the specific needs of a society and culture. On this view, the imitative arts were not created to address the emotional, intellectual or imaginative needs of humans, as such, for the interests of humans vary, depending on the time, the location and the culture. What universal interests, for example, would African Baule figure carvings and the paintings by Michelangelo on the ceiling of the Sistine Chapel have in common? We might, perhaps, say that both are fine examples of works of art, but they would seem to be addressing viewers with different interests and needs.

Recently, philosophers of art have begun to reverse the view of art as a purely cultural phenomenon. They present a variety of considerations to show that there is a universal instinct to make art and that works of art engage aspects of our minds that are universal features of all humans.[2] Aristotle is the philosophical ancestor of these arguments because in *Poetics* 4 Aristotle argues that poetry and the imitative arts originated in human nature. On Aristotle's picture of human beings, there is a shared essence or nature that is common to all humans, in virtue of being human. This means that there are certain activities in which humans engage that stem from and serve the ends of our nature. For example, human beings, Aristotle says, are political animals and, therefore, the state or *polis* comes into existence by nature, meaning that it developed to serve the human instinct for political association.[3] In the same way, poetry and other forms of imitation came into existence by nature as well.

> Because *mimēsis* comes naturally to us, as do melody and rhythm (that metres are categories of rhythm is obvious), in the earliest times those with special natural talents for these things gradually brought poetry into being from improvisations.
>
> (4.1448b18-24)

Central to the argument that poetry and the mimetic arts are a natural development is the claim it is in our nature to imitate. What is Aristotle's argument in *Poetics* 4 for this?

Human beings are the most mimetic of animals (4.1448b5-7).[4] Elsewhere Aristotle notes that certain kinds of animals, such as the owl and the anthus, are capable of mimicking behavior.[5] But humans are capable of more than mimicry, which is a form of unconscious, non-inferentially based behavior. They are capable of making as well as appreciating imitations, and Aristotle thinks that humans tend towards imitation more than other animals. These are unique feature of human beings, and if a feature or capacity uniquely characterizes something, then this is good reason to think that it is part of that thing's essence or nature.[6]

It is more likely that something comes naturally to humans if they start to do it at an early age. So Aristotle notes that imitation is present in humans, starting in childhood. It is not clear if he means that children appreciate imitations, make their own mimetic objects or engage in imitative behavior. He likely means all of these things. Children engage in imitation when they play games of make believe.[7] Youngsters amuse themselves by imagining they are pirates in search of sunken treasure. Or a child dresses up and talks like her mother, pretending she is an adult going off to work in the morning. In addition, children sing, dance and take delight in all forms of music and nursery rhymes. Aristotle argues in *Poetics* 4 that the predisposition for imitation, rhythm, and melody found in children is just a more elementary form of the same instincts that gave rise to poetry and other mimetic arts.

THE PLEASURES IN THE EXPERIENCE OF A WORK OF IMITATIVE ART

Imitation not only comes naturally to human beings: it is also a source of natural delight to them (4.1448b3–5). It is this pair of causes that gives rise to poetry, Aristotle argues. What sort of pleasure does a work of imitation provide? Aristotle answers this question in a central passage in *Poetics* 4:[8]

It can be seen that poetry was broadly engendered by a pair of causes, both natural. For it is an instinct of human beings, from childhood, to engage in mimesis (indeed, this distinguishes them from other animals: man is the most mimetic of all, and it is through mimesis that he develops his earliest understanding): and equally natural that (a) everyone enjoys mimetic objects. A common occurrence indicates this: (b) we enjoy contemplating the most precise images of things whose actual sight is painful to us, such as the forms of the vilest animals and of corpses. (c) The explanation of this too is that understanding (*manthanein*) gives great pleasure not only to philosophers but likewise to others too, though the latter have a smaller share in it.

(d) This is why people enjoy looking at images, because through contemplating them it comes about that they understand (*manthanein*) and
infer (*sullogizesthai*) what each element means, for instance that "this
person is so-and-so" (*houtos ekeinos*). For, (e) if one happens not to have
seen the subject before, the image will not give pleasure *qua* mimesis
but because of its execution or colour, or for some other such reason.

(4.1448b1–18)

First, we consider an overview of the structure of Aristotle's
argument. In this passage, Aristotle starts with the observation
that:

a) Everyone enjoys imitations.

    He reasons that this is so because:

b) Everyone enjoys precise images of things even when the
    objects imitated are visually repugnant, such as vile looking
    animals or corpses.

    a) and b) are true because:

c) Learning and understanding (*manthanein*) are a source of great
    pleasure, for philosophers and non-philosophers alike, and
d) Even in relation to images of unpleasant looking things, the
    viewer takes pleasure in understanding (*manthanein*) and
    inferring (*sullogizesthai*) what each element means, for
    instance that "this person is so-and-so" (*houtos ekeinos*).

    d) is supported by:

e) If the viewer is not acquainted with the subject in the image,
    it will not afford pleasure *as* an imitation or *mimēsis* but
    because of some other reason, such as its craftsmanship or
    color.

There are several pleasures that an artistic image of some individual gives to everyone. First, there is *imitative pleasure*: this
is pleasure in the work, considered *as* an imitation (4.1448b18).

Aristotle argues for (a), the claim that everyone enjoys imitations, by showing that (b) even when the imitative content of a precisely done picture is visually repelling, viewers still can take pleasure in the work. For viewers can take pleasure in an image that is an imitation of a corpse or a vile looking animal, when they would not take pleasure in looking at the object imitated. This is evidence that viewers take pleasure in works *as* imitations, for it cannot be the content, that is, the corpse or animal imitated, that is the source of the pleasure viewers feel in response to such works. The source of the pleasure must come from some pleasure the work provides as an *imitation* of the object.

Second, there is *sensory pleasure* in the work of art, indicated by Aristotle's brief remark that when a viewer does not recognize the subject in a portrait, the viewer can take pleasure in its color. If the viewer is not familiar with Socrates, for example, the picture will not be a source of mimetic or imitative pleasure. But it can give pleasure because of its color or other of its sensory qualities.

Aristotle finds great value in the exercise of the senses; all human beings, he says, take delight in the senses apart from their usefulness in navigating their environment.[9] Because the exercise of sense perception is a natural function, the senses give pleasure when they are exercised merely for their own sake, and not for some other means. Not only portraits, but also other forms of mimetic art, offer the pleasures of sensory experience, including the sounds, sights, and rhythms of music and dance, and the recitation of rhythmic verse in various forms of poetry.

There is, perhaps, also a third pleasure mentioned in the passage. This is the pleasure in craftsmanship (*apergasia*). There is enjoyment found in the "precise images" of things (*Poetics* 4.1448b10). Aristotle does not explain his meaning, but it would appear he is referring to the quality of an image when it is well executed. Perhaps Aristotle is observing that the viewer can take pleasure in the workmanship that is displayed in the work when the subject is accurately represented.

In other places when Aristotle discusses the appreciation of the skill or craft (*technē*) of the mimetic artist, this comprises more than just accuracy. It involves the creation of a work with a discernible form. The work of the mimetic artist is an instance of a skill or art (*technē*). The skill of the craftsperson is often compared to the productive activity of nature. "Art imitates nature," Aristotle says, because the craftsman draws on his know-how to create a work whose elements form a unified structure that parallels the unity found in living things.[10]

In *Parts of Animals*, Aristotle talks of how the pleasure in the skill of the mimetic artist can compensate for an unpleasant subject matter:

> For if some have no graces to charm the sense, yet nature, which fashioned them, gives amazing pleasure in their study to all who can trace links of causation, and are inclined to philosophy. Indeed, it would be strange if mimic representations of them were attractive, because they disclose the mimetic skill of the painter or sculptor, and the original realities were not more interesting, to all at any rate who have eyes to discern the causes. We therefore must not recoil with childish aversion from the examination of the humbler animals. Every realm of nature is marvelous . . . so we should venture on the study of every kind of animal without distaste; for each and all will reveal something beautiful. Absence of hazard and conduciveness of everything to an end are to be found in nature's works in the highest degree, and the end for which those works are put together and produced is a form of the beautiful.
>
> (*Parts of Animals* 1.5.645a4–26; Barnes 1984)

In this passage Aristotle makes a comparison between the pleasure available in a work of art that imitates animals that are unpleasant from a sensory point of view, and the pleasure that students of philosophy can find from a study of these humble animals, when they persist in studying them in spite of their unpleasant appearance. Aristotle is perhaps suggesting that well-executed works of art are like the products of nature. In living things, the parts of an animal are not there by accident, for Aristotle thinks that nature does nothing in vain. Each part in a living thing is there for the sake of some end, which is the principle of organization for the creature. The same goes for skillfully done works of imitation. A painter or other mimetic artist draws on her art (*technē*) to create a work whose elements are arranged to form a unified structure whose organization parallels the arrangement of parts in living things.

Works of imitative art, therefore, are like livings things, in that both have a discernible structure or form, which is the means by which all of the elements in the work are related into a coherent whole. A work's form is distinct from its subject matter, so viewers can derive pleasure in Caravaggio's *Judith Beheading Holofernes*, even if witnessing beheadings in real life would disgust them. It is possible, then, to take pleasure in the form of a work, such as the Caravaggio painting, even when the subject represented is visually repugnant.

If this is correct, the pleasure in form and craftsmanship is a third sort of pleasure, distinct from taking delight in the work's sensory qualities, and also distinct from the pleasure in a work as an imitation. The pleasure in craftsmanship involves delight in the artist's skill more broadly and it includes an appreciation of the work's form or the organization of its parts.

I said that *perhaps Poetics* 4 notes this third kind of pleasure, the pleasure in craftsmanship, because Aristotle may instead be lumping the pleasure in craftsmanship alongside the pleasure in color, as a sensory pleasure (*Poetics* 1448b18). Even if *Poetics* 4 does not clearly recognize the pleasure in craftsmanship as a distinct pleasure, there is reason to think that this pleasure in a work's organization or structure is needed to make sense of the argument of the *Poetics*, as a whole. For the pleasures in the organization or structure of the work, which contemporary philosophers of art call the work's "form," is an independent source of pleasure that viewers take in tragedy.[11] Indeed, in *Poetics* 7 Aristotle makes this point when he elaborates the way in which, in both living things and in tragedy, the source of beauty is found in the size and arrangement of its parts.[12]

Like contemporary aestheticians, Aristotle, therefore, recognizes that there is pleasure to be taken in a work's form apart from its sensible qualities such as color.[13] If this is correct, then the pleasure in craftsmanship involves delight in the artist's skill more broadly and it includes an appreciation of the work's form or the organization of its parts.[14]

To summarize the argument of *Poetics* 4 so far: when we view an image of someone, there are several distinct pleasures involved: First, there is the pleasure in the work *as* an imitation (1448b18). Second, there is sensory pleasure in the work, for example pleasure in its colors and shapes. Finally, perhaps, there is also a third pleasure in the craftsmanship of the work, which comprises an appreciation of the artistic technique of a work when it is well done, as well as pleasure in a work's structure, form, or organization of its parts.

PLEASURE IN IMITATIONS AS PLEASURE IN LEARNING

Of these three pleasures, the pleasure in the work *as* an imitation is by far the most central pleasure that Aristotle examines in *Poetics* 4. What exactly is involved in taking pleasure in the work *as* an imitation? The pleasure viewers take in mimetic works as imitations, he says, is a cognitive one: it is an interest in learning and understanding (*manthanein*).

Humans have a natural tendency to engage in imitation (*mimēsis*) and to enjoy imitations (4.1448b5–9). In *Poetics* 4 Aristotle uses the term "imitation" (*mimēsis*) to refer to: (a) a behavior that arises naturally in humans at an early age; and (b) to works of art that are produced by more complex mimetic activities, such as a portrait that creates a likeness of someone. He says that imitation is naturally pleasant to human beings and the pleasure that humans take in imitations is linked to learning and understanding (*manthanein* 1448b12, 1448b17).

Aristotle illustrates the learning that everyone takes from works of mimetic art with reference to the example of an image of an individual. The viewer of the portrait delights in "understanding and inferring" what each element in the work is, for instance that "this is so-and-so" (1448b15–17). We know that the mental process Aristotle is describing here must involve more than just a grasp of colors and shapes. For Aristotle is describing the delight in mimetic works *as* imitations, and he says if a viewer has not seen the subject of the image before, it cannot give pleasure *as* an imitation, but pleasure can be taken in its execution or color (1448b17–18). His point is that any viewer can appreciate a picture as an experience of certain colors and shapes. To appreciate the picture as an imitation of a cat, for example, a viewer will need to have previously acquired the concept of a cat. If the viewer has no idea what a cat is, she cannot appreciate the image of a cat *as* an imitation. Taking pleasure in an image as an imitation, then, at least involves having an idea of what one is looking at.

To enjoy the picture as a precise or accurate imitation of its subject (1448b10) more is involved than just having previously acquired the concept of a cat. To discern if the picture is an accurate imitation of a cat, the viewer must compare her perception of the image with her perceptions of cats that she has previously encountered. In appreciating the picture as an accurate imitation, memory comes into play because memories are the recording of past observations. As an imitation or likeness of a cat, the picture calls to mind one or more cats that the viewer has perceived in the past.[15] Appreciating a work as an imitation of a cat involves recognition of something familiar, for example that one has seen either that particular cat before or that the figure in the picture resembles one's memories of cats one has seen before.

Thus, the viewer who appreciates the picture of a cat *as* an accurate imitation must activate her previously acquired concept of a cat, and she must use her memory to compare the image in the picture with her recollection of previous cats. What more is involved in taking pleasure in a work *as* an imitation? Aristotle says, "This is why people enjoy looking at images, because through contemplating them it comes about that they understand (*manthanein*) and infer (*sullogizesthai*) what each element means, for instance that "this person is so-and-so" (4.1448b15–17). The two key terms in this passage are "understand" (*manthanein*) and "infer" (*sullogizesthai*). What is the mental process involved when one "understands and infers" what each element in the work means so as to arrive at the conclusion "this" (the image in the picture) is "that" (some subject with which one is previously acquainted)?

As the passage in *Poetics* 4 indicates, "understanding" (*manthanein*) can refer to the learning and knowledge of the world that philosophers seek, as well as the understanding that all humans, philosophers and ordinary folk, delight in. In the famous opening lines of *Metaphysics* 1.1, Aristotle says that *all* humans desire and take delight in understanding the world around them, a claim that Aristotle repeats in *Poetics* 4. Here Aristotle uses a simple example of the elementary recognition of a figure in a painting to indicate that the pleasure in a work as an imitation is available to all human beings.

Indeed, as he says, "it is natural that everyone enjoys mimetic objects" (1448b9). Of course, there are more complicated processes of recognition and understanding involved in more sophisticated forms of imitation, such as tragedy. In *Poetics* 4 Aristotle is describing a pleasure in learning from imitations that is available to all human beings, even those who do not engage in the deeper learning about the causes of things in the universe that philosophers seek.

While Aristotle sometimes uses the term "inference" (*sullogismos*) to refer to the more formal notion of logical deduction within an established framework of logical reasoning, he also uses it in a less formal sense, as in everyday reasoning from some truth claim to what follows from this.[16] Since in *Poetics* 4 he is describing a process of inference available to everyone, not just logicians, it must be a process of informal reasoning that is engaged when someone views a picture.

Further, since the mental process Aristotle is describing involves reasoning, it is a rational process: it involves giving reasons that lead to a certain conclusion. As Malcolm Heath notes, this means that the recognitions that imitations call for involve more than just identifying the subject by noting perceptual resemblances to a previously encountered object.[17] Aristotle is describing an activity of viewing the picture that engages the spectator in some sort of reasoning that involves the pleasure of learning (*manthanein*).

We can understand the mental process of recognizing the painting as an imitation of a cat as reasoning out the similarities and differences between the figure in the painting and cats we have previously experienced. The figure in the picture has four paws, whiskers, a tail, is furry, and so on. These features are like the other cats that the viewer has experienced. On the other hand, the figure in the picture is different than other cats the viewer has seen. For the former is flat and two-dimensional, and is missing the details that one perceives when one sees a cat in real life. The real life cats one has seen, on the other hand, are three-dimensional and have a number of features that are omitted in the picture of the cat.

There is understanding and learning involved in this process of reasoning out the similarities and differences. For the viewer needs to mobilize her concept of a cat as she discerns likenesses between the figure in the painting and the cats she is familiar with. Her reasoning involves her looking for what is common to both the figure in the painting and the cats she has known. She reasons:

> This figure reminds me of cats I have previously met. Is it really a picture of a cat? A cat is an animal with such and such features., e.g. a tail, whiskers, four paws. The figure in the painting has these features, just like the cats I have known. Therefore, that (figure in the painting) is this (a cat or an instance of the concept "Cat.").

This discussion of the pleasure in a work as an imitation has established an important point: Aristotle holds that the pleasure in a work *as* an imitation is a cognitive one. It involves a mental process in which the viewer reasons out the similarities and differences between the imitation and the original, and in the process takes delight in recognizing something familiar while also learning and understanding about the subject that is imitated.

Schematically, the process in which a viewer contemplates an image of a cat can be broken down as follows:

1) The viewer *recognizes* that the figure in the painting is familiar to her: it resembles cats she has seen.
2) Drawing on her *memories* of previous cats, the viewer notes certain similarities and differences between the figure and her retained past experiences of cats.
3) The observation of similarities and differences prompts the viewer to *reason* out that the figure is a cat by drawing on her concept of a cat as an animal with such and such features.

It should be clear why this process involves reasoning and inference. It is less obvious why the process involves learning and understanding (*manthanein*). Aristotle is part of a tradition in ancient Greek philosophy, starting with the pre-Socratic philosopher, Xenophanes and then later Plato, according to which there is a difference between true belief and knowledge or understanding.[18] Knowledge involves more than having a correct belief that something is the case. It involves an account or explanation of the reasons *why* something is the case. In *Poetics* 4 Aristotle makes the point that even the elementary process of recognizing a figure in an imitation as a cat involves understanding, for the viewer needs to give an account or explanation of the reasons why the figure is an imitation of a cat, in spite of the differences between the imitation and the original.

THE DEBATE AROUND "UNDERSTAND AND INFER" IN *POETICS* 4

At this point in the argument, in *Poetics* 4, Aristotle is concerned only to illustrate the pleasure in learning from imitations that is available to everyone (1448b13–15). At least this is how I am reading the argument, and here I am in agreement with other commentators such as Jonathan Lear, G. F. Ferrari, Malcolm Heath, and Pierre Destrée.[19] An alternative interpretation is possible and should be noted here. Stephen Halliwell has been a strong advocate for the view that in *Poetics* 4 Aristotle is talking about more than an elementary process of recognition and reasoning.[20] Halliwell agrees with Martha Nussbaum, who argues that in *Poetics* 4, "Aristotle is here speaking very generally of human delight, at all ages, in works of art of many types."[21] Halliwell develops this point by arguing that in *Poetics* 4 the relevant sense of "understand and infer" is a philosophical reasoning out about the causes of the subject that is imitated.[22]

Halliwell's interpretation of *Poetics* 4 is disputed and has been the subject of much debate. The discussion has centered around whether or not the process Aristotle describes of "understanding and inferring" from a precisely rendered image is intended to be an *elementary* process of learning that is available to *everyone*. Jonathan Lear and G. R. F. Ferrari argue that *Poetics* 4 is confined to describing the most elementary learning ("this is a picture of a cat") from elementary works of art and it is meant to describe a cognitive process that is available to everyone. Ferrari uses this interpretation of *Poetics* 4 to support his larger interpretation of the *Poetics* that the pleasure that we take in fiction is not the pleasure of learning. Lear argues that because the learning described in *Poetics* 4 is cognitively trivial, it cannot sustain the view that pleasure in tragedy is a species of cognitive pleasure.

On the other hand, Heath, while agreeing with Lear and Ferrari that *Poetics* 4 is examining the pleasure in learning available to everyone, argues that in *Poetics* 4 Aristotle does not *limit* the sort of learning that is available from imitative art. Rather Aristotle examines the elementary processes of recognition involved in grasping an image so as to better understand the cognitive underpinnings that are the basis for a range of possibilities, from more simple to more sophisticated forms of recognition and understanding when engaging with works of art.[23]

Halliwell maintains that there is an implicit reference to a *philosophical* concept of "understanding and inferring" at play in *Poetics* 4. This reading of *Poetics* 4 secures Halliwell's larger reading of the *Poetics* according to which poetry imparts a quasi-philosophical understanding of the causes, reasons, motives, and intelligible patterns of human life.[24]

Halliwell's argument is quite complex, but there are several central points he makes. First, there is a linguistic point: in *Poetics* 4, the terms "understand and infer" (*manthanein kai sullogizesthai*) are used to describe the mental process involved in recognizing the subject of an image. Halliwell argues that in *Poetics* 4 and elsewhere Aristotle uses these terms in connection with the deep learning about causes that Aristotle associates with philosophers.

Second, Halliwell argues that there are passages outside of the *Poetics* that can illuminate the point that the pleasure in viewing described in *Poetics* 4 is meant to encompass the pleasure that philosophers take in a deeper and weightier sort of understanding.

First, we can consider Halliwell's linguistic point. While Aristotle mentions the pleasure in learning and understanding that philosophers take, he stresses that learning is not pleasant only to philosophers. He echoes the point made in the opening lines of *Metaphysics* 1.1 that all human beings desire to learn, though he adds that non-philosophers have a smaller share in it, meaning that their learning is more rudimentary than grasping the final and pure causes of things in the universe (*Poetics* 4.1448b13).

The aim of the passage is then to explain the learning that is available to all, philosophers and ordinary folk alike, which accounts for why Aristotle uses the simple recognition of a figure in a picture.[25] His point is one made by Malcolm Heath, that the mental process involved in such an elementary identification is an intellectual and cognitive process, for it involves justifying the insight that the figure is of a certain subject through a process of reasoning and understanding that can take either simple or complex forms. In some respects, a picture of a cat does not really closely resemble a cat at all for, for example, the picture is two-dimensional while the real life cat is three-dimensional, the picture is 25 pounds, while the cat is 12 pounds, and so on. There are certain points of similarity as well. By grasping these common features, the viewer mobilizes her understanding of "cat" and then reasons her way to the conclusion that the subject of the picture is a cat as follows: "cats have whiskers, a tail, a furry coat, paws and so does the figure in the picture. Therefore, the subject is a cat."[26]

Second, Halliwell argues that several other texts contain related lines of thought that support the view that the learning at issue in *Poetics* 4 encompasses the more sophisticated philosophical learning that is made possible by more complex forms of art.[27] For example, he considers *Parts of Animals* (1.5.645a7–15), discussed above, where a contrast is made between things that fail to please the senses, vile looking animals, and the pleasure that philosophers take in being able to discern the organization and unity that is found in such creatures. Contemplating the structure of these animals is a source of pleasure for those who are able to discern the explanation of why the parts are organized and function as they do (*PA* 1.5.64a15). Likewise, contemplating the organization and structure of the likeness of such animals in painting and sculpture is also a source of pleasure, owing to the skill of the artists. Halliwell concludes the point of the analogy may be to suggest that mimetic artists also provide pleasure by offering some insight into the causes of the parts of the animals.[28]

This conclusion does not seem to follow. Halliwell acknowledges that in the *PA* passage Aristotle does not say that the pleasure a viewer takes in a sculpture or painting of a vile looking animal is traced to a philosophical pleasure in causes. The evidence is just too weak in the passage to support the view that the pleasure viewers take in the skill of the artist derives from a philosophical understanding of why the parts of the animal depicted are organized as they are. It is more reasonable to instead interpret the passage as speaking about the pleasure in form and organizational structure, as discussed above, rather than assimilate this pleasure to the pleasure in a work *as* an imitation.

To elaborate, as Halliwell observes, Aristotle often makes an analogy between art (*technē*) and nature.[29] Both art and nature are: (1) teleological or goal-directed; and (2) involve the imposition of a form or structure on matter. Painting and sculpture are examples of art (*technē*), an activity in which a person with knowledge, the artist, imposes a form, a structure, on some matter so as to realize some end (e.g. the making of a house for shelter). Natural processes also involve the imposition of some form on some matter, for example the shaping of some matter so that it takes on the species form of a frog and is able to develop into an adult member of the species.

The mimetic artist's goal is to bring the viewer's attention to a form and organization in some subject, for example an animal. In doing so she distills the animal to certain basic or essential features, enabling the viewer to contemplate them. This highlighting of structure or form is something that mimetic art has in common with the philosophers' activity of discerning the organization and structure of an animal so as to understand its causes and how it works. While there is a loss of detail, for example, in a painting of a vile looking animal, it is this loss of detail that makes it possible for the viewer to recognize the form that is shared by the representation and its subject. The artist's focus on making evident a form or structure in the animal is something like the attention to organization and structure that the philosopher brings with her as she contemplates the structure of the animal, as the analogy in the *Parts of Animals* passage indicates.

Still, Aristotle does not say that the form or structure that the artist imposes on matter is the *same* form or structure that the scientist or philosopher studies. The painter or sculptor, after all, is not a scientist or philosopher. There are similarities between the mimetic artist and the philosopher in that both are concerned with something more universal and general. In this sense, mimetic art and philosophy share a similar concern with form and structure.

In the *Parts of Animals* passage, Aristotle does not assimilate the pleasure in the skill of the artist to the philosophical pleasure in grasping the ultimate causes of natural phenomena; rather, he distinguishes them. He argues *if* one takes a pleasure in grasping the organization of parts in a painting of a vile appearing animal, then the pleasures of a philosophical understanding of the causes of the animal and its parts will be even more rewarding. The implication is that philosophy is sure to give the philosophically inclined observer a greater insight into the workings and pure causes of nature than painting or sculpture. This is no surprise, as painters and sculptors need not do the work of philosophers!

Taking all these points together, it follows that while both the mimetic artist and the philosopher are interested in the form and structure of things, this does not mean that the imitative artist (e.g. painter or sculptor) is doing the work of the philosopher in searching for the final causes of things in the universe.

To return to the *Poetics*, how does this conclusion bear on *Poetics* 4? The viewer who grasps the likeness between the image of a cat and the cats she has encountered may do so in virtue of grasping a shared form or structure that the painting of the cat makes evident. The form or structure in the painting may facilitate the mimetic pleasure she takes in recognizing and understanding that the image is a likeness of a cat. But this does not mean that the mimetic works, more generally, are like

philosophy in providing an understanding of the causal principles that philosophy articulates.

At the same time, there is a good reason that *Poetics* 4 mentions that understanding gives delight to both philosophers and
others (4.1448b112–15). For the viewer who reasons out that
the figure in the picture is an imitation of a cat has some small
share of the understanding that philosophers seek.[30] The simple recognition of a figure as an imitation of a cat, Aristotle is
saying, calls on the same cognitive process of reasoning and
understanding that a philosopher seeks when she attempts to
understand the ultimate causes of living things.[31] Thus, appreciating something *as* an imitation involves the pleasure of
learning (4.1448b12–17). This point is secured by the argument
of *Poetics* 4 and the door is left open that more complex forms of
imitative art call for more complex and sophisticated forms of
understanding and learning.[32]

MIMETIC ART AS A KNOWLEDGE-SEEKING ACTIVITY

The argument of *Poetics* 4 is, then, that even the most uncomplicated forms of imitative art call for an intellectual process of
recognition and understanding.[33] For to delight in the work, *as*
an imitation (*mimēsis*) the viewer must not only recognize *that*
the portrait is an imitation of a cat. She must also draw on her
understanding of the features that comprise a cat as she reasons
her way to the conclusion: "This is a picture of a cat."

The viewer need not have the understanding of "Cat" that
a scientist has, science (*epistēmē*) being a knowledge-seeking
activity that, like philosophy, searches out knowledge of the
first causes of things, for its own sake. While the viewer may,
for example, correctly recognize that the figure in the picture is
a cat, and she may identify features that belong to all cats, for
example whiskers, four paws, tail, fur, and so on, not all of these
may be features that science reveals as essential, defining traits
of the species cat.

Nonetheless, Aristotle stresses that the person who exercises her understanding of cats to identify the subject in the picture is engaging in the same general kind of process of reasoning and understanding that philosophers do, but at a more elementary level. This is why he says: "understanding gives great pleasure not only to philosophers but likewise to others too, though the latter have a smaller share in it" (4.1448b13). It follows that *all* forms of imitative art are opportunities for learning and understanding. For the ability to reason out, even at a rudimentary level, the ways in which the image of a cat is similar to and different from cats the viewer has seen before is essential to the pleasure the viewer takes in the image *as* an imitation.

Aristotle's view that the pleasure in imitation is the pleasure in understanding can be usefully contrasted with those of the character Socrates in Plato's *Republic* 10 (595a–608b). Like Aristotle, Socrates also uses an example from the visual arts to illustrate his view about the nature of imitation. Socrates also operates with a view that a painting is an imitation of some reality, but by this he means that it is a copy of the appearance of a sensible particular. The problem is that appearances are misleading:

> The mimetic art is far removed from truth, and this, it seems, is the reason why it can produce everything, because it touches or lays hold of only a small part of the object and that a phantom, as for example, a painter, we say, will paint us a cobbler, a carpenter and other craftsmen, though he himself has no expertness in any of these arts, but nevertheless if he were a good painter, by exhibiting at a distance his picture of a carpenter he would deceive children and foolish men, and make them believe it to be a real carpenter.
>
> (*Republic* 10.598b; Hamilton and Cairns 1961)

If we think, as Socrates does, that a painting just reproduces the appearance of some sensible thing, we can see why he worries that it just lays hold of a "small part" of the object. Appearances are partial and incomplete when we are trying to understand the object as a whole. A painter might depict how a bed looks, for example, from one perspective, but this will not give the "big picture" of how the bed looks from all angles. From Plato's perspective, sensible objects are just poor imitations of the true objects of knowledge, the Forms, which are immaterial, eternal objects whose stability and constancy suit them to be the proper objects of knowledge. The unchanging nature of the Forms enables us to have true knowledge of them, in contrast to the nature of sensible objects that are subject to decay and do not present a constancy in appearance. Knowledge of the Forms is accessed through the intellect, according to the Platonic view that Socrates develops. So it is a futile attempt for a viewer to get knowledge of reality by looking at a painting that inevitably operates at the level of sensation and not by engaging the viewer's intellect.

Aristotle has several major disagreements with Socrates' arguments.

First, Aristotle is an empiricist. He agrees that knowledge is of something that is universal, "Cat" or "Human Being" rather than this particular cat or that particular human being. But according to his metaphysics, or account of the nature of reality, the universals that are the proper objects of knowledge do not exist separate from the sensible particulars that exemplify them. He thinks that by studying particular sensible things, for example particular cats, we can come to understand the common form or species (*eidos*) that they all share. He would not, therefore, be concerned that the sensible representations in an image can lead the viewer away from knowledge, for the delight that all humans take in sensation is the starting point for a deeper understanding of the world.[34]

Second, Socrates raises the worry that mimetic art can deceive some viewers, so that, for example, a foolish person at a distance might confuse a picture of a carpenter for a carpenter. Unlike Socrates, Aristotle is not worried that a painting of a cat will take in and deceive the viewer. If it were to deceive a small child, for example, it would not give pleasure as an imitation. For the pleasure in a work of mimetic art requires recognizing that the work *is* an imitation of some original (4.1448b18). In relating the imitation to the subject imitated, the viewer needs to differentiate the two (e.g. the picture is two-dimensional, a real life cat is three-dimensional) and reason out the differences.

This point is brought out especially well by Aristotle's discussion of the delight the viewer takes in a picture of a vile looking animal or corpse (*Poetics* 1448b9–12). To take pleasure in such an image, the viewer needs to, on the one hand, relate the image to the original, but also, on the other hand, differentiate it, or she will feel the same revulsion towards the image that she has to the original. The pleasure in a work, as an imitation, will therefore be nullified if the viewer is deceived to the point where she takes the image for the original.[35]

Third, the crux of Socrates' argument is that painting and poetry are imitations of the appearance of things, and appearances are misleading and not a proper object of knowledge. Aristotle disagrees that what an image of a cat imitates is the sensible appearance of a cat. Instead, the painting imitates a sensible object, a particular cat that is the embodiment of a universal or kind, Cat. The way in which we come to know about the universals is, indeed, through the sense perception of particulars that exemplify them. If we come to have knowledge of universals via the sense perception of particulars that embody them, then there is no reason to think that representations of sensible objects must necessarily lead us away from knowledge of the universals that are the proper objects of knowledge.

Aristotle's comparison between art (*technē*) and nature suggest that the artist works by imposing some form or structure on matter, and this is also, as we saw in the *Parts of Animals* passage, true of the mimetic artist as well. In the case of a simple picture of a cat, this form might be something as simple as the outline of the figure of a cat (see *Poetics* 6.1450a37). It is not correct, then, to say that the artist reproduces the appearance or look of the cat from a certain perspective. Art aims to reveal something more universal, a common structure, form or pattern that gives shape to human experience. This point will be central to the argument of the Poetics, as Aristotle turns his to attention to the way in which the plot organizes and reveals a unified and coherent pattern of human action.

Aristotle's concern, then, in *Poetics* 4.1448b3–19 is to explain how the pleasure in even the most elementary form of imitation involves a recognition and understanding. There is a sense, however, in which Halliwell's view that *Poetics* 4 is talking about more than just the pleasure in learning found in recognizing a figure in a picture can be vindicated. For if there is pleasure in learning to be found even in the elementary recognitions of a figure in a picture, we can see how more complicated forms of mimetic art, that call forth more complicated processes of recognition and reasoning, can also provide some kind of pleasurable understanding.

In other words, the argument in *Poetics* 4 that there is a pleasurable understanding available in the most rudimentary forms of mimetic art secures the more general point that the pleasure in a work, as a *mimēsis*, may involve the pleasure of recognition and understanding. This is not to say that the pleasure in more complex forms of mimetic art, such as tragedy, can simply be *reduced* to the generic pleasure in learning that is available in all forms of imitation. The emotional experience is essential to producing the distinctive pleasure in tragedy (*Poetics* 24.1453b10–11). Still, this observation does not undermine the point that all forms of mimetic works offer a cognitive pleasure, for they are the occasions for the viewer or audience to reason out the similarities and differences between the subject of the work and the original.

Indeed, Aristotle makes the point that poetry, as well as other forms of mimetic art, engage the viewer in a process of recognition, reasoning, and understanding:

> Since learning and wondering are pleasant, it follows that such things as acts of imitation must be pleasant—for instance, painting, sculpture, poetry—and every product of skillful imitation; this latter, even if the object imitated is not itself pleasant; for it is not the object itself that here gives delight; the spectator draws inferences (*sullogismos*) ("That is a so-and-so") and thus learns (*manthanein*) something.
>
> (*Rhetoric* 1.1371b4–10; Barnes 1984 Vol. Two)

This passage in *Rhetoric* 1.1 is a parallel passage to *Poetics* 4 in that it says that the mimetic arts more generally prompt the pleasure of learning (*manthanein*) through having the viewer draw inferences ("that is a so-and-so").

While it is clear that Aristotle holds that all forms of mimetic art, including poetry, prompt the audience to engage in a process of reasoning out and understanding, it is less clear exactly what he might mean in saying that the audiences for these works learn something. This problem can be seen by considering the case of a simple recognition of a figure in a picture. What is it that the viewer who looks at a picture of a cat in a painting learns that he did not already know before? He must have some idea of what a cat is and/or have experience with particular cats in order to grasp that the subject of the work is a cat. This viewer *mobilizes* her understanding of "Cat" to identify the figure as a cat. In what sense does the viewer of the painting learn something about cats that he did not know before? Applying this point more generally: if a work of mimetic art calls upon the audience to relate the work to something previously known and familiar to them, how does the audience learn something new?

FROM RECOGNITION TO FRESH UNDERSTANDING

In general, there is no problem with understanding on Aristotle's account of knowledge how an inquiry might presuppose as well as advance our understanding of something. In *Posterior Analytics* 1.1 Aristotle says, "All teaching and all intellectual learning come about from already existing knowledge."[36] By this he means understanding must start from somewhere; it does not just begin from scratch.

If one inquires into what virtue is, for example, one must at least start with some examples of virtue that are brought together in one's experience, and then refine one's understanding to arrive at a more proper understanding of the boundaries of the concept. Otherwise, one ends up with the paradox of inquiry made famous in Plato's *Meno*: inquiry into some subject x becomes either pointless or futile.[37] If one knows all about a subject, x, then there is no point in inquiring into it and if one knows nothing about x, then an investigation into x is futile, for you will not even be able to recognize that which you seek.

Aristotle addresses this problem by arguing there are degrees and different levels of understanding:

> Nothing, I think, prevents one from in a sense understanding and in a sense being ignorant of what one is learning: for what is absurd is not that you should know in some sense what you are learning, but that you should know it in *this* sense, i.e. in the way and sense in which you are learning it.
>
> (*Posterior Analytics* 1.1.71b6–9)

Viewed from the perspective of Aristotle's theory of knowledge, then, there is no problem in understanding how a work of mimetic art presupposes some knowledge of the subject, but can end up transforming and advancing the audience's understanding of it as well.

How might Aristotle think that when we view imitative art, our knowledge gets transformed or deepened? One suggestion for how this can happen is found in *Rhetoric* 3.10, where Aristotle discusses metaphors, a topic he also discusses in the *Poetics*.[38] In that text Aristotle discusses how Homer in *Odyssey* XIV 213 conveys learning with the use of a metaphor. This text is, therefore, a useful parallel passage for understanding the argument in *Rhetoric* 1.1 that the mimetic arts, more generally, engage the audience in learning something through a process of reasoning and understanding.

Metaphors involve a comparison between two distinct things in which there is transference of meaning from one term to a second term, thereby facilitating recognition of a likeness. Aristotle thinks that metaphors also prompt, "This is that" reasoning in which the reader searches for the common notion that unites the two terms (*Rhetoric* 3.10.1410b18). Aristotle considers an example of metaphor in Homer's *Odyssey* in which Odysseus, now an older man after his long travels, compares himself to a "withered stalk":

> Now strange words simply puzzle us: ordinary words convey what we know already: it is from metaphor that we can best get ahold of something fresh. When the poet calls old age "a withered stalk," he conveys a new idea, a new fact, to us by means of the general notion of "lost bloom," which is common to both things.
>
> (*Rhetoric* 3.10.1410b12–15)

Homer's metaphor prompts the viewer to search for and reason out the larger group or kind that is common to old age and a withered stalk, "lost bloom."

Lost Bloom (common grouping)
Withered Stalk   Old Age

The listener must already be familiar with the concept of "old age" or otherwise the metaphor would have no meaning for her. But the metaphor deepens her understanding of what old age is because it gives her a new orientation or point of view on it.

If the answer to the search is obvious and "plain to everyone," then the pleasure is diminished. On the other hand, the search for the common thread in a metaphor should, Aristotle says, be neither too long, nor too hard to grasp; nor should it be too superficial or teach nothing. Metaphors whose meaning comes at once or a little later, after some reflection, are the ones that provide knowledge.[39]

Metaphor, then, involves a "this is that" inference in which there is pleasure in learning something new, provided that this learning is not too difficult and does not take too long to acquire.

Aristotle's discussion of metaphor is a useful parallel to the process described in *Poetics* 4 of recognizing a figure in a painting.[40] As we see with the example of Homer's metaphor, the process of reasoning and understanding may mobilize a previously acquired concept while also transforming it by giving us a new perspective on it. This new understanding is available even in an elementary work of imitation, for while a painting of a cat is an imitation of a particular cat, it requires the viewer to grasp something more general and more abstract, a form that is common to the cat in the painting and cats the viewer has previously encountered. This has the potential to deepen the viewer's understanding of cats by requiring her to call upon and apply what she already knows to the situation.

CONCLUSION: THE PLEASURE IN IMITATION AS IMITATION

What can we conclude then about what *Poetics* 4 is saying about the nature of the pleasure in learning from imitations? Aristotle uses the example of an elementary recognition of a figure in a painting to emphasize the point that even the most uncomplicated work of mimetic art, such as a painting of a cat, engages the viewer in a rational process in which she infers a correspondence between the figure in the work and the object that is imitated on the basis of similarities and differences. The process of recognition of a figure in a painting is a source of pleasurable understanding, because the viewer must mobilize and apply her understanding of what it is to be a cat as she reasons her way to the identification of the figure in the painting.

If there is pleasurable understanding available in the most elementary forms of imitation, the general point is secured that all works of imitation, even those of vile and unpleasant looking things, offer the pleasure of understanding. Because all humans, by their very nature, desire to know and take pleasure in doing so, the argument in *Poetics* 4 establishes the point with which we started the chapter: the pleasure in imitations has its origins in our nature as human beings.

Pleasure, Aristotle says, is the unimpeded exercise of a natural capacity in human beings, such as sense perception or reasoning

(*Nicomachean Ethics* 7.12.1153a10 and 10.4.1174b23–33). Works of mimetic art are pleasurable, then, because they call on the audience to exercise the natural functions and capacities of a human being. The unimpeded, perfect exercise of these natural capacities is a source of pleasure. Given that all forms of *mimēsis* provide the opportunity for the audience to exercise natural capacities such as sense perception, understanding, and reasoning, it is understandable that humans would engage in these activities from an early age.

The argument of *Poetics* 4, therefore, brings to light an important contrast between the *Poetics* and the way in which an influential strand in modern (seventeenth–twentieth century) philosophy has thought about the pleasure available from works of art. In the eighteenth century Alexander Baumgarten coined the term "aesthetic" (from the Greek word *aisthēsis*, sense perception) to refer to the experience of beauty and sensory pleasure available in works of art and in nature.

The notion that works of art offer a distinct and special sort of experience, *aesthetic* experience, became the focus of philosophers' attention and a new field of philosophical inquiry, aesthetics, was born. Along with the notion of the aesthetic came the idea that the experience of a work of art is valuable "for its own sake" and not as a means to some further end. This led to the school of thought according to which art is separate from and autonomous from life, and we should seek it out because it offers a distinctive kind of experience, separate from the experiences we have in our daily lives.

More recently, philosophers of art have argued against the autonomy of art and life, arguing instead that the experiences works of art offer are in an important respect continuous with those available in real life.[41] Their arguments center on the idea that mimetic arts, arts that aim to represent life-like human situations and predicaments, draw on the same psychological and cognitive capacities, such as the ability to comprehend a narrative, that human beings exercise in their daily lives.

Aristotle is very much an intellectual ancestor of this more recent trend in philosophy of art. Works of mimetic art are pleasurable because they enable the viewer to exercise the natural capacities that human beings put into effect in their daily lives. This point is brought out in the discussion of the pleasures of imitations in *Poetics* 4 and is evident in the characterization of *mimēsis* in Chapter 2 as an artifact or behavior that elicits and then completes or perfects some of the natural effects that could be produced by experiencing something in real life.

The pleasures, then, that are available from works of imitation are multiple and diverse. There is the pleasure we take in the exercise of the senses: pleasures in the sounds, sights, and rhythms of music and dance, and the recitation of rhythmic verse in various forms of poetry. Works of imitation offer the pleasure in craftsmanship, which is the pleasure of recognizing that the parts of the work are organized into a discernible whole. But the pleasure that gets special attention in *Poetics* 4 is the pleasure in the work *as* an imitation, and this pleasure is linked to the recognition and understanding that all works of imitation, even the most elementary ones, provide.

NOTES

1 Reading for this chapter is *Poetics* 4. Recommended texts: *Metaphysics* 1.1; *Parts of Animals* 1.5.645a4–26.
2 See Noël Carroll 2005; Denis Dutton 2010; Stephen Davies 2013; and the essays in Elisabeth Schellekens and Peter Goldie 2013.
3 *Politics* 1.1.1253a1–18.
4 As Malcolm Heath notes (2009: 62), this implies that other animals also imitate.
5 *History of Animals* 8.12.597b23–29 and 9.1.609b14–18.
6 Compare Aristotle's argument in *Nicomachean Ethics* 1.7 that reason is the function that uniquely characterizes human beings and therefore, being rational is the final end or purpose of humanity.
7 For an analysis of *mimēsis* as a form of make believe, see K. L. Walton 1990, especially Chapter One.
8 I have added (a)–(e) into the text to facilitate the breakdown of Aristotle's argument.
9 *Metaphysics* 1.1.980a23–27.

10 *Physics* 2.8.199a11–15.
11 For example, Monroe Beardsley (1967: 167) understands a work of art's form as the organization of the elements of the work.
12 *Poetics* 7.1450b32–35.
13 For helpful discussions of the notion of form in modern aesthetics see Beardsley 1966: 363–364 and John Andrew Fisher 1993: 245–267.
14 See also Chapter 5 for a discussion of magnitude and beauty in the plots of tragedy and how this relates to the goal of the work.
15 See Aristotle's *De Memoria* 1.450b21–25 where he discusses the mental processes involved in recognizing that a painting is a picture of an animal and grasping it as an accurate likeness of an animal.
16 See, for example, later on in *Poetics* 25.1461b2.
17 Heath 2009: 10–11 and Heath 2013: 67–71.
18 Aristotle *Posterior Analytics* 1.33.
19 Jonathan Lear 1992: 322–323; G.R.F. Ferrari 1999: 184–188; Malcolm Heath 2009: 64–64; Malcolm Heath 2013: 67–71; and Pierre Destrée 2013: 10 and especially 11. I disagree, however, with Lear, Ferrari, and Destrée when they then conclude that the pleasure in works of mimetic art is not the pleasure in learning. My reasoning is made clear in what follows, and also see Chapter 11 where I engage more fully with their concerns.
20 See Stephen Halliwell 2002: 186–193; Stephen Halliwell 2003: 91–95; and Halliwell 1998: 70–74.
21 Nussbaum 1986: 388.
22 Halliwell 2002: 192.
23 Heath 2009: 73. As will become clear, I agree with Heath's reading of *Poetics* 4.
24 Halliwell 2002: 195.
25 As Heath observes, there are other places where Aristotle uses the term "*manthanein*" to denote the understanding that ordinary folk seek from imitations (see Heath 2009: 64). Indeed, in *Poetics* 4, Aristotle uses the term "*manthanein*" to refer to animal learning and to the learning experiences of children (4.1448b7f.). This means that when Aristotle uses the term "*manthanein*" he does necessarily mean to mark out the advanced learning about causes that philosophers seek.
26 Heath 2009: 62–68 and Heath 2013: 66–72.
27 Halliwell 1998: 74–77. This argument is also made in David Gallop 1990.
28 Halliwell 1998: 74.
29 See *Physics* 2.2.
30 See also James Redfield 1994: 53.
31 The continuum model is supported by Aristotle's comment that non-philosophers have a "smaller share" of understanding than philosophers (4.1448b14). See also James Redfield 1994: 52–53.
32 Here I am in essential agreement with Malcolm Heath's reading of *Poetics* 4, when he says that Aristotle's reasoning is that "it is not possible to understand the more cognitively sophisticated forms of engagement with poetry without acknowledging the elementary processes on which they rest" (2009: 73).

33 Heath 2009: 62–68; and Heath 2013: 66–72.
34 See *Metaphysics* 1.1.980aa23–28.
35 See also *Poetics* 24.1453b10–11.
36 *Posterior Analytics* 1.1.71a1.
37 *Posterior Analytics* 1.1.71a30.
38 For Aristotle's main account of metaphor in the *Poetics* see 21.1457b7–32 and 22.1459a6f. For the difference between metaphor and simile see *Rhetoric* 3.10.1410b15–24. For a useful discussion of metaphor in the *Poetics* and *Rhetoric* see Fran O'Rourke 2006.
39 *Rhetoric* 3.10.1410b24–25.
40 This point is noted in Malcolm Heath 2009: 65–66.
41 See especially Noël Carroll 2005 and the essays in Schellekens and Goldie 2012.

WORKS CITED

Barnes, Jonathan (ed.) 1984. *The Collected Works of Aristotle*. Volumes One and Two. Princeton, NJ: Princeton University Press.

Beardsley, Monroe 1966. *Aesthetics from Classical Greece to the Present*. New York: Macmillan.

_____ 1967. *Aesthetics*. New Haven, CT: Yale University Press.

Carroll, Noël 2005. "Art and Human Nature." *Journal of Aesthetics and Art Criticism* 62 (2): 95–107.

Davies, Stephen 2013. *The Artful Species: Aesthetics, Art and Evolution*. Oxford: Oxford University Press.

Destrée, Pierre 2013. "Aristotle and the Paradox of Tragic Pleasure," in Jerrold Levinson (ed.), *Suffering Art Gladly*. Basingstoke: Palgrave Macmillan: 3–27.

Dutton, Denis 2010. *The Art Instinct: Beauty, Pleasure and Human Evolution*. London: Bloomsbury Press.

Ferrari, G. R. G. 1999. "Aristotle's Literary Aesthetics." *Phronesis* 45 (13): 181–198.

Fisher, John Andrew 1993. *Reflecting on Art*. Mountain View, CA: Mayfield Publishing Company.

Gallop, David 1990. "Animals in the *Poetics*." *Oxford Studies in Ancient Philosophy* 8: 145–171.

Halliwell, Stephen 1998. *Aristotle's Poetics: With a New Introduction by the Author*. Chicago: University of Chicago Press.

_____ 2002. *The Aesthetics of Mimesis: Ancient Texts and Modern Problems*. Princeton, NJ: Princeton University Press.

_____ 2003. "Aristotelian Mimesis and Human Understanding," in Øivind Andersen and Jon Haarber (eds.), *Making Sense of Aristotle: Essays in Poetics*. London: Duckworth: 87–108.

Hamilton, E. and H. Cairns (eds.) 1961. *The Collected Dialogues of Plato*. Princeton, NJ: Princeton University Press.

Heath, Malcolm 2009. "Cognition in Aristotle's *Poetics*." *Mnemosyne* 62 (1): 51–75.

_____ 2013. *Ancient Philosophical Poetics*. Cambridge: Cambridge University Press.

Lear, Jonathan 1992. "*Katharsis*," in Amélie Oskenberg Rorty (ed.), *Essays on Aristotle's Poetics*. Princeton, NJ: Princeton University Press: 315–340.

Nussbaum, Martha 1986. *The Fragility of Goodness: Luck and Ethics in Ancient Greek Tragedy and Philosophy*. Cambridge: Cambridge University Press.

O'Rourke, Fran 2006. "Aristotle and the Metaphysics of Metaphor." *Proceedings of the Boston Area Colloquium of Ancient Philosophy* 21 (1): 155–190.

Redfield, James 1994. *Nature and Culture in the Iliad*. Durham, NC and London: Duke University Press.

Schellekens, Elisabeth and Peter Goldie 2012. *The Aesthetic Mind: Philosophy and Psychology*. Oxford: Oxford University Press.

Walton, Kendall 1990. *Mimesis and Make-Believe. On the Foundations of the Representational Arts*. Cambridge, MA: Harvard University Press.

RECOMMENDED READING

Rorty, Amélie Oskenberg 1992. "The Psychology of Aristotelian Tragedy," in Rorty (ed.), *Essays on Aristotle's Poetics*. Princeton, NJ: Princeton University Press: 1–22.

Wolff, Francis 2007. "The Three Pleasures of Mimēsis According to Aristotle's *Poetics*," in Bernadette Bensaude-Vincent and William R. Newman (eds.), *The Artificial and the Natural: An Evolving Polarity*. Cambridge, MA: The MIT Press: 51–66.

5

TRAGEDY DEFINED

INTRODUCTION: HISTORICAL ORIGINS AND PHILOSOPHICAL INTEREST[1]

Although the opening of the *Poetics* promises to talk of poetry "in general," tragedy is the central focus of most of the work, showing Aristotle's high regard for the genre.[2] Tragedy, in Aristotle's view, encompasses the achievements of the other poetic forms, but surpasses them in what it accomplishes. Tragedy (*tragōidia*, meaning "goat song")[3] derived from the dithyramb, a processional and choral lyric performance in honor of the god Dionysus, that was enacted in a circular arena, known as the orchestra, where the chorus acted, danced, and sang.[4] Prior to the development of tragedy and comedy, there was an earlier innovation in which the choral leader became the first actor (*hupocritēs*, the source for the English word "hypocrite"), a figure who answered questions from the chorus, thus making dialogue possible (4.1449a1–19). Tragedy and comedy may then have emerged out of dithyramb and phallic songs by retaining the chorus, but advancing the earlier innovation through Aeschylus' increase of actors from one to two (4.1449a18; 4.1449a24), followed by Sophocles' introduction of three actors and scene painting (4.1449a19). This introduction of a second and then third actor substantially reduced the role of the chorus. When tragedy emerged out of the dithyramb, the content of tragedy was widened to include themes from the old myths about gods and heroes.

The fifth century BCE is the age of classical Greek tragedy and although it is thought that numerous plays were produced, only the tragedies of three playwrights, Aeschylus, Sophocles, and Euripides, remain, with only seven complete plays of the first two poets remaining and eighteen complete tragedies of Euripides left.[5] Aristotle says that there is a natural appropriateness of meter to a poetic genre, and tragedy came into its own nature when it introduced a meter, iambic trimeter, that has the rhythm of ordinary speech (4.1449a23–25).

Philosophers have a long history of being interested in tragedy. One reason is that tragedy is thought to reveal some deep insight about the human condition, for it shows the role that luck and necessity play in a human life, leading to unsettling reversals of fortune in which characters must, nevertheless, try to do the best they can. Tragedy can reveal truths to us about human nature because it shows the possibilities for a human life, and so offers some insight about the human condition.[6] A second source of interest in tragedy is the thought that it offers a distinctive sort of experience. Aristotle marks this out by referring to the idea that the poet should "create the pleasure which comes from pity and fear through mimesis."[7] Tragedy has, therefore, attracted the attention of philosophers because (a) it seems to offer the opportunity for learning important truths about our lives; and (b) it offers a distinctive emotional experience.

Aristotle talks about tragedy having evolved for a certain end, the realization of its nature (*phusis*):

> When it [tragedy] came into being from an improvisational origin . . . it was gradually enhanced as poets developed the potential they saw in it. And after going through many changes tragedy ceased to evolve, since it had reached its own nature.

(*Poetics* 4.1449a8–15)

Yet, there is some confusion as to the end for which tragedy evolved. Is it to be a source of learning? Is it to provide a *catharsis* of pity and fear, as the famous definition of tragedy in *Poetics* 6 suggests?[8] Or is it to give a distinctive sort of experience, "the pleasure which comes from pity and fear through *mimēsis*"?[9] To answer these questions, we must examine the definition of tragedy in *Poetics* 6, consider the disputed notion of *catharsis* that figures in that definition, as well as examine the emotional experience tragedy provides and consider how or if the viewer learns from tragedy. These tasks will be the focus of this chapter and several that follow.

POETICS 6: DEFINING TRAGEDY

Aristotle's practice is to offer an adequate definition of the subject of inquiry, since a sound definition helps to understand what a thing is, in its essential nature. So, in *Poetics* 6, Aristotle offers a definition of tragedy that pulls together his earlier remarks as well as identifies the effect of tragedy, bringing about a *catharsis* of pity and fear:

> Tragedy, then, is a *mimēsis* of an action that is elevated, complete, and of magnitude; in language embellished in distinct forms in its sections; employing the mode of enactment and not narrative; and through pity and fear accomplishing the *catharsis* of such emotions.

(6.1449b24–28)[10]

Tragedy					
Imitation (*mimēsis*) of an action that is:					
Serious	Complete	Magnitude	Embellished language	Dramatic mode	*Catharsis* of pity and fear

Some definitions:

Serious: action that is admirable or good.

Complete: a plot that has a beginning, middle, and end and is unified by necessary or probable connections.

Magnitude: the size of the plot that enables it to follow through the necessary or probable consequences of an action to its natural completion, in a way that allows for a change from good fortune to bad or the reverse (6.1451a15).

Embellished language: words with rhythm, melody, and song.

Dramatic mode: the story is enacted by performers rather than recited by a narrator.

Catharsis of pity and fear: literally, the cleansing, purification, or purgation of the emotions of pity and fear.

The concept in the definition of tragedy that has received the most critical attention in this definition is *catharsis*, largely because the term occurs at the end, the place in a definition that many think Aristotle reserves for the goal or final end of the thing being defined. Just what Aristotle means by "*catharsis*" is hotly debated. "*Catharsis*" is mentioned in just two places in the *Poetics*, but Aristotle offers no definition of it.[11] The most influential accounts of what Aristotle may mean by the term have followed the main root meanings of the it: purgation, cleansing, or purification. There are further debates about the objects of *catharsis:* is it the emotions of pity and fear, as we are lead to believe from the standard translations of the definition quoted above? Or is *catharsis* a purification or clarification of the pitiful and fear-inspiring incidents in the plot, as some have contended?

Sometimes discussions of the *Poetics'* account of tragedy start with *catharsis*, making this the centerpiece of Aristotle's analysis of tragedy. I will proceed a bit differently. Students do need to be familiar with the debates around the concept because it is so central to how many readers of the *Poetics* approach the work. But we will be in a better position to examine these disputes, and to draw our own conclusions about their significance, if we first get a handle on the other central concepts in the definition. At least, this is my operating assumption going forward. So we examine the debates about *catharsis* in Chapter 9, after we consider the other elements in Aristotle's definition of tragedy.

There is one thing that is, on Aristotle's view, an indisputable goal of tragedy. This is that tragedy evokes emotions, especially the emotions of pity and fear. Besides occurring in the definition of tragedy, Aristotle mentions elsewhere that tragedy is an imitation of an action that evokes pity and fear (*Poetics* 9.1452a2–3). Aristotle's ranking of tragic plots in *Poetics* 13 and 14 is based on the idea that to be good and proper tragedy, the characters and actions must evoke pity and fear (*Poetics* 13.1452b30–1453a8, b10–22). In addition, Aristotle says (in *Poetics* 14.1453b12–13) that the poet should "create the pleasure which comes from pity and fear through *mimēsis*." Aristotle clearly thinks that a goal of tragedy (if not *the* final goal) is to produce a certain psychological effect in the audience: to have experiences (*pathēmata*) of pity and fear. The terms used to define tragedy can, therefore, be understood in light of the broader goal of evoking this specific kind of emotional experience in the audience.

SERIOUS OR ADMIRABLE ACTION

Tragedy is an imitation of action and life (6.1450a19), but especially of action that is serious or admirable (*spoudaios*). An action is good provided that a good or admirable person performs the action.[12] This condition on tragic action, therefore, in part refers back to the point made in *Poetics* 2 that the characters in tragedy must be good or admirable, in contrast to the characters in comedy. In ancient Greek thinking, the *spoudaioi* are people who are outstanding in excellence (*arête*), where this refers both to a superior social standing as well as to excellence in the sense of moral virtue. Aristotle also refers to the admirable characters of tragedy in both the moral and the social sense. For example, the requirement that the characters of tragedy are admirable because they are morally virtuous is suggested at *Poetics* 2.1448a1–4, while the social sense is evident when Aristotle says (at *Poetics* 13.1453a7–12) that the ideal character of tragedy belongs to the class of those who are "illustrious men" and "enjoy great renown and prosperity."

Why does Aristotle think that tragedy should focus on the actions of morally good individuals? Tragedies show an assortment of agents striving for happiness, but then meeting with profound reversals of fortune: going from good fortune (*eutuchia*) to bad fortune (*dustuchia*), or the reverse (7.1451a13–14; 13.1452b35–37; 13.1453a13–14; 18.1455b27f.). To merit the audience's fear, the characters must be "like ourselves" (*Poetics* 13.1453a3–5), not in terms of social standing and wealth, but in that they are basically good and decent people. Further, pity is felt for the undeserving victim of adversity and fear is felt for "one like ourselves" (*Poetics* 13.1453a3–5). When the character is a morally good individual, who errs, but is not guilty of any grave moral failing, his change of fortune prompts pity, for his suffering is out of proportion to any error he commits.

It is harder to understand why it is characters that are people with "great good reputation and good fortune" that especially evoke pity and fear (*Poetics* 13.1453a10f.). One answer might be a deflationary one: such individuals, as a matter of fact, were the characters that featured in ancient Greek tragedy. Yet this cannot be the complete solution. For Aristotle is not simply describing the characters that did, as a matter of fact, feature in ancient Greek tragedy. His goal is normative: to prescribe the sorts of characters that *ought* to figure in tragedy if it is to accomplish its objective.[13] Aristotle does not think that money and social status equate with or constitute happiness (*eudaimonia*). A figure in tragedy will be happy or flourish depending on her actions, and actions in turn spring from a fixed and settled character (*Poetics* 6.1450a7). Further, when in *Rhetoric* 2.8, Aristotle explains the mental conditions under which we feel pity, he mentions a variety of evils, such as the loss of friends, lack of food, and bodily injuries, but he does not mention loss of riches or exalted social status (*Rhetoric* 2.8.1386a4–13).

A promising answer is found in Aristotle's view that *surprise* enhances pity and fear. He puts this by saying that pity and fear are most strongly evoked when "events occur contrary to expectation yet on account of one another" (*Poetics* 10.1452a2–4). Aristotle appears to mean that the events are related as cause and effect, though in a way that defies the expectations of the audience, pity and fear are enhanced, so such a juxtaposition of the unexpected yet causally linked is astonishing. When an individual such as a king, queen, or a mythic hero undergoes a reversal of fortune, this turning of the tables is surprising, and provided the change of fortune is not gratuitous or out of the blue, but follows as the result of events that preceded it, this enhances the feeling of pity and fear for the characters.

In addition, in the *Rhetoric* Aristotle observes that fear is felt when the audience can be made to believe that some destructive evil *might* happen to *them* (*Rhetoric* 2.5.1383a7–12). This can happen, he says, when the audience listening to a speech can be made to believe that someone more socially secure than they suffers some destructive evil. For the audience will reason if such a person can experience a reversal of fortune, they can as well. Characters such as kings, queens, and those with great social status and honor, drive home the possibility to the audience that they, also, are vulnerable to the reversal of fortune that tragedy depicts. If the rich and famous can come to such a change of fortune, the audience reasons, why can't we?

COMPLETENESS AND MAGNITUDE

Completeness. The plot is the organization or arrangement of events (*Poetics* 7.1450a15) and it is the means by which the incidents are rendered intelligible. To evoke pity and fear, the plot must have a certain sort of structure: it must imitate a sequence of actions that is complete. To be complete, a plot must have a beginning, middle, and end (7.1450b22–28). The beginning of the plot is, "that which does not itself follow necessarily from something else, but after which a further event or process naturally occurs" (7.1450b26–28). The middle is that which, "both follows a preceding event and has further consequences" (7.1450b29–31). The ending is, "that which itself naturally occurs, whether necessarily or usually, after a preceding event, but need not be followed by anything else" (7.1450b28).

Now it is a metaphysical truth, we can suppose, that every event has a cause, so the idea that there could be an event that occurs without a cause is incoherent. Similarly, unless the end of the universe comes, every event is followed by another event, so the idea of an ending being that which is not followed by anything else is also puzzling. How can Aristotle's account of the notions of beginning and end make sense?

This objection brings out the need to think of the plot, not as the totality of all the things that a character says or does in some possible world, but as the ordering of a *selection* of these events into a self-contained narrative, with well-defined endpoints. To make a plot of your life, for example, in the way Aristotle is thinking of it, you must select some subset of the events from your larger life story that can intelligibly and coherently hang together as a single unified action. Suppose on your seventeenth birthday you ardently declare yourself a vegan, but the next day you go out and enjoy a steak dinner! While every human life has its contradictions (!), this sequence of events would be eliminated from the plot of your life's story, for as it stands, such a change of heart would be incoherent. Thus, the poet must not include any and all events of a character's life story in the plot, as Homer, being the superior poet that he is, realized (*Poetics* 9.1451a22–30).

We can see how to build a plot so that it is complete, in Aristotle's sense, as follows. First, we need a self-contained beginning event that kicks the story off (7.1450b25–27), for example, "Sam claimed that the neighborhood stray black cat was his cat, so he took the cat from Felicia, who had also been feeding him." The middle consists of an action that follows from the beginning event and has at least one event that follows it as a consequence (7.1450b29–30), for example, "When Sam was away for two weeks, Felicia started feeding the cat again, and the cat became Felicia's loyal companion for the rest of his life." The end is an action that follows from the middle and brings the story to completion or closure, for example, "Sam was so upset with Felicia for taking the cat that they never spoke again."

Aristotle distinguishes the plot (*muthos*) from the drama. We can think of the plot as the events that occur in the story. The drama is how the story is *told* or presented on the stage. Sometimes the events in the plot and the events in the drama are identical, but Aristotle suggests that the events in the plot and the events in the drama can diverge.[14]

To illustrate, an action that is crucial to the story of Sophocles' *Oedipus the King* is Oedipus' unknowing killing of his father at the crossroads: this is something that takes place before the staged drama starts. It is part of the plot or story, but it is "outside of the drama." There are, then, events that are "outside the drama" but are essential to the plot.[15]

The standards for poetic unity require that every component event in the plot makes a vital contribution, to the point where if even a single one is removed or put in a different place in the plot, the sense of the plot forming a complete whole is spoiled (9.1451a30–35).

The plot should not go on for too long, for several reasons. First, there are practical limits on what an audience can be expected to retain in memory (this relates to the *magnitude* of the plot, a point we soon return to). Second, the ending must bring about a sense that the action that started the play is brought to its natural completion. This gives the audience a sense of having a complete experience by having the plot reach what is often called "narrative closure."

Magnitude. Closely related to completeness is the requirement that a tragic plot have a sufficient magnitude (8.1451a9–15). A tragedy is an imitation of an action that is carried through to its natural end of happiness or unhappiness. Magnitude is the size of the plot that enables it to follow through the necessary or probable consequences of an action to its natural completion, in a way that allows for a change from good fortune to bad or the reverse (6.1451a15). The length, in temporal terms, must be short enough to hold all the events in memory (8.1451a5), while its scale, in spatial dimensions, must be of an order that allows for coherent observation and does not exceed the spectator's range of perception (8.1451a5).

Aristotle does not think that the length of the plot should be dictated by contingent events, for example, the fact that a playwright is just given a twenty-minute slot in which to perform her play at a festival (8.1451a8–9). The plot should take into account the limits of the audience's memory and perceptual ability, while also providing sufficient time for a development and resolution of the action.

So, for example, imagine a variation on the plot of Sophocles' *Oedipus* in which the messenger arrives at the start of the plague with the news that Oedipus caused the plague because he killed his father, Laius, at the crossroads and married his mother, Queen Jocasta. Oedipus quickly accepts his role in bringing the plague on his city, plucks out his eyes, and goes into exile. This plot has some magnitude, for it contains some events, but it is what Aristotle calls "slight": there is not a sufficient length for the action to develop a proper emotional response based on a grasp of the events' significance (8.1451a12–15). The audience might, for example, respond with shock upon hearing the bad news from the messenger and seeing Oedipus' reaction, but a fitting emotional response, which includes pity and fear for the characters, must develop over some time. Plots that are too short do not allow for the development of the serious action that made later tragedy acquire dignity (4.1449a19).

Magnitude is what gives the plot its beauty (7.1450b35). Here beauty is related to proportion and size (see *Metaphysics* 13.3.1078a31–b5; *Politics* 7.15.1248b8–10), not to what we might think of as the aesthetic appeal of its sensible properties. It is the design of a thing that enables it to carry out its natural function, and the design or organization of its parts is, in its own right, an object of beauty, even when the sensory appearance of something is unsightly (*Parts of Animals* 1.5.645a23–25).

EMBELLISHED LANGUAGE AND DRAMATIC MODE

The fourth aspect of the definition of tragedy is embellished language. Rhythm, melody, and song are the "seasonings" or embellishments (*hēdusmata*) of the language of tragedy (6.1449b28–31). The term "seasonings" or "sweetenings" is a metaphor used in cooking to refer to the addition of spices, condiments, and other additives to enhance the flavor of the food. One might take Aristotle's point to be that embellished language is a non-essential item, because it is a sensory pleasure and does not pertain to tragedy's function as an imitation. In contrast, in *Poetics* 2, Aristotle cites rhythm and melody, along with language, as three basic media that tragedy uses to achieve the imitation of human life and action. So while plot, the organization of events in the play, is the central component of tragedy, embellished language is nevertheless a component of tragedy that contributes to its function as an imitation of human action.

The fifth aspect of the definition of tragedy is its distinctive mode of storytelling. Tragedy is an imitation of action that accomplishes its purpose through the *dramatic* mode of storytelling, with imitation proceeding by characters that are actively doing things. On the one hand, Aristotle thinks that the dramatic form is the superior form of imitation, for he commends Homer for departing from the method of other epic poets and keeping narration to a minimum and to "bring on stage" characters who speak and act out the drama.[16] Nevertheless, there is also an advantage to the narrative form, for it allows many parts of the action to be presented simultaneously, and if these events are all relevant to the overall theme, they enhance the poem's seriousness and weight.[17]

UNIFIED ACTION: THE NECESSARY OR LIKELY CONNECTION BETWEEN EVENTS

Closely related to the completeness of the plot is the requirement that it imitates a single unified action (7.1451a1; 7.1451a16 –17; 26.1462b4). For a plot to be unified, the events must be linked by *necessity or probability*.[18] These connections are the cement that binds together the events in the plot into an integrated whole. This means that a well-ordered plot does not simply line up one event after another, as in the sequence of events, "The king died and then the queen died."[19] Aristotle calls a plot that threads one event after another episodic and disjointed.[20] If the poet instead writes, "The king died and then the queen died of grief," the reader can grasp what brought on the queen's death and the significance of the king's death to the queen's passing.

This illustrates a fundamental constraint that Aristotle places on the plot. This is the idea that in the plot, things happen *because of*, and not only after, their antecedents (11.1452a20–22). In the properly constructed plot, whether it is in tragedy, comedy, or epic, imitated events are to follow one another "by necessity or probability." When the plot is so composed, the plot reveals causal connections between the events that a mere list or chronicle of events does not.

Why does Aristotle insist on such a connection between the events in the plot? A necessary or probable connection between events is a way to make the plot: (1) believable; (2) coherent; and (3) capable of evoking in the audience amazement and a sense of wonder that enhances the pity and fear for the characters and their predicaments.[21]

First, tragedy is an imitation of human life and action. It is a distinctive feature of tragedy that the characters find themselves in highly unusual circumstances. While unusual, the plot must still be believable in terms of how things go for these types of people in their circumstances. Given that there is not, in reality, an Oedipus, *if* there were *and* he was in this particular situation, is it credible that things would happen as they do in the plot? Having the events follow one another according to probability or necessity is a way to achieve the requirement of believability (*Poetics* 9.1451b15–32; 17.1455a30).

Second, the plot must make sense as a narrative: this means that the events must be *coherent* and fit together in an understandable way. Creating causal connections between events in the plot is a way to achieve a coherent plot. Imagine a sequence of events that is not coherent: your beloved family cat, Fluffy, dies and then after examining Fluffy's body, your vet tells you and your family that there was no cause for Fluffy's death. You would surely demand an explanation for your dear cat's passing! This is because you believe that relations of cause and effect regulate events in the world, including the death of cats. It is simply not coherent that Fluffy's passing has no cause.

Necessity and probability govern events that are related as cause and effect. Given that one event occurs, another, necessarily or probably, follows. A necessary connection between events is the highest standard that a scientist seeks when she strives to understand just why it is that an event of a certain kind regularly and routinely follows another of some other kind. For this is indicative of a causal connection that helps explain not just why an event occurred, but also why it is necessary, in the sense that it "could not be otherwise."[22] Two events (e.g. the use of iPhones and an increase in heart disease) could be spatially and temporally conjoined, yet not reveal an underlying causal connection, just an accidental correlation. So a scientist can only be certain that she has uncovered a causal relation when she discovers that two classes of events are necessarily conjoined.

Yet when one kind of event is conjoined with another, almost always or for the most part, this can still indicate a causal connection. Some causal connections in the realm of physical things only hold for the most part, because matter is capable of being otherwise, and deviations can occur that make it the case, for example, that men usually, but not always, grow hair on their chins.[23] Still, there can be a causal connection even when an event takes place "for the most part," provided we have good reason to think that the link is not temporary or accidental.[24]

Tragedy, and indeed comedy as well as epic, can concern characters that are made up (9.1451b20–25), as did Agathon's *Antheus*, in which the poet invented the names and the events in the play (9.1451b22). Or the plot can make use of names that the audience believes to exist, as when some tragic playwrights used the names of characters from traditional myths, to give an air of authenticity to the story (9.1451b20–22). Whether actual or made up, the plot should develop out of how the audience expects that characters like this talk and act. Connecting the events in a probable or necessary sequence is the means to achieve the required level of believability and coherence.

Third, and perhaps most importantly, Aristotle thinks that when events occur on account of one another, but also take the audience by surprise, this prompts amazement:

> Given that mimesis is not only of a complete action but also of the fearful and pitiable matters, the latter arise above all when events occur contrary to expectation and yet on account of one another. The awesome will be maintained in this way more than through show of chance and fortune, because even among chance events we find most awesome those which seem to have happened by design (as when Mitys' statue at Argos killed the murderer of Mitys, by falling on him as he looked at it: such things *seem* not to occur randomly.
>
> (*Poetics* 9.1452a1–9)

In this passage Aristotle reveals a *third* reason for requiring that the events in the plot have a necessary or probable connection. For Aristotle observes that tragic pity and fear are evoked especially by turns of events that take the audience by surprise, and give them a sense of wonder or awe, but in retrospect reveal an underlying causal connection. This is because there is a connection between amazement and learning:

> Learning things and wondering at things are also pleasant for the most part: wondering implies the desire of learning, so that the object of wonder is an object of desire; while in learning one is brought into one's natural condition.
>
> (*Rhetoric* 1.11.1371a30–32 in Barnes 1984)

When a sequence of events occurs by surprise, this is astonishing, and it produces a desire to understand why this unexpected event happened.[25] When the events are linked via a necessary or probable connection, the audience can reflect back on the structure of the plot and come to understand, in retrospect, why the events, while unexpected, were a result of what went before.[26]

To illustrate, the news that Oedipus caused the plague by killing his father and marrying his mother takes the audience, at least somewhat, by surprise; yet the connections in the plot, with one event happening *because of* the actions that preceded it, should make sense, in retrospect, so that the outcome is understandable to the audience. The organizing principle for the plot, then, is "the causally connected yet unpredictable outcome."

CHANCE, THE IRRATIONAL, AND "OUTSIDE THE DRAMA"

The situation in which Mitys' statue kills his murderer is a chance event, for Mitys' murder and the accident that brings about the death of his murderer are not related.[27] It does seem like poetic justice that the murderer would be killed in this way, and chance events that give the semblance or *appearance* of purpose are more amazing than chance events that appear completely random. Still, Aristotle thinks that it is a mistake to include any chance events in the plot if the unity and coherence of the plot is to be maintained.

This point is confirmed from an examination of Aristotle's natural philosophy, where chance is incompatible with and set against what happens in accordance with the necessary and the probable.

First, events that are related as cause and effect involve the working out of purpose and some end, while chance is what comes to pass accidentally and in a way that impedes the regularity of natural processes. Chance events are not random and uncaused: they occur "for the sake of something" or for some end, but not the goal that is naturally connected with the process in question.[28]

For example, Maria goes to the market place to collect provisions for a feast and she meets Harry who is there to do some shopping of his own. Harry owes Maria money and ends up repaying his debt. If Maria had known she could get the debt repaid, she would have gone for that reason, but as it is, her shopping trip is not connected with that goal and the outcome is a type of chance event that Aristotle calls "luck."[29] This outcome is an accidental or chance intervention for it is not the result of a process that occurs always or normally: we do not usually get our debts repaid when we go food shopping!

Second, the necessary and the probable, or what holds for the most part, are things that can be given an account (*logos*) or rational explanation, while what occurs by chance or luck is "a cause incalculable to human reasoning" (*Eudemian Ethics* 7.14.1247b8). While actions that occur necessarily or usually can be rationally understood, chance events are unaccountable (*paralogos*), for it is not humanly comprehensible why one action that was aimed at a certain outcome (collecting food for dinner) ends up accomplishing another, completely unrelated end (having a loan repaid).

Given the opposition between chance and the irrational, on the one hand, and what occurs, necessarily or usually, it seems to follow that there is no place for chance or the irrational in the properly constructed plot. The problem with chance events is that they undermine the regularity and sense of purpose that is a primary source of the causal connections among events in the plot. Irrational events are to be excluded as well, unless there is some over-riding reason to include them.[30] The poet should not make a plot where you are a vegan one day, then enjoying a steak dinner the next, for such a turnabout is not comprehensible, unless intervening events are added that make the change of heart explicable.

For the same reason, Aristotle faults plots in ancient Greek tragedy in which the poet resorts to irrationalities and improbabilities to resolve the plot. Euripides' use of the *deus ex machina* (from the Latin "God from the machine"; the Greek is "*theos apo mēkhanēs*") device in his *Medea is* unwarranted, for Medea is spirited away in a chariot at the end of the play when this is an ad hoc resolution to the build up to the conclusion (*Poetics* 15.1454a37).[31]

Irrationalities also occur in epic poetry, as Aristotle alleges is true in Homer's *Iliad* 22.131ff. Hector flees when Achilles approaches him, and Achilles' army obeys him when he orders them not to intervene (14.1460a14–16; 14.1460a15). In Homer's *Odyssey* 12, Odysseus is conveyed to the shores of Ithaca in a supernaturally swift boat, yet he fails to wake up when he is put ashore (14.1460a34–36).

Yet, Aristotle thinks there is a way for the poet to handle irrationalities, when this is needed. This is by referring unaccountable happenings to the class of events that are "outside the tragedy" or "outside the drama."[32] These are events that are outside the dramatized events. So, to illustrate, it is not understandable how Oedipus could have ascended to the throne and remained ignorant of how the previous king, Laius, died (*Poetics*

15.1454b5–7). For it stands to reason that a curious individual like Oedipus would have inquired as to the manner of the king's passing, and would have then learned that Laius died in an altercation with an unknown man at a certain crossroads. Since these were the very circumstances in which Oedipus found himself killing a strange man, he surely would have put two and two together.

As it is, Oedipus' ignorance is unaccountable, or if you will, a gap in the story line. It does not threaten the unity and coherence of the tragedy, however, because Aristotle says that it is referred to the class of events that are "outside the play" or "outside the drama." By this he means that how it is that Oedipus managed to stay ignorant of how King Laius dies is not raised as part of the dramatized events. It is, however, part of the plot that Oedipus was, in fact, ignorant of the manner of the former King's death.

One might wonder why Aristotle would allow improbable or irrational events in the plot, but not the play. The reasoning behind eliminating chance events from the play is that they would undermine the coherence and unity that makes possible the appropriate emotional response to the characters and events in the play. If chance events (and other irrational incidents) are relocated to the plot, some further explanation is needed as to why improbable events need to be excluded from the *play* but need not be excluded from the *plot*.[33]

Now the connection between the events in the plot and the events in the drama is a close one. For the play is an actualization or dramatization of a selection of some of the events in the plot.[34] Still, as we said before, the drama and the plot typically follow distinct temporal orders. There can be events in the plot that predate, and are then followed by, events in the play. Aristotle thinks the key to evoking an emotional response of pity and fear is making the events seem to the audience not distant, but close at hand.[35] The temporal distance of the events that begin the plot from the dramatized action that is part of the tragedy might be one explanation why chance or irrational events could be included in the plot, but not the dramatized events in the play. While such events are part of the plot, and so part of the larger story that the audience imagines, they may not command the audience's attention in the same way as events that are portrayed in the text of the tragedy.

The events that precede the play, while crucial for its development, are in this respect like events that are reported in epic. Aristotle says that epic can get away with the use of an improbable or irrational event more easily. So in Homer's *Iliad* 22.131ff. Hector loses his courage as Achilles approaches him. He flees and is pursued by Achilles, who orders his army to stand down and not interfere. Aristotle says this pursuit of Hector, with the soldiers refraining from pursuit, would appear ridiculous if put on the stage, but because it is reported instead of dramatized on stage, the absurdity has a better chance of escaping the notice of the audience.[36]

Similarly, incongruities in the plot, especially those that precede the action of the play, may fail to capture the audience's imagination in quite the same way that they would if they were included as events that are dramatized on stage, and so performed in front of the audience. Aristotle may then think that placing irrational and chance events outside the drama, but in the plot, may be more acceptable than if these events were included as part of the events are included in the drama. For what is fully enacted in the drama commands the audience's attention to a greater extent than what is reported rather than dramatized.[37] If Sophocles' *Oedipus* play, for example, were to include the scene in which when Oedipus is asked to be king, the absurdity that an inquisitive person like Oedipus would not put two and two together and realize that he killed Laius would be too blatant to ignore. But if Oedipus reports that he was ignorant of how the former king died, there is less of an impact because the audience does not see the scene with the incongruity, so to speak, with their own eyes.

THE *POETICS* AND THE GODS

The gods play a large part in ancient Greek tragedy. For example, the god Apollo arrives in Euripides' *Orestes* to resolve what looks like an irresolvable conflict. The goddess Artemis in Euripides' *Hippolytus* is central to resolving the conflict by explaining to Theseus Hippolytus' innocence. In Aeschylus' *Eumenides*, the Erinyes, goddesses of vengeance, torment Orestes by hunting him down for killing his mother, Clytemnestra, after she kills Orestes' father, Agamemnon.

Stephen Halliwell has argued that in the *Poetics* Aristotle regards the gods and their actions as an irrational element that needs to be banished from the events in the tragedy.[38] One of Halliwell's prime examples comes from *Poetics* 15, where he gives two examples of irrational action that make use of the gods to resolve the dramatic action: the divine assistance given to Medea, which allows her to spirit away at the end of play, and the intervention of Athena in the *Iliad* 2, where the goddess acts to prevent the departure of the Greeks for home (15.1454a36–b2).

But, as other commentators have maintained, it is more reasonable to think that the problem Aristotle is objecting to is not the use of the gods *per se*, but a particular way of bringing in the actions of the gods that appears inconsistent and unmotivated by the preceding action.[39] All looks hopeless for Medea, for instance, until the Sun god's chariot appears and she spirits away in it. As O. B. Hardison, Jr. maintains, "The criticism of *Medea* is not that the play ends with a Sun-chariot but that 'magical powers' have not been stressed sufficiently in the earlier scenes to provide a convincing and effective cause for the final miracle."[40]

Imagine, for example, that a beloved character, Harry Sotter, is in a tight fix from which there looks to be no escape. Suppose he then pulls out his magic wand and reveals he is a wizard with magical powers. He then uses a special method of magical transportation to get himself away from his predicament. This introduction of magical powers would be an ad hoc resolution to the events that preceded it. Contrast this with how magical powers figure in the fiction of the Harry Potter books. It is assumed to be true in the world of these fictional stories that there are wizards with magical powers and that Harry, Hermione, Professor McGonagall, and so on, are wizards. It would not be unmotivated, then, for Harry Potter to use his magical powers to get out of a sticky situation.

Aristotle, then, leaves open that the actions of the gods can be brought in, provided that they occur in a causally coherent way.[41] The poet also has other ways of bringing the gods into the story. The gods' pronouncements could occur, outside the tragedy or dramatized action, in a prologue or epilogue in which a god predicts what will happen or what will follow the action in the play (15.1454b1–3). Or the belief in the gods can come in as, "the kinds of things that people believe and say" (25.1460b10), that is, as things that are supposed to be true in the world of the fiction, in the way that magical powers are thought to be true in the fictional world that the J. K. Rowling novels depict.

OBJECTIONS AND REPLIES

To conclude this section, we can take stock of Aristotle's requirement that the plot proceed according to probability and necessity, which is the central way of achieving the unity needed in tragic plots. Does Aristotle's reasoning stand up? We can consider some objections to the conclusion that it does not.

1) *Is a necessary connection between events in the plot feasible?*
The idea that the actions in the plot follow necessarily from earlier events has struck some as quite puzzling. Humans are so hard to predict, even for the experts such as psychologists who study them for a living. Is a necessary connection between events in the realm of human action even possible?

We might look to Aristotle's *Nicomachean Ethics* to answer this, since ethics is the science that is concerned with action (*praxis*). On the one hand, the fundamental principle of ethics is that all humans desire happiness or flourishing (*eudaimonia*).[42] This has the status of a necessary truth about human beings, and it is highly relevant to understanding tragedy, as well, for the plots of tragedy show human agents striving for happiness and either failing or succeeding in getting it (*NE* 6.1450a20).

Yet Aristotle also says the discipline of ethics must be content to formulate first principles that hold only "for the most part," since more precision is not possible for a science that discusses human action.[43] What he appears to mean is that in the realm of human action as it relates to happiness (*eudaimonia*), it is difficult to make iron clad generalizations that hold without exceptions for all people, for example, "material wealth destroys happiness" or "courageous people die young." Perhaps there is some wealthy person whose happiness is not marred by a lot of money or a courageous person whose bravery does not lead her to die prematurely from performing valiant actions.

Nevertheless, it is possible to know what a specific person will do in a certain circumstance, provided one has a grasp on that person's character. Aristotle believes that through a combination of habit, upbringing, and individual choices, individuals develop a fixed character that shapes how they think and what they do.[44] The origin of human action is choice (*prohairesis*), where choice is a reasoned desire with a view to some end.[45] Aristotle thinks that human agents necessarily act in accordance with their desires,[46] which are in turn determined by their moral character. For, to illustrate, once a person develops an unjust or self-indulgent character, certain desires and actions necessarily follow from this.[47]

The key to saying what someone, for example Bob, will necessarily do in a certain situation, therefore involves knowing what kind of character Bob has. In real life, this can be a challenging task, for we may not be able to amass enough evidence about Bob's behavior and motives to place him as a certain *kind* of individual. Here it may make more sense to speak in terms of what Bob is likely to do based on our best estimate of what sort of person Bob is.

The poet is in a different sort of situation: she *creates* the characters and their predicaments and so she can fill out the episodes in the plot in a way that makes it comprehensible, at least in some cases, that a necessary connection holds between events. It may be that this is not possible for all plots and characters, which explains why Aristotle sometimes just speaks of the poet creating a series in which one action follows from previous ones according to what is usually or probably the case.[48] Where a necessary connection between plotted events is feasible, it will create a greater sense of unity in the action, and as we will examine in greater detail later, this is key to tragedy prompting appropriate emotional response in the audience.

2) *Is a causal connection necessary for the audience to feel for the characters?* Aristotle holds that the emotional engagement of the audience with the drama depends on their grasping a causal connection between events in the plot. David Velleman argues that provided the plot makes emotional sense to us, it does not matter whether or not we grasp *why* the events occurred as they did.[49] We might, to illustrate, grasp *that* the king died and then the queen died, without knowing *why* she died. Yet if the sequence of events makes emotional sense to us ("Of course," we might think, "That is what queens do after their partners die. They die of grief!"), then this succession of actions can elicit an emotional response, even if we don't know *why* the events really happened as they did.

Here Aristotle has a fundamental disagreement with Velleman. Yes, he would reply, the audience can have *an* emotional response to the story about the queen even when it fails to understand *why* things happened as they did. Yet they will not have the *appropriate* emotional response if they fail to grasp the real emotional import (or lack thereof) of the events. If the queen's passing is not related to the death of the king, then the audience imports an emotional significance to the events that is not, in reality, objectively there in the dramatic actions. A proper emotional response to the characters must, therefore, be based on grasping a causal connection between events in the plot.

Why is this so, and what is meant by a "proper" emotional response here? Aristotle thinks that the experience of amazement (*to thaumostos*) and astonishment (*ekplēxis*) is a part of the audience's response to tragedy and epic. He thinks that the arousal of amazement is just as important in epic as in tragedy;[50] epic has more scope for irrational and improbable events because when events are narrated (the mode of imitation made use of in epic) it is easier for the audience not to notice the absurdity. While chance events that *appear* or *strike* the audience as purposeful (Mitys' statue killing Mitys' murderer) can create a sense of awe at the unexpected turn of the action, Aristotle prefers that the awesome is prompted by a plot with necessary and probable connections. He also holds that wonder and awe are best inspired by a reversal of fortune that is contrary to expectation, but is, in retrospect, understood as a necessary or probable result of the event that preceded it (*Poetics* 10.1452a3-5). This is because wonder and awe inspire the desire to know the explanation for that which you do not understand. So a plot with a surprising twist, yet where events are connected by necessity or probability, is the best way to satisfy the desire to understand. Such a plot inspires an emotional response that is accompanied by an understanding as to why things happened as they did.

CONCLUSION

Aristotle's reply, while understandable, raises further questions that we need to address. Science tracks necessary and probable connections between events in the world, but why think that the plots of poetry must do so as well? The poet is, after all, an artist, not a social scientist or psychologist. Further, the scientist and the philosopher seek out causal principles because they aim to investigate the truths about the world. Is this also the goal of poetry? These questions will be addressed in the coming chapters.

NOTES

1 *Relevant texts: Poetics* 6, 7, and 8; *Poetics* 9 1452a1–9; *Poetics* 18.1455b23–32.
2 Internal and external evidence, however, also suggests that there was a lost second book of the *Poetics* devoted to comedy.
3 The origin of the name is not entirely certain. Some think tragedy was so named because in the poetic competitions the winner received a goat. Others speculate that the name derives from the fact that the actors wore the skins of goats (along with masks).
4 For an accessible, historical overview of what is known about the beginning of ancient Greek tragedy, see Albrecht Dihle 1994: 91–108.
5 Peter Levi 2001.
6 For this view of tragedy, see Martha Nussbaum 1986; Malcolm Budd 1995: 83–123; and James Shelley 2003. For a useful overview of some themes in tragedy in the Western philosophical tradition see Aaron Ridley 2003 and Alex Neill 2005.
7 *Poetics* 14.1453b10–12.
8 *Poetics* 6.1449b22–30.
9 *Poetics* 14.1453b12–13.
10 All quotations from the *Poetics*, in Greek and in English, are from Stephen Halliwell 1999, unless otherwise noted.
11 In addition to the definition, *"catharsis"* occurs for a second and final time in *Poetics* 17, where Aristotle makes an incidental reference to a ritual of purification or *catharsis* in a play by Euripides.
12 *Nicomachean Ethics* 2.
13 This is quite evident especially in *Poetics* 13–14.
14 See *Poetics* 14.1453b29–34, where Aristotle suggests that an action that is central to the plot or story may be outside the drama, and *Poetics* 18.1455b23–26, where Aristotle says that the plot **complication** (*desis*) will typically include things that are outside the tragedy or drama. For discussions of the distinction between plot and drama in the *Poetics* see Heath 1991: 394; Roberts 1992: 136–137.
15 The temporal independence between what the *Poetics* calls "plot" and "drama" has been recognized by contemporary narratologists, including Seymour Chatman, although he uses the terms "story" versus "discourse" to mark out the difference. See Chatman 1980: 19–21, 121–123.
16 *Poetics* 24.1460a10f.

17 *Poetics* 24.1459b26–28. For a more extensive discussion of the difference between narrative and dramatic modes, see Chapter 3.

18 *Poetics* 9.1451a37–38; 9.1451b9; 11.1452a17–21; 15.1454a33–36.

19 E. M. Forster 1927: 30.

20 *Poetics* 1451a37–38; 1451b9; 1452a17–21; 1454a33–36.

21 Such connections between events may not be the *only* way to make the plot believable (see *Poetics* 24.1460a26–27 where he describes the other techniques that Homer uses to make implausible events in the plot believable) but Aristotle thinks that necessary and probable connections between events are by far the *preferred* way to prompt the audience to find the action believable.

22 See *Metaphysics* 5.5-5.6.1015a35–b15.

23 Aristotle *Posterior Analytics* 1.30.87b19–27.

24 *Physics* 2.8.

25 See *Metaphysics* 1.1, where Aristotle says that philosophy comes out of the astonishment and amazement that we feel at the world and our desire to learn and understand the ultimate causes of why things are as they are.

26 Astonishment is part of epic as well as tragedy, but epic can use incidents that are either contrary to reason or improbable to produce a sense of amazement because the audience does not actually see the improbable events dramatized on the stage (*Poetics* 24.1460a11–18).

27 *Poetics* 10.1452a5–10.

28 *Physics* 2.5.196b18f.

29 *Physics* 2.5.197a3–5. Luck is chance that occurs to humans, that is, natural beings capable of thought and decision.

30 See *Poetics* 25.

31 Euripides was known for using the theatrical maneuver of the *deus ex machina* in a number of his plays. As the play comes to a conclusion, an actor playing a god is hoisted up on a machine (*machina*, Latin) or crane and settles scores and restores order. Some literary critics think that Euripides is deliberately playing with the expectation that the ending will, miraculously, "wrap up" all the problems raised in the play. In *Medea*, it is the title character, not a god, who is hoisted above the stage in the sun god's chariot and spirits away.

32 See, for example, *Poetics* 14.1453b30, where Aristotle uses "*drama*" (*drama*) and "tragedy" (*tragōidia*) synonymously. Other references to "outside the tragedy" or "outside the drama" occur at 15.1454b6–9 and 24.1460a11–17 and 27–32.

33 Commentators have also been concerned that Aristotle's relegation of improbable events to those that occur outside the play is arbitrary. See Cynthia Freeland 1992: 115; Stephen Halliwell 1998: 150–151; and H. D. F. Kitto 1964: 88. By developing the different ways the plot and the play affect the audience (in what follows) it is possible to address these scholars' concerns.

34 In one passage, *Poetics* 24.1460a28–20, Aristotle even appears to equate the plot (here referred to as "plot structure" (*mutheuma*)) with the drama, but this passage may be an anomaly. For a comment on the significance of the association between "plot structure" and "drama" in this passage, see R. Janko 1987: 144.

35 For this point see *Rhetoric* 2.8.1386a34f.

36 "In tragedy one needs to create a sense of awe, but epic has more scope for the irrational (the chief cause of awe), because we do not actually see the agent" (*Poetics* 24.1460a12–14).

37 See *Poetics* 24.1460a3–11 where Aristotle praises Homer for keeping the use of his "own voice" to a minimum and introducing the characters to tell their own story. The implication is that acting out the scene rather than reporting it by using a narrator has a greater effect on the audience. On the distinction between narrative and dramatic modes, see *Poetics* 3 and Chapter 3.

38 See S. Halliwell 1987: 150–151 and S. Halliwell 1998: 231–234.

39 See Leon Golden and O. B. Hardison, Jr. 1981: 209–210; M. Heath 1991: 396–397; D. Roberts 1992: 138–140.

40 Golden and Hardison 208.

41 This discussion is, by necessity, brief and it does not do full justice to the controversy. For the full debate see the references to Halliwell in note 38, and for replies to his concerns see Golden and Hardison, Jr., Heath, and Roberts, cited in note 39.

42 *Nicomachean Ethics* 1.1.

43 *Nicomachean Ethics* 1.2.1094b14–22; 2.2.1103b34–1104a10.

44 *Nicomachean Ethics* 1.1.

45 *Nicomachean Ethics* 6.2.1139a30f.

46 *Metaphysics* 9.5.1048a10–16.

47 For this point see also Dorothea Frede 1992: 203 and Paul A. Taylor 2008: 269.

48 What holds "for the most part" is mentioned at *Poetics* 7.1450b29 and what is probable (*eikos*) is mentioned at 1451b11–15 and 29–32. What holds "necessarily or probably" is mentioned at 1451a37–38; 1452a17–21; 1454a33-36; 1455a16–19; 1461b11–12.

49 David Velleman 2003: 21.

50 On amazement in epic see *Poetics* 24.1460a11–18 and on astonishment in epic see 24.1460b25.

WORKS CITED

Barnes, Jonathan (ed.) 1984. *The Complete Works of Aristotle*. Volume Two. Princeton, NJ: Princeton University Press.

Budd, Malcolm 1995. *Values of Art: Pictures, Poetry, and Music*. London: Penguin Press.

Chatman, Seymour 1980. *Story and Discourse: Narrative Structure in Fiction and Film*. Ithaca, NY: Cornell University Press.

Dihle, Albrecht 1994. *A History of Greek Literature: From Homer to the Hellenistic Period*, translated by Clare Krojzle. London and New York: Routledge.

Forster, E. M. 1927. *Aspects of the Novel*. New York: Harcourt Brace and Company.

Frede, Dorothea 1992. "Necessity, Chance, and 'What Happens for the Most Part'," in Amélie Oskenberg Rorty (ed.), *Essays on Aristotle's Poetics*. Princeton, NJ: Princeton University Press: 197–220.

Freeland, Cynthia 1992. "Plot Imitates Action: Aesthetic Evaluation and Moral Realism in Aristotle's *Poetics*," in Amélie Oskenberg Rorty (ed.), *Essays on Aristotle's Poetics*. Princeton, NJ: Princeton University Press: 111–132.

Golden, Leon and O. B. Hardison Jr. 1981. *Aristotle's Poetics: A Translation and Commentary for Students of Literature*. Tallahassee: University Presses of Florida.

Halliwell, Stephen 1987. *The Poetics of Aristotle*. Chapel Hill: University of North Carolina Press.

—— 1998. *Aristotle's Poetics: With a New Introduction by the Author*. Chicago: University of Chicago Press.

—— 1999. *Aristotle's Poetics Edited and Translated by Stephen Halliwell*. Cambridge, MA: Harvard University Press.

Heath, Malcolm 1991: "The Universality in Aristotle's *Poetics*." *The Classical Quarterly*, New Series 41 (2): 389–402.

Janko, Richard 1987. *Aristotle, Poetics: With the Tractatus Coislinianus, Reconstruction of Poetics II, and the Fragments of the On Poets*. Indianapolis, IN and Cambridge: Hackett Publishing Company.

Kitto, H. D. F. 1964. *Form and Meaning in Drama*. Second Edition. London: Methuen.

Levi, Peter 2001. "Greek Drama," in John Boardman, Jasper Griffin and Oswyn Murray (eds.), *The Oxford Illustrated History of Greece and the Hellenistic World*. Oxford and New York: Oxford University Press: 150–179.

Neill, A. 2005. "Tragedy," in Berys Gaut and Dominic McIver Lopes (eds.), *The Routledge Companion to Aesthetics*. Oxford and New York: Routledge: 415–424.

Nussbaum, M. 1986. *The Fragility of Goodness: Luck and Ethics in Ancient Greek Tragedy and Philosophy*. Cambridge: Cambridge University Press.

Ridley, Aaron 2003. "Tragedy," in Jerrold Levinson (ed.), *The Oxford Handbook of Aesthetics*. Oxford and New York: Oxford University Press: 408–420.

Roberts, Deborah H. 1992. "Outside the Drama," in Amélie Oskenberg Rorty (ed.) *Essays on Aristotle's Poetics*. Princeton, NJ: Princeton University Press: 133–154.

Rorty, Amélie Oskenberg (ed.) 1992. *Essays on Aristotle's Poetics*. Princeton, NJ: Princeton University Press.

Shelley, James 2003. "Imagining the Truth: An Account of Tragic Pleasure," in Matthew Kieran and Dominic Lopes (eds.), *Imagination, Philosophy and the Arts*. London: Routledge: 177–186.

Taylor, Paul A. 2008. "Sympathy and Insight in Aristotle's *Poetics*." *Journal of Aesthetics and Art Criticism* 66 (3): 265–280.

Velleman, David 2003. "Narrative Explanation." *The Philosophical Review* 112 (1): 1–25.

RECOMMENDED READING

Carroll, Noël 2007. "Narrative Closure." *Philosophical Studies* 135: 1–15.

6

THE SIX ELEMENTS OF POETIC COMPOSITION[1]

FOCUS ON THE PLOT

Do you read or watch plays and movies primarily because of your love of plot, story, and action? Do you especially love the performance of the actors? Do you delight in the special visual effects in movies? Or is it character and character development that gives you the greatest pleasure? Some may say they especially love the characters in great fiction and they delight in seeing them change, develop, and progress. Fans of movies such as *The Lord of the Rings* and the *Matrix* will tell you that the special effects in these movies are a special source of pleasure for them. Lovers of the theater will tell you that they especially like drama for the performance and movie aficionados may say they seek out films with great acting. This suggests that there are many, diverse sources of pleasure that readers and spectators find in drama and fiction.

Given this, it is surprising to find Aristotle's arguments in *Poetics* 6 for the importance of plot and action over character, performance, and the other elements of tragedy, such as music. These arguments have perplexed readers and divided commentators. Character (*ēthos*) is the second-ranking qualitative part in tragedy, coming second in importance to plot, the arrangement or composition of the incidents in the drama. It is that element of the tragedy that reveals the nature of a dramatic agent's moral choices, what sorts of things an agent chooses or rejects (6.1450b7–9). Given the important connection between action and character in Aristotle's ethics, some commentators resist the idea that we should take Aristotle seriously when he says that there could be a characterless tragedy. Readers of the *Poetics* often fail to understand why Aristotle would give such central importance to plot, when other aspects of drama, as noted in our opening discussion, give such pleasures to readers and spectators of fiction. In this chapter, we try to come to terms with Aristotle's arguments for the centrality of plot. We will see there is a plausible way of interpreting him as giving central importance to the plot, without underestimating the contribution made by the other elements of tragedy.

THE SIX QUALITATIVE ELEMENTS OF TRAGEDY

After offering his definition of tragedy, Aristotle goes on to list six necessary elements that give tragedy its qualities: plot, character, reasoning, diction, spectacle and lyric poetry or song (*Poetics* 6: 1450a7).

Tragedy					
Six qualitative elements					
Plot	Character	Reasoning	Diction	Lyric poetry (song)	Spectacle

Elements that pertain to the object of imitation, action:[2]

- **Plot** (*muthos*): the composition or arrangement (*sustasis*) of the events (6.1450a4 and 15).
- **Character** (*ēthos*): the fixed and settled disposition of an individual, in virtue of which she makes a moral choice, that is, chooses or rejects something (6.1450b6–7).
- **Reasoning** (*dianoia*, sometimes translated as "thought"): the parts of the tragedy in which a dramatic personality demonstrates or reasons about something and expresses her views (6.1450b8).

Elements that pertain to the means of imitation (rhythm, language, and melody):

- **Diction** (*lexis*): the spoken verses in the play, excluding the lyrics in the songs (6.1449b35).
- **Song** (*melos*, *melopoiia*, sometimes called "lyric poetry"): refers to the parts of the play that are sung.

Elements that pertain to the mode of imitation (as an enacted drama):

- **Spectacle** (*opsis*): refers to the aspects of the play that relate to performance, for example its stage apparatus, acting, and visual effects.

Tragedy has what we can call "quantitative" parts into which a play can be divided, such as the prologue, epilogue, choral songs, and the acts or episodes (*Poetics* 12.1452b15f.). There are also other parts that tragedy has, "qualitative" parts that contribute to its overall function and purpose. Why does Aristotle discuss the qualities of tragedy? If he has already defined tragedy, aren't these qualitative parts redundant?

Tragedy, Aristotle says, is an imitation of action and is performed by certain dramatic personalities (6.1449b37). Aristotle proceeds to list the qualitative elements because he wants to crack open, so to speak, tragedy, as an imitation of an action, to see what it necessarily includes or involves. As an analogy, a philosopher might hold that a person, by definition, has a mind, but then go on to inquire as to what aspects of the mind (e.g. consciousness) contribute to a person's functioning so that he can be rational, intelligent, and so on. So after defining tragedy (6.1449b22f.), Aristotle goes on to list the qualitative parts of tragedy that contribute to its goal of arousing pity and fear in the audience.

First, there are three qualitative parts (plot, character, and thought, in descending order of importance) that pertain to the *object* of imitation, *action*. Each tragedy, first and foremost, must have a plot (*muthos*), which is the arrangement of the incidents or events (6.1450a4). It is not identical with the actions that are imitated (6.1452a13). We could have a string of actions imitated in a tragedy, but there is no plot until those actions are given an order or structure. Plot is so important, that it is the "originating principle and, as it were, soul of tragedy" (6.1450a38–39). It is the plot that animates the elements in the play, in the way that the soul (*psuchē*) brings life to the body of an animal, enabling it to carry out the life functions that characterize a particular species.[3] Why is plot given such a pre-eminent place? More on this question shortly.

Next there are two other qualitative parts that pertain to action. Character (*ēthos*) and reasoning (*dianoia*, sometimes translated as "thought"), which are the two causes of action (6.1450a1–2).[4] Here some caution regarding Aristotle's terminology is needed. By "character" (*ēthos*) in *Poetics* 6 Aristotle is not talking about a character's personality or temperament, for example what Harry Potter thinks, what he likes, dislikes, his attitudes towards his friends, family, and so on. Instead, he refers to a concept that comes out of his discussion of virtuous action in his ethics. Character is "that which reveals moral choice" (*Poetics* 6.1450b7): it is a fixed and established disposition to choose and to avoid certain actions. Character (*ēthos*) is the source of a person's motivation and desires (1450a12; 1450b8).[5]

"Reasoning" is a second cause of action and is brought about by what an agent chooses to do on the basis of what her practical wisdom tells her is the best course of action to accomplish her goals. "Reasoning" or "thought" (*dianoia*) refers to the rational thoughts of the dramatic personalities, including arguments and deliberations they make, as well as the views they hold. Together, character (*ēthos*) and reasoning reveal how the *agent* views the action: what she hopes to accomplish as well as what deliberations motivated her to act as she did.

There are two qualitative parts, diction and song, that relate to tragedy's *means* of imitation: rhythm, language, and melody. Imitation in tragedy occurs either by means of speech or by song (6.1449b32). Diction (*lexis*), the fourth-ranking qualitative element of tragedy, refers to the composition of all the spoken verses in the dialogue (*Poetics* 6.1449b35). A poet must know how to distinguish a syllable from a verb or noun and other parts of speech. He must also know the different ways in which a character can deliver a speech, for example as a prayer, a command, a narrative, a threat, a question, a reply, and so on (19.1456b9–10).[6] Aristotle does not have much to say about this element of tragedy in *Poetics* 6.

Song (*melos*, *melopoiia*, sometimes called "lyric poetry") is the fifth-ranking qualitative part of tragedy and it also pertains to tragedy's *means* or media of imitation: (*Poetics* 6.1450b15). For song makes use of rhythm, language, and melody (or music) in the service of imitation (1447a22). Aristotle does not say much about song here, except to call it the greatest "embellishment" (*hēdusmata*), a metaphor from cooking meaning "seasoning" or "sweetening." Later (in *Poetics* 26) Aristotle says that in tragedy there is a substantial role for music, through which the most vivid pleasures are produced (26.1462a16).

The songs performed by the chorus should enrich, rather than compete with, the plot. As Aristotle observes:

> The chorus should be treated as one of the actors; it should be a part of the whole and participate, not as in Euripides but as in Sophocles. With the other poets, the songs are no more integral to the plot than to another tragedy—hence the practice, started by Agathon, of singing interlude odes.

(*Poetics* 19.1456a22–29)

Here Aristotle seems to be saying that the chorus, a group that sings, dances, and serves as a moderator and observer of the actions of the characters, should itself be regarded as a character. He appears to mean that the singing and dancing of the chorus should be integrated into the action of the play, rather than providing an interlude that has nothing to do with the plot, in the manner of a National Football League half-time event.

In this regard, Aristotle holds out Sophocles as a model for how to use the chorus, and is critical of the chorus' contribution in Euripides' plays. He does not say what he has in mind, but we can imagine why Aristotle thinks that Sophocles integrates the chorus into the action of the play. For example, the chorus in *Oedipus the King*, speaking for the people of the city, begs Oedipus to help determine the cause of the plague on Thebes; they correct Oedipus when he is off track, telling him to stop arguing with Creon, and they plead with the gods for leniency as Oedipus' true identity is revealed. This contributes to the overall unity and coherence in the elements of the tragedy, rather than having the chorus doing its own thing, distracting the audience from engaging with the incidents in the plot.[7]

The sixth and least integral qualitative part of tragedy, spectacle (*opsis*) pertains to the *mode* of imitation: tragedy is an imitation of action that is performed or enacted through actors on stage, so there is a visual aspect that spectacle (*opsis*) addresses. Spectacle is the least integral part of tragedy, for Aristotle maintains that it is possible to feel fear and pity without seeing the play performed, just by hearing the events read out as they occur in the plot:[8]

> For the plot should be so structured that, even without seeing it performed, the person who hears the events that occur experiences horror and pity at what comes about (as one would feel when hearing the plot of *Oedipus*). To create this effect through spectacle has little to do with the poet's art, and requires material resources. Those who use spectacle to create an effect not of the fearful but only of the sensational have nothing at all in common with tragedy.

(14.1453b3–10)

Clearly, if Aristotle were around today, he would have little appreciation for works of fiction, whether novel, film, or drama, that come up short on plot construction, but instead try to please the audience through, as we would say, "special effects" or rely on the strength of the performance of the actors. While spectacle has an emotional power (14.1453b1–3), it is an inferior way to arouse emotions in the audience, and it belongs more to the art of the costumer, or what we would nowadays call the stage director (7.1450b15–20).

Yet, Aristotle acknowledges that spectacle (along with other aspects of the performance of tragedy, including music and dance) can be an effective way to arouse emotions in the audience, when it is integrated into the mimetic content of the plot.[9] Aristotle even recommends that the poet, when composing plays, work out the plot in gestures, suggesting how performance can enhance the emotional impact of the plot:

> So far as possible, one should also work out the plot in gestures, since a natural affinity makes those in the grip of emotions the most convincing, and the truest distress or anger is conveyed by those who actually feels these things.
>
> (*Poetics* 17.1455a29f.)

If performance enhances the ability of the poet to feel the emotional impact of the plot, perhaps, then it is possible that performance for an audience can have the same effect. This suggests that spectacle can have a place in drama when, like the chorus, it enhances, rather than replaces, the work done by the plot. Aristotle is clear, however, that there is no place for a play that works simply on the level of the visual, with no regard for the plot as the primary vehicle for arousing emotion in the audience.

ARISTOTLE ON THE POSSIBILITY OF A CHARACTERLESS TRAGEDY

Aristotle presents several arguments in *Poetics* 6 to establish the centrality of the plot as the primary element of tragedy. He even goes so far as to argue that there could be a successful tragedy that omitted character provided the plot was well constructed (6.1450a23–25). This argument has perplexed readers and divided commentators. Character (*ēthos*) is the second-ranking qualitative part in tragedy, coming second in importance to plot, the arrangement or composition of the incidents in the drama. It is that element of the tragedy that reveals the nature of a dramatic agent's moral choices, what sorts of things an agent chooses or rejects (6.1450b7–9). Given the important connection between action and character, in the sense of a fixed disposition to make certain choices, in Aristotle's ethics, some commentators resist the idea that we should take Aristotle seriously when he says that there could be a characterless tragedy. We now investigate Aristotle's central arguments regarding the primacy of plot.

There are several different challenges we face when we read these arguments in *Poetics* 6. There are problems of interpretation: how do we interpret his claim that there could be a characterless tragedy? And there are critical questions as to how he thinks a plot that omits character (*ēthos*) can succeed in moving the audience. First, we consider the questions of interpretation.

The first argument for the primacy of plot runs as follows (6.1450a15–22)

Argument #1:

1) The end or goal of all human life is happiness (*eudaimonia*).
2) Happiness depends on human actions.
3) Plot is the imitation (*mimēsis*) of action.
4) Therefore, plot is the most important feature of tragedy.

Premise (1), the claim that the end of human life is happiness or flourishing, is central to Aristotle's ethics.[10] It is also a key assumption in the construction of a plot, for happiness is what the tragic characters are aiming for (6.1450a30). People are happy or not according to their actions (premise (2); 1450a19). Therefore, plot, which is the imitation of action, is the most important feature of tragedy.

Even if we grant the premises (1)–(3), we might still balk at drawing the conclusion in (4)). For character (*ēthos*), along with reasoning (*dianoia*), are two causes of action (6.14549b38–39). If there is no cause, then there is no effect. So how could there be action, if a play omits the causes of action?

If Aristotle's second argument is successful, it will answer this question. For it attempts to show that plot is the essential ingredient in tragedy, while character (along with the other elements) are not essential. This means, appearances to the contrary, it is possible to have a play with action, but no character. Aristotle's second argument is that "without action there could not be tragedy, but there might be without character (*ēthos*)" (6.1450a23–24):

Argument #2:

1) Plot is the imitation of action.
2) A tragedy that had action, but lacked the element of character (*ēthos*) could still be a successful tragedy.
3) A tragedy that had the element of character (*ēthos*), but no action could not be successful.
4) Therefore, plot is essential to tragedy, while character (*ēthos*) is not.

Plot is, by definition, the imitation of action (premise (1)). It is possible, Aristotle argues, for a tragedy that has action but is deficient in character to evoke pity and fear in the audience (premise (2)). On the other hand, a tragedy that had character (*ēthos*), for example through a string of speeches by the dramatic actors, but no action, would not be successful at evoking the right emotional response from the audience (premise (3)). Therefore, it follows that plot is essential to tragedy, while character is not (the conclusion, (4)).

What does it mean to say (as in premise (2)) that there could be a tragedy that "lacks character" but has action? Some commentators think that premise (2) must mean that the play does contain "character," but it is revealed through the action, and not, for example, by speeches the character makes. For the notions of character and action are correlated in Aristotle's ethics. Virtuous actions build up a virtuous character, and the virtue is the active realization of one's character in action.[11] Following along with this idea, a characterless tragedy would be one in which character (*ēthos*) is displayed through consistent patterns of *actions*. Along these lines, John Jones says, "He is saying that the human self is present in its acts—present, moreover, with a fullness and effectiveness attained nowhere else."[12] So, when spectators see dramatic agents repeatedly performing just or temperate actions, they infer that the cause of these actions is a fixed and stable virtuous character (*ēthos*).

The problem with this interpretation is that character need *not* be revealed explicitly through the action: "Character is that which reveals moral choice—that is, when otherwise unclear, what kinds of things an agent chooses or rejects" (6.1450b7–9). This suggests that while some action reveals a person's moral choices, others (e.g. a king giving out food to the poor) need not.

A second line of interpretation proposes that we take Aristotle literally: that there could be a play with action, but not character.[13] This interpretation has the advantage of taking Aristotle as true to his word, for in the passage quoted above, he suggests that it is possible for tragedy to succeed without character. Yet, to say that there is action without character would, as said before, be metaphysically incoherent. This would be like saying there could be an effect without its cause.

What then does he mean in saying that a characterless tragedy is possible? Aristotle's point in premise (2) must be an epistemological one: a "characterless" tragedy is one in which the ethical qualities and dispositions of the dramatic agents are not made known clearly or fully to the audience through the actions or the speeches in the play.[14] For example, suppose a king repeatedly does good things for the people of his city. This tells us something about his character, but if the nature of his moral choice is not completely clear from his actions or speeches in the play (e.g. is his action motivated by the desire to help the citizens or just to give the appearance of being a just ruler?), then his motivations and choices will not be clear. In this sense, the play has action, but not character (*ēthos*). Interpreted in this way, Aristotle's argument #2 is that a tragedy could be successful that did not make known the character (*ēthos*) of the dramatic agents, provided that it had a well-constructed plot. But it is not possible for the reverse to be true: a play that revealed character (*ēthos*) through a string of speeches, but lacked action, would not successfully evoke pity and fear in the audience.

If it is possible for character to be omitted from a tragedy, this raises some critical questions about the overall consistency of the argument in the *Poetics*. Elizabeth Belfiore, in particular, has pressed several points.[15] In *Poetics* 2 Aristotle distinguishes tragedy from comedy by saying that the former imitates the action of people who are elevated or admirable (the *spoudaioi*), while comedy imitates the action of those who are "base" (*phaulos*), where these two types of people differ in their character (1448a1–3). Here admirable action is determined by the nature of the agent's character. How then is it feasible to think a tragedy can omit a dramatic agent's character? Would it even be possible, without the dramatic agent's character, to determine if the play was a tragedy or a comedy?

In addition, in *Poetics* 13 Aristotle characterizes the ideal dramatic agent as someone who is intermediate, but "not preeminent in virtue and justice, and one who falls into adversity not through evil and depravity, but through some kind of error" (1453a7–12). Elizabeth Belfiore asks, how can a tragedy imitate such an individual without including character (*ēthos*) in some way? Finally, we can add a third, related, point of concern. Pity is felt for the undeserving victim of adversity (13.1453a2–3).

Don't we need to know the nature of the dramatic agent's moral choices to know if he does not deserve to suffer? It is because, to illustrate, Oedipus kills his father unintentionally, without knowing what he is doing, that the audience feel for him. Pity appears to involve some kind of evaluation of the agent's actions that requires knowing what he chose and what he intended to do.

Taken all together, then, how can Aristotle be serious in saying that a characterless tragedy is possible? Short of saying that Aristotle is confused on this point, some other option is needed. To start, we can think of Aristotle's ranking of the qualitative parts of tragedy as like a pyramid, with the action and the plot forming the base. There is no pyramid without the base. Once this is established, the other parts of the tragedy, character, reasoning, diction, song, and spectacle, build on the emotional basis of the tragedy that is provided by the plot.

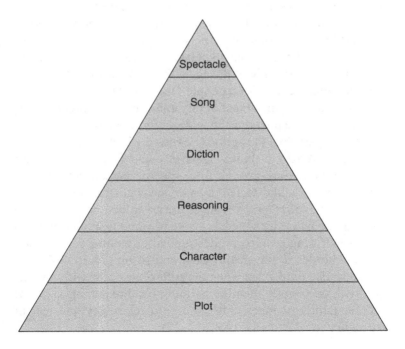

The plot is the emotional ground floor for tragedy because the plot is like the soul of tragedy (6.1450a37). The soul is the creature's essence: it is that which makes possible and explains the presence of all the stable characteristics, including the necessary ones that characterize the animal as a certain kind of being. The soul, then, is not a part of an animal that can in principle be dispensed with: it is the basic nature or essence of a thing that makes possible all of its stable and fixed characteristics. The comparison, then, of the plot with the soul of tragedy (6.1450a37) tells us that not only is the plot a necessary element of tragedy: it is the essence of tragedy, that which makes possible all of the other qualitative parts of tragedy.[16]

Following along with this point, Aristotle maintains that tragedy is an imitation of an action, and only secondarily an imitation of an agent who acts (6.1450b3–4; 6.1450a20–22). Actions are not abstract things, but are particulars that are performed in specific circumstances and by a specific agent (*Nicomachean Ethics* 3.1.1110b6–7). It would make no sense, then, if Aristotle argued that there could be a tragedy that had an action without an agent. There is no action without the agent that can perform it, and it is the individual agents, for example Oedipus, Alcestis, Antigone, and so on, that are the object of pity and fear. So, in order to imitate an action, the poet must include an imitation of the dramatic agent who performs the action (*Poetics* 6.1450b3–4).

No one, Aristotle thinks, feels pity and fear for a faceless mob; these emotions are felt for a specific person. So pity and fear are felt for and directed towards the characters in a tragedy (*Poetics* 13.1453a1–3). Yet there are basic components of the plot that are naturally suited to evoke pity and fear. One component is suffering (*pathos*), a destructive or painful action, such as a public death, physical agony, and so on (11.1452b7–10). Aristotle also thinks that when the sufferings occur within families, with one family member harming (or threatening to harm) another family member, this naturally evokes pity and fear in the audience (*Poetics* 14.1453b13–22):

Since poets should create the pleasure from pity and fear through mimesis, obviously this should be built into the events. Let us, then, take up the question of what sorts of incidents strike us as terrible or pitiable . . . What tragedy must seek are cases where the suffering occurs within relationships, such as brother and brother, son and father, mother and son, son and mother—when the one kills (or is about to kill) the other, or commits some other such deed.

(14.1453b10–22)

Aristotle suggests that pity and fear for characters in this set of circumstances are possible just on the basis of grasping the events, without needing to know anything about the moral character of the dramatic agent. Certain situations, such as family-on-family violence, are, then, by their very nature a trigger to the audience feeling pity and fear for those involved, regardless of the moral character of the person who inflicts or almost inflicts harm.

Several other components of the plot, reversal and recognition, also prompt pity and fear as well. Reversal (*peripeteia*), is a change of fortune that is opposite to what is expected, yet a turn of events that happens in accordance with probability and necessity (1452a22–29); recognition (*anagnōrisis*) is when there is a change from ignorance to knowledge (1452a29–32). These two components are features of the structure of the plot, and so have nothing to do with the audience grasping the full nature of the character (*ēthos*) of the dramatic agents.

Aristotle's argument that there can be a characterless tragedy that evokes pity and fear appears to be coherent. Certain events, such as situations where one family member harms or threatens to harm another, are by their nature scenarios that dispose people to feel pity and fear for the dramatic agents. The poet connects a plot around such events by building a plot based on what likely or necessarily happens to the dramatic agents when they are in this situation. This is the base of the tragedy. Next, the poet proceeds to build on this base structure by explicitly revealing the character (*ēthos*) and reasoning of the dramatic agent. The remaining elements, diction, song, and spectacle, are coordinated to build on and develop the emotional power in the plot.

This way of explaining the poet's method of composing a story raises a final potential problem for the idea of a characterless tragedy. For Aristotle indicates that the plot is built around what it is likely or necessary that a certain kind of character will say or do. Poetry is based on the "universal . . . the kinds of things which it suits a certain kind of person to say or do, in terms of probability or necessity" (*Poetics* 9.1451b5–7). This suggests that the poet composes the play by developing the plot out of the character (*ēthos*) of the dramatic agents.

Given that the agent is a certain kind of person, how will she act? For instance, suppose that the plot is to involve the series of events in Sophocles' *Oedipus:* the poet draws on the dramatic agent's character to construct the plot. What is the king likely to do when he discovers that he may be somehow involved in the destruction of his city? What is he likely or necessarily to do when he discovers the truth about his identity? And so on. The poet, it would seem, must make essential use of character in order to establish that certain events follow, necessarily or probably, from previous events. How, then, can there be a characterless tragedy, if the character (*ēthos*) of the dramatic agent is essential to constructing the plot?

In a discussion of character in *Poetics* 15, Aristotle clarifies that there are two independent steps in poetic composition: first, the structure of events in the plot should follow by necessity and probability; and second, what the dramatic agents say and do should also follow according to what is necessary or likely that such persons say and do.

> With character, precisely as in the structure of events, one should always seek necessity or probability—so that for such a person to say or do such things is necessary or probable, and the sequence of events is also necessary or probable.

(15.1454a32–33)

This is what we would expect Aristotle to say if he is thinking that poetic composition proceeds as in the pyramid model, with the composition of the events in the plot coming first, and then a second layer being added, with speech or action revealing the nature of a moral choice by the dramatic agent (see 15.1454a17–18).

Perhaps, to illustrate, the poet starts with the basic plot where it is necessary or likely that any person would react with horror when finding out that he unintentionally killed his father and married his mother. When the poet adds in that Oedipus is a morally decent person, a person "intermediate in virtue and justice," whose change of fortune is caused by an error (*hamartia*), not a vicious character or depravity (13.1453a5–7), it is then likely that other actions follow, for example that he will pluck out his eyes in shame and exile himself from the city he loves.

Aristotle is careful to argue that a characterless tragedy will have *some* degree of success, while a tragedy with character, but without plot and action cannot succeed whatsoever. But he does not claim that a characterless plot will have the full success that a play with character, reasoning, and the other qualitative parts has:

> If someone lays out a string of diction and thought, he will not achieve the stated function of tragedy: much *more* successful will be a tragedy which, though deficient in these other elements, has a plot and structure of events.
>
> (6.1450a28–32, my emphasis)

CONCLUSION

Thinking of the six qualitative elements of tragedy as forming a pyramid, with the plot forming the basis and the other elements contributing to the effect of tragedy, provides a way to take Aristotle seriously when he stresses the primacy of plot over the other elements of tragedy, without thinking that he misunderstands the contribution that the other parts make to tragedy. It is coherent why he thinks that character is secondary to plot, and why there could even possibly be a characterless tragedy.

Further, as the pyramid model suggests, there is no reason to think he is being insensitive to the important role that character, reasoning, and the other elements such as diction, thought, song, and even spectacle play in producing the emotional qualities of tragedy. Indeed, he lists these as necessary elements that every tragedy ought to have (6.1450a8–9).

At the same time, we also can see how Aristotle's argument regarding the primacy of the plot fits into the larger account of poetic unity that he elaborates in books 7–8 of the *Poetics*. It is, above all else, the necessary and probable connections in the plot that make the action believable, understandable, and capable of prompting pity, fear, and awe. The emotional power of tragedy, therefore, does not primarily come from the character of the dramatic agents, their thoughts, their eloquent speeches, nor from spectacle or music, though all these parts of tragedy undeniably contribute to a work's emotional effects.[17] The emotional response to tragedy is grounded in a pattern of understandable human action whose meaning and significance it is the job of the plot to reveal.

NOTES

1 Reading for this chapter is *Poetics* 6 and *Poetics* 19.
2 See the distinction between objects, means, and mode of imitation in *Poetics* 2–3 and discussed in Chapter 3.
3 *De Anima* (On the Soul) 2.1.
4 Character (*ēthos*) is not to be confused with the notion of a "dramatic character" in the play. To avoid a misunderstanding in this discussion I will use the term "dramatic personality" or sometimes "dramatic agent" to refer to the dramatic characters in the play. An "agent" (e.g. Oedipus, Odysseus, Antigone) is someone who has agency, that is, is able to make choices, follow through on these choices in action, and manipulate her environment to accomplish her goals.
5 See *Nicomachean Ethics* 2.6.

6 Later in the text he suggests that diction belongs not properly speaking to the poet's craft, but to the art of delivery or oratory (see *Poetics* 19.1456b10–15).

7 It is generally supposed that in saying that the chorus should not be used "in Euripides' way" Aristotle is making a criticism of Euripides that is often repeated today: that the choral lyrics in his plays are not integral to the action of the play. Aristotle's meaning in saying the chorus should be regarded as one of the actors is investigated in Albert Weiner 1980, especially 208–210. See Rush Rehm 1996 for an interesting, positive re-assessment of the chorus in Euripides' work.

8 As G. M. Sifakis notes (2001: 10), tragedies and epics were not read by the public at the time that Aristotle was writing, so Aristotle is well aware that performance would have been the way members of the public appreciated tragedy, not by reading, as we now do with novels.

9 For the development of this argument see Gregory Scott 2000.

10 *Nicomachean Ethics* 1.1.

11 *Nicomachean Ethics* 2, especially 2.4. An agent develops a virtuous character by the actions she performs, "one becomes just by performing just actions and self-controlled by practicing self-control" (*Nicomachean Ethics* 2.4.1105a17–18). In turn the actions an agent performs are an expression of her character. "When an individual has no ulterior motive, he speaks, acts, and lives his real character" (*Nicomachean Ethics* 4.7.1127a27f.).

12 John Jones 1962: 33. See also Stephen Halliwell 1998: 151–152; and more recently Silvia Carli 2010: 330, footnote 131.

13 See Catherine Lord 1969: 55–62 and Elizabeth S. Belfiore 1992: 108–110.

14 Action and thought are the two ways in which character (*ēthos*) is revealed in the play.

15 Elizabeth Belfiore 1992: 101–107.

16 Cf Catherine Lord 1969 who argues that tragedy is like an organic unity with each part, including the plot, dispensable because the work of one part can be taken over by the other parts.

17 For some good arguments to the conclusion that Aristotle does not downgrade performance as an aspect of tragedy, see Gregory Scott 2000.

WORKS CITED

Belfiore, Elizabeth S. 1992. *Tragic Pleasures: Aristotle on Plot and Emotion*. Princeton, NJ: Princeton University Press.

Carli, Silvia 2010. "Philosophy is More Philosophical than History: Aristotle on Mimēsis and Form." *Review of Metaphysics* 64 (2) (December): 303–336.

Halliwell, Stephen 1998. *Aristotle's Poetics: With a New Introduction by the Author*. Chicago: University of Chicago Press.

Jones, John 1962. *On Aristotle and Greek Tragedy*. London: Oxford University Press.

Lord, Catherine 1969. "Tragedy without Character." *The Journal of Aesthetics and Art Criticism* 28 (1): 55–62.

Rehm, Rush 1996. "Performing the Chorus: Choral Action, Interaction, and Absence in Euripides." *Arion: A Journal of Humanities and the Classics.* Third Series, 4 (1), The Chorus in Greek Tragedy and Culture, Two (Spring): 46–60.

Scott, Gregory 2000. "The Poetics of Performance: The Necessity of Spectacle, Music, and Dance in Aristotelian Tragedy," in Salim Kemal and Ivan Gaskell (eds.), *Performance and Authenticity in the Arts.* Cambridge: Cambridge University Press: 15–48.

Sifakis, G. M. 2001. *Aristotle on the Function of Tragic Poetry.* Herakleion: Crete University Press.

Weiner, Albert 1980. "The Function of the Tragic Greek Chorus." *Theatre Journal* 32 (2) (May): 205–212.

7

PHILOSOPHY, POETRY, AND KNOWLEDGE

ANCIENT AND CONTEMPORARY DEBATES ABOUT ART AND KNOWLEDGE

Do we learn things from art?[1] Going back to Socrates in Plato's *Republic* 10 right up until the present time, philosophers have engaged in a vigorous debate on this question. They have asked, is art a source of knowledge? If so, what sorts of things do we learn from art and just how does this learning take place?

Mimetic art, art that purports to be about or stand for something, is often thought to make a good case for the cognitive value of art.[2] The value of mimetic art, it is argued, rests on its accuracy of representation or imitation. We can learn about people, moments in history, as well as landscapes from an accurate painting; for example, from Jean-Pierre Houël's *Prise de la Bastille* (*Taking of the Bastille*) we can learn about the day in history when ordinary French citizens stormed the Bastille prison, protesting against the tyranny of Louis XVI and setting out events that led to the French revolution. From great novels we can learn about what it was like to live in Victorian England or the conditions of slaves in the eighteenth-century American South. This kind of knowledge is what philosophers call *knowledge of facts*. Perhaps, it has been suggested, we can learn something about the cause of the French revolution and how the storming of the Bastille lead up to this important moment in French history from looking at and studying Houël's painting.[3]

There is a strong challenge to the claim that we can learn about the world from works of art, including works like Houël's painting, that purport to be about events in history. How do we know that the representation or imitation of the event is accurate? We agree that we would not learn from a painting that presented a view of that momentous day in French history that was misinformed, distorted, sentimental, or idealized. Just looking at Houël's painting, how do we know that what we are looking at is an accurate rather than a wildly inaccurate representation?[4] It might even be suggested that it is part of the power of great works of art that they are able to capture our imagination in a way that we (mistakenly) think that by looking at them we are learning what some day in history was really like.[5] As Oscar Wilde wryly observed, lying, the telling of beautiful untrue things, is the proper aim of art.[6]

It is part of the traditional conception of knowledge that it meets three conditions. We say that:

A person, S, knows that p (some state of affairs, e.g. that grass is green) if and only if:

1) S believes p.
2) S is justified in believing p.
3) p is true.

The first condition, belief, captures the idea that a necessary condition for a person knowing that some state of affairs, p, is true, is that she at least believes it. A person who knows something, at the least, takes the world to be a certain way. The second and third conditions express the idea that knowledge builds on belief: there is more to knowing something than merely believing it. Finally, if you tell me that you know that the moon is made of green cheese, I expect to see evidence. This is because knowledge requires support or justification (the second condition). Further, what a person believes must be true (third condition). We do not say things such as "In the sixth century BCE people in Greece knew the earth was flat," for knowledge implies truth.

First, there is a concern about the *truth claims* of art (condition (3)). Does art make claims about the world, and are these claims true? A leading account of truth is the correspondence theory of truth. The idea is that a representation of reality is true provided that it corresponds with reality. This notion of truth captures the idea that truth is objective and mind-independent.[7] Does art convey or impart truths to the audience? Or is art, as Wilde suggests, the telling of beautiful falsehoods?

Second, there is a concern that the evidence or warrant condition for knowledge is not met. Is the audience or viewer justified in believing the ideas about the world that she has gained from art? This is a concern about *justification:* is there some reason to accept and trust the change in one's ideas and feelings that art brings about in the viewer?

This concern about whether art imparts truth and knowledge goes back at least to Plato, Aristotle's teacher. Plato called the universal objects of knowledge, the Forms, and he held that individual sensible particulars, this beautiful rose or that just act, resemble or "participate" in the Forms Beauty-Itself or Justice-Itself. Yet these sensible particulars, Plato argued, are not the proper objects of knowledge because they are not always true examples of the universals they strive to be like. The rose is beautiful today, but in a few days its beauty will fade as it decomposes. An act may appear just to one person or one society and not just to another. This means that Forms, immaterial, eternal, non-sensible abstract objects, must be the proper objects of knowledge and it is only accessible or available via the intellect, not the senses.

The mimetic artist, according to Socrates' battery of arguments in *Republic* 10, works at the level of sense perception, so the poet or painter produces a work that is an imitation of a sensible particular. The mimetic artist might try to imitate the true objects of knowledge, the Forms, but Plato's metaphysics and his view that mimetic artists are limited to copying the sensible appearances of things entail that mimetic art is several times removed from the true objects of knowledge, the Forms.

The worry that we cannot verify that the things we learn from art about the world are in fact true has prompted some cognitivists to look for other ways in which we learn from art.[8] For the talk of "learning" from fiction cannot be justified if the insights that we derive from the work have not been tested.[9] Perhaps art gives us knowledge, not of the factual, but of the possible. Works of art, including tragedy, essentially appeal to the audience's imagination. The artist constructs a make-believe world and asks the audience to imagine what the set of possibilities described in the world is like. Contemplating this fictional world can lead to a kind of conceptual knowledge that is especially relevant to moral understanding. If a reader, for example, imagines the actions of Raskolnikov, the central character in Dostoevsky's great novel, *Crime and Punishment*, she will imagine a fictional world in which Raskolnikov murders a pawnbroker that he says is good for nothing and evil. This contemplation of what is possible, but not actual, can prompt the reader to refine or test her understanding of good and evil, leading to a kind of conceptual knowledge that is key to moral understanding.[10]

While knowledge of what is possible is useful, it has been thought by some that art can give us knowledge not just of what is possible, but what is actual.[11] In particular, some have the sense that through mimetic art it is possible to acquire a more profound sort of knowledge, a deeper understanding of human nature. As noted earlier, some philosophers argue that tragedy, in particular, is especially capable of imparting these deeper truths to its audiences and readers.[12] This view is reflected in language when people read Sophocles' *Oedipus* or Shakespeare's *Hamlet*, for example, and say that these works are "illuminating," "revealing," or "edifying."

We need some explanation of what we mean when we say that works of art impart some deeper insights. We can say that a work gives us some more profound understanding or knowledge when the work is capable of affecting a change in the audience's view of themselves and/or the world.[13] Hence, it is not surprising that the debate around art and knowledge has taken up the question: just what is it that the viewers, readers, or audience of a work of art come to learn or understand that they did not understand before?

This has proven difficult for contemporary art cognitivists to answer. Jerome Stolnitz, among others, has pressed the point that the supposed truths that art offers are either so abstract as to be trivial ("Stubborn pride and prejudice keep two attractive people apart") or truths that apply to just the particular characters in the work of fiction, and so not real truths at all, since there must be a certain level of generality for the insights in a work of fiction to be useful and relevant for our lives.[14] Various art cognitivists have taken up the challenge of responding to Stolnitz's criticisms.[15]

ARISTOTLE AND THE DEBATE ABOUT ART AND KNOWLEDGE

Many contemporary art cognitivists cite Aristotle's *Poetics* in support of their arguments that art can be a source of knowledge and learning. This is because in *Poetics* 9 Aristotle suggests that poetry can move beyond what a particular subject did or said (e.g. what Odysseus or Antigone did) to something that has a higher level of generality, a universal, which he explains as "the kind of thing that it fits a certain kind of person to say or do in terms of probability or necessity" (9.1451b7–8). Poetry is more philosophical than history because it "speaks more of the universal, while history relates particulars" (9.1451b6–7).

In this chapter we focus on understanding just what Aristotle means in saying that poetry "speaks more" of the universal, and how this bears on the comparison that Aristotle makes between philosophy, poetry, and history. To do so, we begin with some background on Aristotle's theory of knowledge.

A BRIEF PRIMER ON ARISTOTLE'S THEORY OF KNOWLEDGE

In Aristotle's metaphysics, the universal (*to katholou*) is that which is by nature predicated on many things (*De Interpretatione* 17a35–37).[16] Aristotle follows a tradition initiated by Socrates and carried on by Plato, according to which knowledge, properly speaking, is not of a particular (this individual human being or individual horse), but is of a universal human being or horse, something that is common to and is the identity shared by many individual human beings and horses, respectively.[17] While Aristotle agrees that knowledge (*epistēmē*) is of the universal and not the particular, his view of where universals are found and how we come to know them radically depart from those of his teacher.

Aristotle rejects the view that universals exist separately from sensible particulars. For he thinks it makes no sense to say that a disembodied Form, Human Being-Itself, is the cause or explanation of why you, Socrates, and I are all human beings. Universals cannot contribute to knowledge, "if they are not *in* the particulars that share in them" (*Metaphysics* 1.991a14). Thus, while Aristotle agrees that knowledge investigates the form and the universal, not the particular, he denies that universals, human being, horse, exist separately from the sensible particulars that embody them.

Because the universals (human being, horse) are embodied in sensible particulars (this human being, that horse), sense perception is the starting point for an individual moving to the universals of knowledge (*epistēmē*). An individual goes through various cognitive stages on the route to such understanding.[18] The sensible world has a certain structure or order: sensible objects belong to natural kinds. The latter are a grouping of particular things under a shared kind based on the fact that they share an essence or basic nature. Examples of natural kinds are the species cats, zebras, seals, and human beings.

Aristotle thinks that human beings have an innate ability to understand the fundamental essence of natural kinds using, as a start, sense perception and memory. At this stage the mind retains sense perceptions and then sorts them into categories based on similarities and differences. There will be some errors as this process gets going, for a child might group together all adult females under the category "mother."[19] The child then moves to a phase where she is able to use the term "mother" correctly.

Next, an individual progresses to the third phase, *experience (empeiria)*, a cognitive state that is unique to humans where there is coalescing of memories of retained sense perceptions of the same kind of object. Here the person who has experience can correctly identify natural groupings, for example that Callias and Coriscus belong to a group that were helped by a certain medicine, but he does not grasp a general principle that explains *why* the medicine cured them. Knowledge and understanding occur when the individual acquires art (*technē*), a state where the physician is able to produce health based on an understanding of the causes: "Patients with such and such kind of symptoms are cured by drug z *because* of factors x and y."

The highest form of knowledge is wisdom (*sophia*), a knowledge of the first and most universal causes of things: this is a cognitive state in which we engage for its own sake, simply out of our desire to attain the truth.[20] Here the person inspects or theorizes (from "*theōrein*") the universal truths that describe the nature of the universe and the kinds of things in it. Philosophy is a form of wisdom, for it is concerned with knowledge of the truth.[21] Wisdom is the purest realization of the human desire to know, a process that starts with the delight that humans take in sense perception and leads to the knowledge of the universal causes of things, for its own sake.

With this background, we can turn our attention to the argument in *Poetics* 9.

FROM POETIC UNITY TO POETIC UNIVERSALS

In *Poetics* 9 Aristotle makes a comparison between poetry, history, and philosophy:

> It is not the poet's function to relate actual events, but the *kinds* of things that might occur and are possible in terms of probability or necessity ... The difference between the historian and the poet ... is this: that the one relates actual events, the other the kinds of things that might occur. Consequently, poetry is more philosophical and more elevated than history, since poetry relates more of the universal, while history relates particulars. "Universal" (*katholou*) means the kinds of things which it suits a certain kind of person to say or do, in terms of probability or necessity.
>
> (9.1451a36–b9)

This paragraph starts with an idea with which we are already familiar from *Poetics* 8: the poet's job is to construct a plot with events that are linked by probability or necessity.[22] The well-formed plot structures a sequence of actions into a coherent and well-structured whole in which the causal and explanatory links between the events are evident. Aristotle's standard for a coherent and unified plot is probability and necessity (1451b25f., 1451a14–15, 1460b12). The events in the plot must, at a minimum, proceed according to what is likely or what happens for the most part. Plots that conform to necessity meet a higher standard of poetic unity: they concern a pattern of events that happen invariably. Aristotle's view that the plot must proceed according to probability or necessity leads him to the view that poetry embodies "universals," the kind of thing that could or might happen, in accordance with probability and necessity (9.1451b7).

POETRY DEALS WITH THE POSSIBLE

In *Poetics* 9 Aristotle develops the implications that the well-formed plot must proceed according to probability and necessity. He draws a contrast between poetry and history, on the one hand, and poetry and philosophy, on the other. The writing of the historian relates the actual, while the plots of the poet convey the possible, the sort of thing that *might* occur (9.1451a38–b1). This is the first central difference he draws between poetry and history.

To illustrate, the historian writes of a battle that did, as a matter of fact, occur between the Greeks and the Persians. The poet writes a plot concerning a battle that could or might have occurred between these two groups. Possible events are the sort of thing that it is plausible to think could occur, even if these events are not, as a matter of fact, known to have taken place. The relevant sense of "could" here is not mere logical possibility, that is, something that is not contradictory or absurd, for example a squared circle. The poet deals with possible events that could occur, in the sense that these happenings are consistent with past human experience, even if they are not known to have actually occurred (9.1454b3).

Here Aristotle draws our attention to a distinction between history and poetry that is readily understandable. While history operates at the level of the factual, poetry uses fiction and the imagination to construct plots. There was not, as a matter of fact, a King Oedipus who brought a plague on his kingdom by unintentionally killing his father and marrying his mother. The poet enlists the audience's imagination in asking them to consider a story that relates what could happen if there were such an individual. While there may not have been such an unfortunate king, Sophocles constructs his plot so that the audience is able to imagine that the events surrounding Oedipus' actions are the sort of things that *could* take place, in keeping with human knowledge and experience.

In a rather difficult section in *Poetics* 9, Aristotle appears to take back his claim that poetry deals with the possible, not the actual. He is trying to come to terms with the fact that some tragedies deal with events that are believed to be historical fact, for example the Trojan War:

> But in tragedy they adhere to the actual names. The reason is that the possible seems plausible: about the possibility of things which have not occurred we are not yet sure; but it is evident that actual events are possible—they could not otherwise have occurred.
>
> (9.1451b13–19)

First, it is not clear whether Aristotle is saying that he, Aristotle, believed that the events told in traditional stories are true or whether he is simply reporting the beliefs of the audience that events such as the Trojan War actually took place. Commentators think that it is the latter, not the former, that is, Aristotle is reporting the beliefs of the average person who accepts the traditional stories as true, rather than saying that events told in these stories actually took place.[23]

Second, a more pressing problem is in understanding the logic of Aristotle's argument. He appears to give this explanation of why tragedians in some cases use the names of characters from the traditional stories, such as Heracles or Oedipus:

1) The possible seems plausible (*pithanos*, credible, believable).
2) That which has actually happened is possible.
3) Therefore, that which has actually happened is plausible.

That which is possible is believable, for the possible is the sort of thing that could happen, within the realm of human experience (premise 1). That which is actual is also possible, presumably because impossible events cannot occur (premise 2). Therefore, the actual is plausible (conclusion in 3). The tragedians, in other words, use the actual names in the service of what is possible and believable.

The problem commentators have is with premise (2) of the argument. Is Aristotle saying that everything that actually happens is possible, in the sense of being coherent with past human experience? Surely this is false, as random and freakish sorts of things do happen that are outside the scope of human experience. Aristotle recognizes this point a little later on in *Poetics* 9:

> The poet should be more a maker of plots than of verses, in so far as he is a poet by virtue of *mimēsis*, and his *mimēsis* is of action. So even should his poetry concern actual events, he is no less a poet for that, as there is nothing to prevent *some* actual events from being probable as well as possible, and it is through probability that the poet makes his material from them.
>
> (9.1451b26–32, my emphasis)

Here Aristotle makes clear his own view, that there is no problem if a poet makes a plot that deals with actual events. For he reasons that *some* actual events will be possible, that is something that is not outside the scope of human knowledge and experience, as well as probable, in that these events conform to a pattern of what is likely to take place. This implies that he recognizes that at least some actually occurring events will *not* be possible or plausible in the requisite sense. Therefore, Aristotle's reasoning in the passage above implies that he would reject premise (2) above.

It is more likely, then, that the argument he is relaying above is not his own: rather, he is constructing the reasoning of the poets who endeavor to use "actual names" (that is the names of characters from traditional stories) in the service of believability. Why would he repeat their arguments if those poets' reasoning about *why* adherence to the traditional names works is false? Aristotle's empirically based method of proceeding requires that he take the poets' observations about what works seriously. For if the poets who use traditional stories routinely succeed, there may well be an underlying reason for their success, even if the poets' *account* or explanation of *why* the traditional stories work is faulty.

To these poets he says, "Adherence to the traditional plots of tragedy should not be sought at all costs" (9.1451b23). Instead, he suggests that the traditional stories would only be known to a minority and even plays that deal with made-up characters and events please the audience just as much as those dramas based on the stories drawn from ancient mythology.

Taking these points together, we see that Aristotle's overall point is clear, which is that history deals with actual events, while poetry constructs a plot with causal connections between events, either actual or possible. Some actual events can be possible and probable, that is, they are events that display a causal connection with what went before, occurring not just after previous events but *because* of them (9.1450b27–28; 9.1452a20–21). So the poet is not barred from drawing from the same material about which the historian writes. But the poet deals with this material differently, by incorporating the events into a plot that proceeds according to probability or necessity. Aristotle commends the comic poets for recognizing this point well, for they "construct the plot on the basis of probability, and only then supply arbitrary names" (9.1451b12–14).

POETRY "SPEAKS OF" THE UNIVERSAL

In *Poetics* 9 Aristotle draws a second point of contrast between history and poetry. Poetry is more aligned with the interests of philosophy because poetic plots "speak of" the universal, whereas history is concerned with particulars. The universal "means the kinds of things which it suits a certain kind of person to say or do, in terms of probability or necessity" (9.1451b7–9), while a particular is what a specific individual, for example Alcibiades, did or experienced (9.1451b11). Poetry is closer to philosophy than history because the plot constructs the actions and interactions of the characters in terms of a larger pattern of what a certain kind of person will say or do in a specific situation, according to probability or necessity (1451b8).

This means that poet is capable of conveying something more universal than history, which is more aligned, in Aristotle's view, with the reporting of particular events, for example this battle between the Greeks and the Persians that occurred on such and such a date. Poetry does not just say or report what has happened, at the level of specific events. The unified structure of the plot puts events into a coherent and unified whole so that the audience grasps a universal pattern of human experience through understanding the causal connections that are built into the structure of the well-formed plot.

This does not mean that the poet leaves the particular characters and situations behind while focusing on composing a plot whose actions conform to a larger pattern of action that conveys a causal connection between events. For actions, in Aristotle's metaphysics, embody particulars (*Nicomachean Ethics* 2.6.1107a31; *NE* 3.1.1110b6–7; *NE* 6.4.1140a1–23). Poetry is an imitation of human action and life, so it follows that it must be an imitation of particular individuals acting in specific circumstances. There is no sense, then, in which we should understand Aristotle as saying that poetry is an imitation of universals.

In addition, emotions, on Aristotle's view, are directed towards specific individuals. That is, they have specific objects or targets. We feel pity, fear, and fellow feeling (*philanthrōpos*), for the characters in a tragedy (13.1453a3–5), not for a general sort of situation. In *Poetics* 17 Aristotle describes the importance of the poet working out the material as much as possible "in the mind's eye" and "most vividly" as if present at the actual events (1455a22–23). The emotions of the audience are, therefore, directed towards characters that are vividly described and fleshed out. For Aristotle recognizes that it is convincingly drawn characters that are capable of gripping the audience's emotions. If the characters are presented as "types" or "stereotypes" the plot will fail to move the audience in the required manner.

Yet, particular objects are the bearers of universals. There are no individual basic entities or "substances" that are not embodiments of some general kind of thing.[24] This is a general principle of Aristotle's metaphysics.[25] This means that we do not encounter individual dogs and zebras as "bare particulars." Our minds are structured so as to be capable of seeing these particulars as instances of the general kinds or universals that they are (dog and zebra). Aristotle thinks that the same cognitive faculties that come into play when we encounter sensible particulars in real life are also marshaled when the audience watches a play or hears an epic poem. It follows that the audience is primed to see the characters and actions in poetry as instances of larger kinds or patterns as well.

While the plot is an imitation of human action and life, it gives an order and structure to human action that is often not apparent in real life. In everyday life things can appear to happen randomly and for no apparent reason, especially situations that involve human suffering. In contrast in the poetic plot, events have been structured into a unity, a complete whole with a beginning, middle, and end, where events are linked by causal connections. Poetic unity makes possible the grasp of this larger pattern of causally coherent action, thereby helping the audience to understand the sense in which events in the plot happen *because* of what went before.

Towards this end, in *Poetics* 17 Aristotle advises the poet to start composing with a sketch of the general structure of the plot in mind (1455b1–3).[26] The poet starts to compose with a general outline of the events in mind and then proceeds to add names to the characters as well as work out the necessary and probable connections between episodes in the plot. Aristotle illustrates the idea of how the poet starts with a general structure in mind with the example from Euripides' *Iphigenia in Tauris*:

> A girl was sacrificed, and vanished without trace from her sacrificers; settled in a different country, where it was a custom to sacrifice strangers to the goddess, she became priestess of this rite. Later, the priestess' brother happened to arrive there (that the god's oracle told him to go there, and for what purpose, is outside the plot). Captured after his arrival and on the point of being sacrificed, he caused his recognition . . . and hence was rescued. The next stage is to supply names and devise episodes.
>
> (18.1455b3–13)

The poet starts with a general structure in mind and then supplies the names of characters and composes episodes that are linked by necessity or probability. When the full plot is fleshed out, it will embody a causally coherent pattern concerning human experience that enables the audience to make sense of the action and understand its significance.

It is important to clarify the sense in which poetry "speaks of" universals. We have said that it does not mean that the plot "imitates" universals; rather, the plot is an imitation of particular actions, but it embodies or instantiates a universal pattern pertaining to human experience. The audience must grasp this pattern to make sense of the action. Yet this does not mean that the universal generalizations that are embodied in the plot are explicitly articulated, either by a narrator or a character. A character can use speech to prove or refute something or to convey her emotions. The impression that a sequence of events is important or worthy of pity and fear should be evident without speech (19.1456b3–5). The universal patterns are implicit in the structure of the events.

The audience of poetry recognizes something familiar in the action of the plot and delights in reasoning out what is common to the sequence of actions in the poem or play and items in their past experience. If the poet comes out and directly tells the audience, through a narrator or the speech of a character, the common pattern that is shared, this is didactic and diminishes the audience's sense of having worked out a puzzle on their own.[27]

In addition in *Poetics* 9, Aristotle argues for the important role that "amazement" or "wonder" (*to thaumaston*) plays in prompting the audience's pity and fear. Events that evoke these emotions "arise above all when events occur contrary to expectation yet on account of one another" (9.1452a3). When, in particular, a plot features an unexpected reversal of fortune (*peripeteia*), this evokes a sense of awe in the audience and prompts them to search for an implicit pattern of action that can render the turn of events explicable. It is important, for the aspect of surprise, that the universals concerning character and action that the audience searches for are not explicitly articulated.

This point is brought out a bit later, in *Poetics* 10, where Aristotle praises the "complex" plot, which has recognition (*anagnōrismos*), a change from ignorance to knowledge, or reversal (*peripeteia*), or a combination of both (10.1452a16–17). Aristotle says:

> These elements (recognition and reversal) should emerge *from the very structure of the plot*, so that they ensue from the preceding events by necessity or probability; as it makes a great difference whether things happen because of, or only after, their antecedents.
>
> (10.1452a17–22, my emphasis)

POETRY AS A FORM OF KNOWLEDGE

What is the point of Aristotle's comparison between history, poetry, and philosophy? The answer to this question is not obvious. At the least, Aristotle seems to want to commend poetry for achieving a degree of seriousness (*spoudaios*, also translated as "noble") that history lacks. The reason for the greater degree of nobility in poetry than in the reports of the typical historian has to do with the fact that poetry deals with the possible and the universal. This brings its concerns closer in line with those of the philosopher and scientist who are interested in articulating the universal causes of things, for the sake of understanding, for its own sake.

We see in *Poetics* 4 that the pleasure we take in a work *as* an imitation is the pleasure in learning.[28] Yet, there is no evidence either in *Poetics* 4 or in related passages in *Parts of Animals* 1.5.645a5–25 or *Rhetoric* 1.11.1371b4–12 that Aristotle is associating the understanding available from mimetic works with the study and learning that philosophers seek.[29] Things seem to be different, however, when we consider *Poetics* 9. Aristotle does not say that poetry does the work of philosophy; but in saying that poetry is "more philosophical" (*philosophōteron*) he is at least saying that poetry is more like philosophy than history, and the reason for this is linked to the nature of the universals that are embedded into the structure of the well-formed poetic plot.

There are several pressing questions about this comparison between poetry and philosophy that need to be addressed. First, what is the point of poetry embedding these universals into the plot? Second, what is the more exact nature of the universals in plots? Do they approximate to the universal generalizations concerning human life and action that it is said in *Nicomachean Ethics* 10 are what the philosopher seeks to comprehend and contemplate?

First, why are the universals embedded in the plot? There are several reasons. First, through a plot that is unified by necessary and probable connections, the audience is able to take pleasure in the recognition that the action has been constructed into a well-formed whole. As Amélie Rorty explains "Because it represents a story that is complete in itself, uninterrupted by the irrelevant flotsam and jetsam accidents of everyday life, drama brings the pleasure of the sense of closure."[30] The sense that one is admiring something that has been well structured and unified is a pleasure taken in the work's form and structure, and it is made possible by the internal coherence of the plot.[31]

Second, this appreciation of the action as structured into a complete whole also makes possible an intellectual or cognitive pleasure. Pleasure for Aristotle occurs when there is the perception that one is settling down into one's natural state.[32] All human beings, Aristotle says, naturally take delight in learning and understanding.[33] This pleasure in seeing the larger causal pattern in which an action occurs makes possible an intellectual pleasure that is seldom available in everyday life, when people act not knowing fully the consequences of their actions and how what they do will reverberate as well as come up against the actions of others.

When events occur "contrary to expectations yet on account of one another" (9.1452a3), there is also an important *affective* response that the plot makes possible: this is a sense of wonder and amazement, which Aristotle thinks is, in and of itself, pleasant. Wonder inspires the desire to know the explanation for that which you do not understand. Aristotle says, in fact, that philosophy was born out of the wonder that the humans had about their surroundings.[34]

> For it is owing to their wonder that men both now begin and at first began to philosophize; they wondered originally at the obvious difficulties, then advanced little by little and stated difficulties about the greatest matters, e.g. about the phenomena of the moon and those of the sun and the stars, and about the genesis of the universe. And a man who is puzzled and wonders thinks himself ignorant . . . therefore . . . they philosophized to escape from their ignorance.
>
> (*Metaphysics* 1.2.982b12–20; Barnes 1984)

Since the desire to know is part of what it is to be human, any activity that facilitates the viewer's desire to understand a puzzle will bring one into one's natural state. Plots that jolt the viewer with a surprising development that he did not foresee give him the pleasure of wonder. The curiosity that wonder inspired is then repaid when the viewer is able to go back and reflect on how the surprising result was contrary to his expectations, yet occurred on account of another event.

Third, and perhaps most importantly, the pleasure in learning that the plot inspires is not a purely abstract or intellectual pleasure that is removed from one's everyday experience and emotions. Essentially bound up with the pleasure of tragedy are the emotions of feeling pity and fear for the characters. Drama evokes these emotions in the audience by having the plot structured according to probability and necessity. As Aristotle explains:

> As it is not every pleasure one should seek from tragedy, but the appropriate kind. And since the poet should create the pleasure that comes from pity and fear through *mimēsis*, obviously this should be built into the plot.
>
> (14.1453b11–13)

It is the structure of the plot in tragedy, in particular the fact that the incidents follow according to a universal pattern of what "it suits a certain kind of person to say or do, in terms of probability or necessity" (9.1451b8–9) that makes possible pity and fear for the characters.

We can say more about why this is so. The audience feels pity and fear for the character when they understand that the reversal of fortune that the character experiences is not fortuitous or random; rather, it follows according to a pattern of necessary and probable action. Now in real life we do not need to grasp this larger pattern to feel pity and fear for others. Why would this be necessary in tragedy? A plot that shows that what happens to the character is the sort of thing that is necessary or likely shows that there is a reason for the reversal that the character experiences, and reasons, by definition, are general and not particular. They apply to anyone who falls under a certain class. Through exhibiting a pattern of action that applies to the character *and* the spectator, this prompts pity and fear for the character. For we feel fear for someone "like ourselves" (13.1453a5) and we pity others for when they suffer a misfortune that we could expect to fall to us or someone close to us (*Rhetoric* 2.8.1385b12–16).[35]

The universals about human action and nature that are embedded in the plot then are not abstract truths that do not bear on one's lived experience. The world that tragedy imitates is *our* world, and when the audience comes to realize this, through the structure of the plot, this brings home the emotional significance of the events in the plot for the audience.[36]

In this sense the pleasure that the audience takes in drama is not simply the pleasure of solving an intellectual puzzle, as happens in a good detective novel or story. For pity and fear are responses to situations that matter to us: the loss of family, friends and community or the threat that these bonds will be severed in the future. It is when the audience is not just intellectually moved, but awakens to the possibility that what happens to the character could happen to them, that tragedy inspires the right emotional response in the audience.

This brings us to our second concern: what is the more exact nature of the universals in plots? Do they approximate to the universal generalizations concerning human life and action that it is said in *Nicomachean Ethics* 10 are what the philosopher seeks to comprehend and contemplate? Both the universals embedded in the plots of poetry and the universals that philosophy seeks concern patterns of human events and action. Yet there is a difference in the degree of what Aristotle calls "intelligibility" between poetic universals and the universals that philosophy discovers.

The simpler and more universal is the object of a belief, the more intelligible and accurate it is (*Metaphysics* 1.2.982a25–27).[37] Aristotle associates greater accuracy and intelligibility with greater explanatory power, something that philosophers seek in their search for the first causes of things. By this reasoning, a principle that concerned the actions of all human beings would have a greater degree of explanatory power than a generalization that concerned the actions of all human beings who have dogs as companions, for example. To get the required degree of clarification that philosophy, as an inquiry into the ultimate causes of things, seeks it is necessary to achieve a certain level of abstraction and a high level of generality. It is this difference in degree of generality and abstractness that distinguishes the universals embedded in poetic plots and the universal first principles that philosophy seeks.

Aristotle supposes that poetry will make use of at least some principles that have a high degree of generality, for example, the principles he discusses in his ethics, that all humans strive for happiness (*eudaimonia*) and that people are happy or not according to their actions (*Poetics* 6.1450a19). But the universals Aristotle mentions that are implanted in the poetic plot are of a more specific kind, "the kinds of things that it suits a certain kind of person to say or do, in terms of probability or necessity."

This can be understood in terms of the different aims of the poet and the philosopher. The latter is interested in understanding the objective first principles of things, an activity that starts with sensible particulars and ends up with first principles that explain the causes of things at a high level of abstraction. The former embeds universals in the plot so that the audience can feel pity and fear for the characters, by recognizing that what happens to the character is the sort of thing that *could* happen to them.

The generalization concerning human action around which the poetic action is structured cannot, then, be too abstracted away from the audience's lived experience, and the plot must proceed at the level of vividly filled out particular actions and characters to have the emotional power that the poet aims for. In this way tragedy is capable of bringing to life some insights that bear on the spectator's lived experience.

OBJECTIONS AND AN ALTERNATIVE INTERPRETATION

It has forcefully been objected by some that the plots of tragedy *presuppose* the audience's understanding of some pattern or principle that governs human action and nature, and so tragedy cannot *advance* the audience's understanding of these matters.[38] It is the case, for example, that the audience who appreciates Sophocles' *Oedipus the King* must already understand the psychological generalization that young men are prone to be rash or that inquisitive people will press to find out answers, even when this spells trouble for them. If the audience of *Oedipus* must be able to recognize that the plot embodies some truth about human nature and action, they must have already grasped that insight, and are simply applying it to the specific situation spelled out in the play.

Aristotle's view that pity and fear arise "above all when events occur contrary to expectation yet on account of one another" (9.1452a3–4) helps us understand several lines of reply to this objection. First, the text quoted suggests that the causal principles that effective tragedy relies on are not obvious or readily discerned in advance of the action unfolding. There may need to be some search for the pattern that makes sense of the action in the plot, and this is in keeping with Aristotle's general view that learning that is too easy or too obvious to all is not a source of delight or pleasure (*Rhetoric* 3.10.1410b10–12 and b23–25).

This point fits with an observation that Dorothea Frede makes, that many ancient Greek tragedies feature individuals in highly unusual circumstances.[39] The figures of tragedy and epic such as Oedipus, Odysseus, Antigone, and the like may be outside the normal range of everyday human experience. It is not simply a matter, then, of the audience applying tried and trite conventional wisdom, such as "young men are rash" or "inquisitive people press for answers even when trouble lurks ahead"; the generalizations concerning human action that drama brings to light may be complicated and unusual ones whose relevance it is the job of the drama to make clear.

Second, when events in the plot occur "contrary to expectations yet on account of one another" (9.1452a3–4) the viewer is prompted to discover novel connections and resemblances between the character's situation and her own, prompting her to look at her life's possibilities in a new way. In this way, tragedy prompts learning and a sense of discovery in the same way that Aristotle says that metaphors do.[40] Metaphors stimulate the reader to discover novel connections, see new resemblances, and forge new connections ("old age is a withered stalk"), thereby deepening what we already know. Metaphors, through the analogies they set up, "place things before the eyes" (*pro hommatōn*), and thereby bring them to life.[41] Similarly, by showing the reader something unexpected that, nevertheless, unfolds according to probability and necessity, this can bring to life the viewer's understanding of some truth about her life that she had previously grasped, but perhaps in an intellectual or abstract way.[42]

One example of a contemporary film drama that illustrates this point is *Twelve Years A Slave* (Steve McQueen, 2013). The plot is based on the true story of Solomon Northrup (Chiwetel Ejiofor), a free African-American man living in antebellum New York, who is abducted and sold into slavery. He lives as a slave for twelve years enduring extremely harsh treatment and the lack of his freedom. The only thing that keeps him going is the hope that he will see his wife and children again. It might be hard for people who have never experienced slavery to understand what it would be like to endure the miseries and indignities inflicted upon slaves during the time that slavery was legal in the United States and elsewhere. But by telling the story of someone who was free and then became a slave, this relates to the average viewer's experiences, and so the plot is able to bring home to him the importance of freedom to a life well lived.

A further line of objection to the idea that the universals in the plot are a source of knowledge has been raised. Paul Woodruff and Malcolm Heath argue that in *Poetics* 24 Aristotle recognizes that the necessary and probable generalizations that ground the plot may also have to be modified or bent into a shape that conforms to what the audience *believes* to be the case, even when this belief is objectively false or impossible.[43] Poetry, in other words, is concerned with what is convincing and plausible. Understanding and knowledge is concerned with what is true and accurate, and the two need not always coincide.

We need to look at *Poetics* 24 more closely, on its own terms, to understand the implications of these points for the claim that poetry offers the pleasures of understanding about the causes of human action.[44] Aristotle recognizes that poetry does not do the work of philosophy. We should not expect to find the same level of accuracy and concern for the truth in poetry as in philosophy. He also recognizes that the poet sometimes makes choices based on whether they will make emotional or psychological sense to the audience or because they make the plot work more effectively.

Aristotle, for example, expresses admiration for Homer's skill in getting away with irrationalities in the plot when, in the *Odyssey*, Odysseus is put ashore on Ithaca asleep and does not wake up (25.1460a25–b2). Aristotle says that the justification for using an irrational event in the plot is that it is acceptable provided that it "achieves its goal" (25.1460b23–26), meaning that it accomplishes the appropriate emotional and cognitive response by the audience. He does say, "If a poet posits an irrationality, and a more rational alternative is apparent, this is an absurdity" (25.1460a33–35). But Heath and Woodruff would likely use this passage to press the point that Aristotle is tolerant of irrational events in the plot, provided that they accomplish the appropriate emotional response.

Going back to our discussion at the start of the chapter, we noted that one might look at Houël's *Prise de la Bastille* and become convinced that what one was seeing was just how the

Bastille was stormed, even though we had no independent evidence that the painting was accurate in its depiction. So also a good poet such as Homer can convince the audience that what they are seeing is plausible and true to life, even when the plot contains irrational and improbable events, and so is false. If Aristotle tolerates some irrational and improbable events in the plot, how could he think that the audience can learn from tragedy or epic? For how can a viewer learn from something that is false?

The concern is then, if Aristotle is willing to tolerate irrationalities in the plot, what the audience takes away from a drama is not genuine understanding: what the viewer gets is the *illusion* of being presented with some truth that applies to her life—the "beautiful lies" of which Wilde speaks. But the appearance of truth in poetry does not amount to genuine learning or knowledge. Knowledge requires truth.[45]

It is true that the poetic plot is based on what is probable or necessary, according to the audience's experience of life. This is why Aristotle stresses that it is better to imitate plausible impossibilities rather than implausible possibilities (24.1460a27). But immediately after making this point, Aristotle stresses that irrational elements should be avoided, and that irrationalities in the plot are something that a skilled poet such as Homer can get away with, not something to which he or any other poet should aspire (25.1460a33–1460b3).

While the poet must work within the audience's sense of what is plausible, it should also surprise, and then repay their sense of wonder by enabling them to see how, in retrospect, the turn of events is connected to what went before (10.1452a1–5). This suggests that the plot should be able to reveal something to the audience that they did not know before, suggesting that the plot draws upon but also unsettles the audience's expectations of how things go.

It is important to consider a final objection: this relates to the point that nowhere in the *Poetics* is Aristotle willing to concede that a poet is a teacher or that she has any knowledge of human behavior to impart. Knowledge (*epistēmē*) implies an understanding that is teachable and capable of being articulated in general terms by the person who has it (*Metaphysics* 1.1), yet as we have seen earlier, Aristotle denies that even a poet that he regards as superior, Homer, has a knowledge of the rules of the art (*technē*) of poetry, in spite of ample evidence that his poems, in general, embody the principles of poetic composition that Aristotle seeks to explain in the *Poetics*.[46]

In keeping with this view of the poet, *Poetics* 9 says that it is the *poems*, *not* the *poets* that are the source of the universals concerning human life and action. Here he is saying that the audience can take pleasure in grasping these universals, even if the poet is not in a position of being a teacher. Indeed, Aristotle's descriptions of the poet in *Poetics* 17 makes him sound less like an apt student of human psychology, and more like a person with an active imagination. "Hence poetry is the work of a gifted person, or of a manic: of these types the former have versatile imaginations, the latter get carried away" (17.1455a32f.).

Aristotle clearly thinks, then, the imagination, which he defines in the *De Anima* as the faculty in virtue of which an image arises in us (3.3.428a1–3), plays an important role in poetry. Yet, he nowhere gives credit to the poet for having some insight into human behavior: the mimetic poet, he says simply, is a maker of plots rather than of verses (*Poetics* 9.1451b26–27).

If the poet cannot be given credit for knowing and understanding the principles that govern human action and psychology, does this undercut the claim that works of poetry cannot be sources of understanding? The answer is no, because Aristotle allows that works of poetry can embody knowledge even when the creators of these works cannot articulate or teach this understanding.[47] Similarly, looking at well-formed poems, we can see that the plots embody universals concerning human action, even if (from Aristotle's point of view) it is doubtful that the poet is able to teach and articulate his understanding of these general patterns. Poetry's status as an occasion for understanding does not, then, depend on the poet being regarded as a purveyor of truths about human nature.

CONCLUSION

In *Republic* 10 Socrates challenges the view that poetry could be considered to be a viable alternative to philosophy, considered as a route to truth and knowledge. How should we understand the argument of *Poetics* 9 in terms of this larger challenge that a philosopher makes to poetry? Aristotle's answer is more nuanced than it might first appear. While poetry shares philosophy's interest in universals, the universals embedded in the plots of well-formed poetry do not in general approximate the basic explanatory principles that philosophy seeks. If one is interested in pursuing the precise and accurate explanatory principles that philosophy seeks, Aristotle seems to be saying that one should not expect to find them in poetry. In this sense poetry is not a viable alternative to philosophy.

On the other hand, Aristotle does not see the poet as aiming for the same level of generality that philosophy seeks. The goal is to move the audience so they have a distinctive sort of emotional experience, and the power to do this will be lost if the universals that are embedded in the plot are too far removed and abstracted from the particulars in the story. The audience must be able to see the characters and actions in the plot as instances of some larger pattern of necessary or probable human action, but to feel for the characters the audience must be able to grasp the universal *in* the particular, and this means that poetry universals cannot achieve the level of abstraction from particulars that philosophy seeks.

In the *Apology* Socrates questions the poets about the meaning of their poems, and he concludes that the poets do not possess wisdom because they are not able to articulate the basic definitions of the most important things addressed in their poems, such as virtue or human excellence (*Apology* 22b). Aristotle does not have a radically different picture of the state of mind of the poet, but he nevertheless suggests that *works* of mimetic art are the occasion for learning even if the poets cannot articulate the understanding of human action that is embedded in the plot.

Going back to the debate about art and knowledge with which we began, our examination of *Poetics* 9 and related texts suggests how Aristotle could reply to Stolnitz's concern that the truths of poetry are either banal or trivial. Aristotle would say that the poet could not stay in business if the plot rested on banal truths that operate at a high level of abstraction (such as the abstract truths of first philosophy, or metaphysics) because the relevance to the audience's lives would be lost. Neither can the plot dwell at the level of the particular characters because then the audience will fail to understand how what happens to the character could apply to them as well. To do their work, the truths embedded in the plot must be somewhere in between the abstract truths of philosophy and the particular events that history (according to *Poetics* 9) records.[48]

How might Aristotle respond to Stolnitz's demand that to learn from tragedy the audience must be able to justify the insights that they take away from watching or reading a drama? The audience may well have, prior to viewing the tragedy, already tested some of the patterns of human action upon which the plot is based through their own life experiences and their observations of others. Even when the audience grasps in the plot some principle concerning life and action that is new to them, the ultimate test will be whether the audience thinks the action unfolds in accordance with their experience of what is humanly plausible. This is not the objective standard of proof that science or philosophy seeks, but it is appropriate to the task of revealing or bringing home to the audience some insight that applies to human life as they experience it.

Aristotle, then, is a forerunner of contemporary art cognitivism: he thinks that works of mimetic art can be a source of understanding and are valuable, in part, because of this. Yet, he also recognizes that poetry offers the viewer something that philosophy does not. This is the opportunity to have a distinctive emotional experience. In the chapters that follow we will examine the nature of this emotional experience in greater depth.

NOTES

1 Reading for this chapter is *Poetics* 9 and 10. Recommended reading is *Poetics* 17 and *Metaphysics* 1.1.

2 In contemporary philosophy, "cognition" is often used to mark out a faculty of the mind that comes into play when we believe, assert, recognize, or imagine some state of affairs. Art cognitivism is the view that: (a) we can learn from art; and (b) part of the value of art lies in the learning that works of art provide. See Berys Gaut 2003 and Eileen John 2005.

3 Elisabeth Schellekens 2007: 45.

4 As David Davies observes (2007: 14), if we want to find out about the goings on, for example, of the British monarchs, we would be better advised to consult works of history rather than works of fiction because we assume that if the latter are reliable, then the authors have consulted the former. This suggests that if we learn from works, the sort of learning in question is not knowledge of facts.

5 I thank Malcolm Heath for this observation.

6 Oscar Wilde 1891: 1–34.

7 This is indeed the account of truth that Aristotle proposed. See *Metaphysics* 9.10 and *Categories* 12.14b18–23.

8 Hilary H. Putnam 1978.

9 Putnam 1978: 89–90.

10 See also Cynthia Freeland 1997 and Noël Carroll 2002.

11 B. Gaut 2003: 437.

12 See the introduction to Chapter 5.

13 Catherine Wilson 2004.

14 Jerome Stolnitz 2004: 318.

15 Berys Gaut (2003: 439–444), for example, maintains that through exercising the imagination, art can provide us with knowledge about what one should choose, self-knowledge and knowledge about others, as well as moral knowledge.

16 Metaphysics is the study of reality, what really exists.

17 *Metaphysics* 999a28–29.

18 See *Metaphysics* 1.1 and *Posterior Analytics* 2.19.

19 *Physics* 1.1.

20 *Metaphysics* 2.1; *Nicomachean Ethics* 10.

21 *Metaphysics* 2.1.993b20.

22 See Chapter 5.

23 See for example, Gerald Else 1957: 316 and Stephen Halliwell 1999: 60, footnote.

24 Aristotle also accepts the principle that there can be no universal kind of thing (e.g. "zebra" or "oak tree") without its embodiment in a particular thing. So the relationship between an individual and a larger kind or universal is correlative.

25 See Aristotle's *Categories* 5.1a15–25. As Gareth Matthews and Marc Cohen explain, "Every individual is an individual so-and-so. For Felix to be an individual is already for him to be a cat. And for Socrates to be an individual is already for him to be a man" (Matthews and Cohen 1968: 635).

26 In *Poetics* 17 Aristotle uses the term "universal" (*katholou*) to describe this structure, but he is not referring to the "universal" (*katholou*) mentioned in *Poetics* 9, that is, the kind of thing that happens according to probability and necessity.

27 See Chapter 4 and *Rhetoric* 3.10.1410b12–15 for an example of metaphor that can facilitate a kind of new insight or recognition through the indirect use of language.

28 See Chapter 4.

29 For an alternative understanding of these texts offered by Stephen Halliwell, David Gallop, and Martha Nussbaum, see Chapter 4.

30 Amélie Rorty 1992b: 17.

31 See the discussion of the pleasure taken in form in Chapter 4.

32 *Rhetoric* 1.11.1370a3–4. "Pleasure is a certain movement of the soul, a sudden and perceptible settling down into its natural state, and pain the opposite" (Barnes 1984).

33 *Metaphysics* 1.1.980a23.

34 *Metaphysics* 1.2.982b12.

35 See also the discussion of tragic emotions in Chapter 8.

36 The plot, therefore, is key to providing a certain kind of emotional understanding to the spectator. The nature of this understanding is discussed in Chapter 11.

37 On this point see Deborah K. Modrak 2001: 105.

38 See Malcolm Heath 1991: 399f. and Paul Woodruff 2009: 618.

39 Dorothea Frede 1992: 209–210.

40 See *Rhetoric* 3.2.1404b10–15.

41 *Rhetoric* 3.10.1411b21–1412a3. For a useful discussion of this function of metaphors see Fran O'Rourke 2006: 172–176.

42 Aristotle recognizes something that contemporary art cognitivists have recently come to terms with: the idea that art is valuable as a source of understanding because it transforms and deepens the knowledge we already possess. See John Gibson 2008: 585–587 and Noël Carroll 1998.

43 "Things probable (*eikos*) though impossible should be preferred to the possible but implausible" (24.1460a25–26). See Heath 1991: 400 and Woodruff 2009: 618.

44 See the discussion in Chapter 10.

45 As Woodruff says, "In the final test, what is *eikos* (probable) is plausible in a particular case, and what may be so in one case may not be (or may not be in the same way) in another" (2009: 618).

46 See *Poetics* 8.1451.21f. and Chapter 2, pp. 24–25.

47 See the discussion in Chapter 2, pp. 26–32.

48 For another route to the argument that poetry aims for "mid-level" universals see Stephen Halliwell 2002: 197–199.

WORKS CITED

Barnes, Jonathan (ed.) 1984. *The Complete Works of Aristotle*. Volume Two. Princeton, NJ: Princeton University Press.

Carroll, Noël 1998. "Art, Narrative and Moral Understanding," in Jerrold Levinson (ed.), *Aesthetics and Ethics: Essays at the Intersection*. Cambridge: Cambridge University Press: 126–160.

_____ 2002. "The Wheel of Virtue: Art, Literature and Moral Knowledge." *The Journal of Aesthetics and Art Criticism* 60 (1): 3–26.

Davies, David 2007. *Aesthetics and Literature*. New York and London: Continuum.

Else, Gerald 1957. *Aristotle's Poetics: The Argument*. Cambridge, MA: Harvard University Press.

Frede, Dorothea 1992. "Necessity, Chance and What Happens for the Most Part in Aristotle's *Poetics*," in Amélie Oskenberg Rorty (ed.), *Essays on Aristotle's Poetics*. Princeton, NJ: Princeton University Press: 197–220.

Freeland, Cynthia 1997. "Art and Moral Knowledge." *Philosophical Topics* 25: 11–36.

Gaut, Berys 2003. "Art and Knowledge," in Jerrold Levinson (ed.), *The Oxford Handbook of Aesthetics*. Oxford: Oxford University Press: 436–450.

Gibson, John 2008. "Cognitivism and the Arts." *Philosophy Compass* 3/4: 573–589.

Halliwell, Stephen 1999. *Aristotle's Poetics: Edited and Translated by Stephen Halliwell*. Cambridge, MA: Harvard University Press.

_____ 2002. *The Aesthetics of Mimesis. Ancient and Modern Problems*. Princeton, NJ: Princeton University Press.

Heath, Malcolm 1991: "The Universality in Aristotle's *Poetics*." *The Classical Quarterly*, New Series 41 (2): 389–402.

John, Eileen 2005. "Art and Knowledge," in Berys Gaut and Dominic McIver Lopes (eds.), *The Routledge Companion to Aesthetics* Second Edition. Abingdon and New York: Oxford University Press: 417–430.

Matthews, Gareth B. and S. Marc Cohen 1968. "The One and the Many." *The Review of Metaphysics* 21 (4): 630–655.

Modrak, Deborah K. 2001. *Aristotle's Theory of Language and Meaning*. Cambridge: Cambridge University Press.

O'Rourke, Fran 2006. "Aristotle and the Metaphysics of Metaphor." *Proceedings of the Boston Area Colloquium of Ancient Philosophy* 21 (1): 155–190.

Putnam, Hilary H. 1978. "Literature, Science, and Reflection," in Putnam, *Meaning and the Moral Sciences*. London: Routledge and Kegan Paul: 83–94.

Schellekens, Elisabeth 2007. *Aesthetics and Morality*. London and New York: Continuum.

Rorty, Amélie Oskenberg (ed.) 1992a. *Essays on Aristotle's Poetics*. Princeton, NJ: Princeton University Press.

_____ 1992b. "The Psychology of Aristotelian Tragedy," in Rorty 1992a: 1–22.

Stolnitz, Jerome 2004. "On the Cognitive Triviality of Truth," in Eileen John and Dominic McIver Lopes (eds.), *Philosophy of Literature: Contemporary and Classic Reading, An Anthology*. London: Blackwell Publishing: 317–323. Reprinted from *British Journal of Aesthetics* 32 (1992): 191–200. Citations are to the 2004 version.

Wilde, Oscar 1891. *Intentions*. London: James A. Osgood, McIllvaine & Co.

Wilson, Catherine 2004. "Literature and Knowledge," in Eileen John and Dominic McIver Lopes (eds.), *Philosophy of Literature: Contemporary and Classic Reading, An Anthology*. London: Blackwell Publishing: 324–328. Reprinted from *Philosophy* 58 (1983): 489–496. Citations are to the 2004 version.

Woodruff, Paul 2009. "Aristotle's *Poetics*: The Aim of Tragedy," in Georgios Anagnostopoulos (ed.), *A Companion to Aristotle*. Chichester, England: Blackwell Publishing: 612–627.

8

THE TRAGIC EMOTIONS, PLOT ELEMENTS, AND PATTERNS

INTRODUCTION

Aristotle is very explicit in placing the spectator's emotional response of pity and fear for tragic characters at the center of his account of tragedy.[1] In his definition of tragedy in *Poetics* 6 he says that tragedy brings about a *catharsis* of pity and fear (1449b27–28). In addition, the structural requirements on the plot are also motivated by the idea that a coherent and unified plot, where events happen contrary to expectations, yet "on account of one another" is the best way to evoke pity and fear in the audience (10.1452a1–2). In *Poetics* 13 the discussion of plot patterns, which is said to concern "how tragedy's effect is to be achieved" centers around the narrative-structures that are best at inspiring pity and fear (1452b26f.). The emotional experience of tragedy is also given center stage when in *Poetics* 14 Aristotle says that the well-formed plot is the means for the poet to create "the pleasure that comes from pity and fear through *mimēsis*" (1453b11). In a number of places, then, Aristotle says that the aim of tragedy is a certain emotional effect, the response of pity and fear.

Yet, as the character of Stephen Dedalus observes in James Joyce's *Portrait of the Artist as a Young Man*, Aristotle's comments on pity and fear in the *Poetics* are far from a worked out account of these emotions, but the *Rhetoric* is useful in this regard. Pity is felt for the undeserving victim of some destructive or painful harm of the sort that we expect could befall us or someone close to us (*Rhetoric* 2.8.1385b13–14f.). Fear is felt for one "like ourselves" (*Poetics* 13.1453a3) and is experienced when one imagines some destructive or painful evil in the future (*Rhetoric* 2.5.1382a22). Suffering (along with recognition and reversal) is a component of the plot; it is a destructive or painful action (*Poetics* 12.1452b11–12). The suffering that is an aspect of the content of tragedy will inspire pity and fear, under the right circumstances. In keeping with our approach to the *Poetics* throughout the book, we can illuminate Aristotle's views about the emotions and about pity and fear, in particular, by placing the *Poetics*' discussion of the emotions within the wider context of his other writings.[2]

Therefore, in what follows, we will, first, look at other of Aristotle's works that offer a larger picture of the emotions, in general, and the nature of pity and fear, in particular. Next, we consider three components of tragedy that are key elements for eliciting pity and fear: recognition (*anagnōrisis*), reversal (*peripeteia*) and suffering (*pathos*). Finally, we consider Aristotle's recommendations in *Poetics* 13–14 for how best to elicit the proper emotional effects of tragedy so that it accomplishes tragedy's goal of evoking pity and fear.[3]

ARISTOTLE'S ACCOUNT OF THE EMOTIONS

Aristotle's writings on philosophical psychology have a lot to say about the emotions in general and about pity and fear, in particular.

First, to the general question of how Aristotle understands the emotions. Philosophical accounts of the emotions have tended to see them in one of three main ways: (1) as involving conscious experience or feelings; or (2) as bodily responses; or (3) as involving cognitive states: thoughts, beliefs, or judgments. Aristotle's account of the emotions is complex, and though it is most often thought of as a cognitive account of the emotions, it also encompasses the feeling and bodily aspects of emotions as well.

First, emotions are intentional: intentionality (from Latin, *intendere*, meaning "to direct") is the power of the mind to be about, represent, or stand for things. Emotions, on Aristotle's view, are intentional in that they are targeted at an object, for example you feel angry with your roommate for eating your peanut butter or you feel sorrow for the homeless person who has lost his job.

Second, emotions involve states of the body: emotions are affections of the soul, and in the *De Anima* Aristotle says that all affections of the soul, such as anger, fear, and pity, involve the body being affected in a certain way (*De Anima* 1.1.403a16–19).

Third, there is a feeling aspect to emotions, for Aristotle thinks that to have an emotion is to experience pleasure, or pain, or both. Pity and fear, for example, involve pain, while anger involves both pleasure and pain.

Fourth, emotions involve some cognition or mental state: this is a perception, judgment, or belief that the object of the emotion satisfies certain conditions.[4] To illustrate, you are angry with Bob because you believe that he has slighted you or you are afraid of the grizzly bear because you think that she is a threat to your wellbeing.

It is accurate to describe Aristotle's account as a *cognitive* theory of the emotions, in spite of the fact that it has elements of the feeling and bodily reaction analyses of emotion.[5] Emotions are not in his view mere bodily reactions: they involve conceptualizing the object of the emotion in certain ways: to illustrate, in the case of anger, the person you feel anger towards is thought of or evaluated as someone who has slighted you; the person or thing that you fear is believed to be the source of future harm; and the person for whom you feel pity is someone that you suppose to suffer undeservedly. This means that emotions are responsive to reasons (*Nicomachean Ethics* 1.13.1102b29–31) and there are grounds for having an emotion.

PITY AND FEAR IN THE *POETICS* AND THE *RHETORIC*

In *Poetics* 13, Aristotle says simply that the tragedy that shows a very wicked person falling from good fortune to bad does not arouse pity or fear, since pity is felt for the undeserving, fear for one like ourselves (1453a4–6). Aristotle's discussions of pity and fear in the *Rhetoric*, in contrast, is extensive and his comments provide much greater insight into the state of mind of the person who feels these emotions and also the sorts of objects and situations that evoke them.

Rhetoric 2.8 explains the sort of person who merits our pity. Pity is a painful feeling directed to the undeserved suffering of others in virtue of our capacity to feel ourselves vulnerable in similar ways (2.8.1385b12–19) and it involves a painful state of mind in which, "we are in the condition of remembering that similar misfortunes have happened to us or ours, or expecting them to happen in the future" (2.8.1386a1–4; Barnes 1984). In addition, pity also has a self-regarding aspect in that we can feel pity for someone only when we are capable of supposing that some such evil may happen to us or a friend of ours (2.8.1385b15–16).

Fear is a painful feeling or disturbance due to imagining some destructive or painful evil in the future (*Rhetoric* 2.5.1386a27–28). Aristotle follows this up with the explanation that, "fear is caused by whatever we feel has great power of destroying us, or of harming us in ways that tend to cause us great pain" (2.5.1382a26; Barnes 1984), which suggests that he is thinking of fear as an emotion that is directed towards *oneself.*

Furthermore, there is a link between pity and fear. We feel pity for others for what we fear for ourselves, and we feel fear for ourselves that which when it occurs we pity in others (*Rhetoric* 2.5.1382b25–26; 1386a27–29). Pity and fear, in other words, are aroused by the same evils when they happen to different people. At the same time, great fear drives out pity, for Aristotle says that people who feel panic-stricken are not able to pity others due to being too preocupied with their own troubles (*Rhetoric* 2.8.1385b32–33).

Pity and fear, therefore, are painful emotions that involve the expectation or remembering of critical harms. Pity is retrospective as well as prospective: the person who is pitied either reminds us of a similar misfortune we have experienced in the past or calls to mind a painful destruction that we feel vulnerable to in the near future. Fear is exclusively prospective: we feel fear when we are expecting some evil to happen in the near future.

In the *Rhetoric* fear is an emotion that is felt for oneself or for those "belonging to oneself," such as "parents, children or wives" (2.8.1385b28–29; 1386a17–19; Barnes 1984). This has led to a disagreement among commentators, with some maintaining that fear for the characters is really a fear that the spectator has for herself, with others arguing that Aristotle's account in the *Rhetoric* allows that fear can be properly felt *for* the tragic characters.[6] Along the former lines, Alexander Nehamas argues that the fear I feel for the tragic character is "really an imaginative fear for myself."[7] Yet this seems to be in conflict with Aristotle's claim in the *Poetics* that fear, along with pity is directed toward the characters (13.1453a3–5).

There may be a way of reconciling Nehamas' reading with the *Poetics*' view that we feel for the characters, as Nehamas seems to recognize.[8] To feel fear and pity for the tragic character the audience must not just recognize that the character's situation conforms to an *abstract* pattern of universal human experience with which they are familiar: the character's situation must resonate with the audience's past experiences and with expectations they have that they, in the near future, could be vulnerable to the same sort of suffering.[9]

On the other hand, the tragic character cannot simply be a *doppleganger* or a psychological stand in for the audience members. The *Rhetoric* says that intense fear for oneself drives out pity: if the play inspires a direct fear for oneself, the specator will be too preoccupied with what she is imagining to be true of their own situation to pay attention to or be concerned with what is going on with the character. In this situation, intense self-directed fear drives out pity for the character. The account of pity in the *Rhetoric* also rules out that the pity the spectator feels could really be a self-directed pity the spectator feels for herself. Pity is not felt for those closely related to us, Aristotle says, for in this case we feel as if we are in danger ourselves and this drives out pity (2.8.1386a16f.).

To illustrate, imagine you attend a performance of Shakespeare's *Othello* and the situation of Othello suspecting that Desdemona is unfaithful brings home your own concerns about the fidelity of your partner. If these are real and live concerns, you might be too preoccupied with your own situation to pity Othello for what he is going through. Further, if the character in a drama suffers some terrible situation that you strongly and directly believe you are highly suspectible to, you may not be able to feel pity and fear for the character, due to being preoccupied with your own situation.

This suggests that a middle position in the debate about self-regarding fear is the most viable one. Aristotle must think that our emotional response to the tragic characters, in some sense, imaginatively takes us outside of ourselves, and that the emotions we feel are directed towards the characters, as he indicates in *Poetics* 13. He is modifying the *Rhetoric*'s account to allow that fear is not merely felt for oneself: in the context of tragedy it can also be felt for the tragic characters. At the same time the belief that the character suffers something that we can recognize *could* happen to us is something that the drama must bring home to us, otherwise the situation will be too remote and the emotional impact of the action will not be felt.

SIMPLE AND COMPLEX PLOTS: REVERSAL, RECOGNITION, AND PATHOS[10]

In *Poetics* 7 it is said that the plot has to have sufficient magnitude to allow a necessary or probable change (*metabasis*) between the two end points of good fortune and bad (1451a13–16). In *Poetics* 11 a further distinction is made on the plot. Some plots are simple (*haplos*). The plot imitates a sequence of actions that is a well-defined whole, with a beginning, middle, and end (1453b23–24), that moves according to probability or necessity invariably in one direction, either from good fortune to bad or from bad fortune to good (10.1452a11–13). Other plots are what Aristotle calls "complex" (*peplegmenos*): the plot is an imitation of a whole and complete action that is characterized by reversal (*peripeteia*) and recognition (*anagnōrisis*), or both (10.1452a14–16).

Reversal is "a change to the opposite direction of events, as was already stated, and one in accord, as we insist, with probability or necessity" (11.1452a22–23). Most scholars think that the "as was already stated" clause refers to Aristotle's view that pity and fear are aroused when events happen "contrary to expectation but on account of one another" (10.1452a4–5). There is a dramatic change in fortune for the character that she, and the audience, could not have anticipated, heightening the audience's reaction of pity and fear. Yet this change of fortune is not causally inexplicable: the incidents are structured in such a way that when the character and the audience reflects back on the sequence of events, they can see that the change of fortune has its causal antecedents in the action that went before.

There is some debate about whether the reversal involves the overturning of the expectations of the character, the audience, or both. Aristotle's example in *Poetics* 11 indicates that reversal involves a change in the expectation of the character. In Sophocles' *Oedipus the King*, the messenger arrives bringing news that Oedipus hopes will remove his fear of incest with his mother, but the opposite happens as the messenger ends up providing information that reveals he is Jocasta's son and that the prophecy that he will marry his mother is true (11.1452a23–25). But the reference back to *Poetics* 10, that the reversal must be "contrary to expectations, yet on account of one another" is to the audience's expectations of what will happen as well, for the juxtaposition of the unexpected, yet probable or necessary outcome is the best way to arouse pity and fear in the audience (10.1452a3–5).

The example of *Oedipus* shows why reversal is more than just a change of fortune (*metabasis*) for the character but involves a reversal of the character's expectations of how things are. Reversal involves a gap between how things are and how they seem to the character, producing astonishment (10.1452a1–3). The messenger gives Oedipus the good news that his father, Polybus, is dead of natural causes, so that the prophecy that he would kill is father cannot be true. The action appears to be moving towards good fortune for Oedipus. Yet Oedipus is still worried about the second part of the prophecy: that he will sleep with his mother. The messenger reassures him that this could not be true, as Polybus and Merope are not his real parents. This news ends up leading Oedipus to learn that the prophecy was fulfilled and that he has unknowingly killed his father, the man he encountered years ago at the crossroads, and married his mother, Jocasta. Here there is action that appears to be moving to good fortune (the prophecy is not true) but then ends up not only overturning the good news from the messenger (that Oedipus could not have killed his father), but also confirming another worst fear: that the second part of the prophecy is true and that he has committed incest with his mother.

Recognition (*anagnōrisis*), "as the very name indicates, is a change from ignorance to knowledge, leading to friendship or enmity and involving matters of prosperity and adversity" (11.1452a25–26). It can involve acquired knowledge of: (1) inanimate objects; or (2) events; or (3) recognition of persons (11.1452a33f.). Recognition of persons is best because it can be integrated into the plot in a way that leads to good or bad fortune (12.1452a33–b3). Oedipus is an example of this kind of recognition of persons, because the news from the messenger that leads to his reversal of fortune also brings about his learning his real identity.

Therefore, "recognition" in the *Poetics* is a narrower notion than the sense in which it is typically used in discussions of dramas or films. It is not simply the acquiring of some information that causes the character to move from a state of ignorance about himself or his situation. It is an incident in the plot that bears (i) on the good fortune or bad of the character and so arouses pity and fear (12.1452a38–b3); and (ii) moves the plot in a new direction, with friends becoming enemies or vice versa, and family ties being revealed, as in *Oedipus the King* or *Iphigenia in Tauris* in which Iphigenia recognizes the true identity of the person she is about to sacrifice: her long lost brother Orestes. As with other incidents in the plot, recognition, like reversal, should occur in accordance with probability and necessity (10.1452a18–21 and 11.1452a23–24).

Poetics 16 discusses six ways in which the poet introduces recognition, going from worst to best. The least skillful is recognition by means of tell-tale signs or external tokens, for example, when Odysseus is recognized by means of his scar (16.1454b26–28). A contemporary example of this sort of recognition is in Alfred Hitchcock's classic movie, *Vertigo* (1958), where Detective John "Scottie" Ferguson recognizes that Judy Barton is Madeleine, the woman he first investigated and then fell in love with, but who then jumped to her death, by the necklace she is wearing.

The best sort of recognition is that which follows by probability and necessity from "the events themselves," as has been stated in *Poetics* 11 and 14. This is in keeping with the principle of poetic unity that events that inspire pity and fear occur "contrary to expectations yet on account of one another" (9.1452a3–4). The examples Aristotle gives are from his two favorite tragedies, Euripides' *Iphigenia in Tauris* and Sophocles' *Oedipus the King* (16.1455a18–20). Iphigenia gives Orestes a letter to take home, and in it her identity as his sister is revealed. This is not like the recognition by a token or sign, an inferior sort of recognition, because it is probable that she would wish to take back such a letter.

While recognition and reversal can happen independently of one another, the best plot involves a combination of both (11.1452a30). Oedipus recognizes the truth from the shepherd that he is the long ago abandoned child of Laius and Jocasta, and that brings about a change to extreme bad fortune for him. Iphigenia recognizes her long lost brother and this averts the extreme bad fortune of killing Orestes: the action moves instead to their plotting an escape. This is a "mutual recognition" as both characters recognize one another: "Iphigenia was recognized by Orestes through the sending of the letter but for Iphigenia to recognize the relation to herself required a further recognition" (11.1452b29–31).

A contemporary example of a film that involves something like an Aristotelian recognition and reversal is *The Sixth Sense* (M. Night Shyamalan, 1999), in which a child psychologist Malcolm Crowe (Bruce Willis) tries to help a young boy, Cole Sear (Haley Joel Osment) who sees and talks with ghosts that haunt the earth because they have unfinished business.[11] The movie ends with a surprising "twist," that unbeknownst to Malcolm, he also is a ghost, having died from a shot inflicted by an angry former patient. The moment of recognition occurs at the very end of the film, when Malcolm sees his wedding ring roll off his sleeping wife's hand, revealing that she has been mourning his death rather than his preoccupation with his work, as Malcolm had previously thought. Therefore, the knowledge that Malcolm acquires about the existence of the ghost world turns out to be an important self-knowledge, that he is one of them. This new information leads to the painful realization that he has died and that for his wife's sake, he must leave earth, so that his wife can stop mourning and get on with her life. Here the recognition, as in *Oedipus* and *Iphigenia*, brings about a reversal of fortune, in Malcolm's case, going from good fortune to bad.

Both reversal and recognition are elements of the plot, then, and Aristotle insists that both should take place according to probability and necessity (10.1452a10–21). This is especially so in that reversal and recognition involve the plot moving in a direction that the audience and the character did not expect, and the poet must create the pity and fear that comes when unexpected things nevertheless occur on account of what went before. This means that the recognition should come in the middle section of the plot, where the events in the middle follow a preceding event and are followed by further consequences (7.1450b29–30). Oedipus' recognition of who he really is and what he has done brings about the further action of his plucking out his eyes in shame and going into self-exile, bringing the action to narrative closure. The poet needs to take care to incorporate recognition and reversal into the plot so as to preserve the causal connections in the plot.

In addition to reversal and recognition, suffering (*pathos*) is a third element in the plot that Aristotle introduces late in *Poetics* 11. Suffering belongs to every plot, whether it is complex or simple. The suffering in question involves a destructive or painful action of violence around which the plot is built, for example public deaths, physical agony, and the inflicting of wounds (11.1452b10–11). Later, in *Poetics* 14, Aristotle says that the best suffering is that which occurs between family members and loved ones (14.1453b14–15).

To illustrate, while the suffering of the Trojan women in Euripides' play of the same name evokes pity and fear, it is not, Aristotle thinks, the kind of *pathos* that most evokes pity and fear from the audience. When there is a "terrible deed" of violence committed by sister against brother, son against father, and so on, this is the sort of destructive act that incites pity and fear the most. When Medea kills her children (1453b28–29), or Oedipus kills his father, or Iphigenia almost kills her brother, this is the best sort of suffering for a plot to include. Contemporary films also use incidents of violence between family members to heighten the emotional effect. In the horror classic, *The Shining* (Stanley Kubrick, 1980) Jack Torrance (Jack Nicholson), the caretaker of the Overlook Hotel, becomes possessed by the spirit of the house, which threatens to prompt Jack into violence against his wife and son.

Aristotle's inclusion of suffering as a third element of the plot implies that every tragedy must have at least one act of suffering (11.1452b11–12). *Poetics* 14 clarifies that the suffering may just threaten to occur and be averted by the end, as with Euripides' *Iphigenia in Tauris* (11.1454a5–6). The terrible act of violence can take place "outside the drama," as Aristotle clarifies in *Poetics* 14, as when Oedipus' slaying of his father at the crossroads is part of the backstory of *Oedipus the King*, but is not included as one of the incidents in the incidents that are dramatized on stage.

HAMARTIA OR TRAGIC ERROR

In *Poetics* 13 and 14 Aristotle gives his assessment of which plot structures are the most effective in arousing fear and pity in the audience. These two chapters have puzzled commentators because they seem to give rankings of plots that are inconsistent. *Poetics* 14 ranks most highly the plot pattern featured in Euripides' *Iphigenia in Tauris*, in which suffering and bad fortune threaten but are at the last moment averted. The plot that involves a character who brings harm to his kin, but does so unknowingly is ranked second-best (14.1453b30). The plot type of Sophocles' *Oedipus the King*, which is ranked second-best in *Poetics* 14 comes out first-best in *Poetics* 13.

Another apparent inconsistency between the two chapters relates to one of the most central, if also most often misunderstood, concepts in the *Poetics*: the notion that it is an error or *hamartia* that brings about (or threatens to bring about) the tragic misfortune for the character (13.1454a13). The meaning of *hamartia* is hotly contested. Commentators have suggested that by "*hamartia*" Aristotle means an error that is either related to the tragic agent's character, for example a "character flaw," or an intellectual error, for example some mistake in calculation or a mistake of fact, or a range of error that includes a moral failing as well as a mistake of fact. Aristotle's discussion of tragic error in *Poetics* 13 appears to link *hamartia* to character, whereas his remarks in *Poetics* 14 appear to favor the view that tragic error is a mistake of fact.

The root meaning of "*hamartia*" is "missing the mark." Aristotle tells us that the error of *hamartia* that leads to the character's change of fortune is distinguished from a morally vicious character and/or malice (13.1453a7). The challenge to understanding the notion of "*hamartia*" is whether the error in question relates to moral character, intellectual miscalculation, or mistake of the facts, and whether or not it is an error for which the character is culpable or blameworthy.[12]

Given that the best plot contains reversal and recognition, it is natural that some commentators have seen a close connection between these two concepts and the notion of *hamartia* that Aristotle presents as a feature of the best type of plot pattern in *Poetics* 13. On this view, the error in question relates to an ignorance of the particulars of the action that involves the terrible deed of violence. On the intellectual error reading, Oedipus' mistake or *hamartia* is acting without the full or correct knowledge of what he is doing. It is not that he is guilty of "hubris" or arrogance, or guilty of excessive anger, which prompts him to kill the man at the crossroads, thereby unknowingly bringing about his father's death. Rather, Oedipus' error relates to the lack of knowledge of what he is really doing when he kills the man at the crossroads.

On this reading, *hamartia*, recognition, and reversal are linking concepts in the best complex plots. The error is caused by lack of an understanding of the facts, understanding that Oedipus needs to have if he is to avoid the terrible deed of killing his father. When recognition occurs that brings this needed information to the character, the tragic agent undergoes a change that is opposite to what was anticipated. Because Oedipus cannot be held responsible for information that was withheld from him by his parents, his suffering evokes the audience's pity and fear.

This is so, because according to Aristotle's account of responsible action, a person acts involuntarily when the action: (1) has its causal origin in the person who performs the action; and (2) is done without full knowledge of the person acted on, the instrument used, or the result intended by the action (*Nicomachean Ethics* 5.8.1135a23–25). Because Oedipus does not realize the identity of the man he encounters at the crossroads, and because upon learning later what he has done, he deeply regrets it, his action is involuntary (1136a5–8).[13]

The problem is that Aristotle does not tell us in *Poetics* 13 that *hamartia* is mistake of the facts or intellectual error. He explains "*hamartia*" as a "great error" that is the opposite of depravity or moral wickedness (1453a10), which means it could be a mistake of the facts or could be an error that is related to the agent's moral character, but one that is nevertheless excusable. The difference between *hamartia* as a moral or intellectual error is vast, and it has dramatic implications for how we read the argument of the *Poetics*.

Arthur Miller's *All My Sons* features a central protagonist, Joe Keller, who is a basically good person but who makes the moral mistake of knowingly shipping damaged aircraft cylinder heads from his factory during World War II, leading to consequences that Keller never anticipated, including the loss of the respect of his children and his own suicide. But this, and many other contemporary films and dramas that we think of as fine tragedies would not properly count as such if the error or *hamartia* of the character is an intellectual miscalculation or mistaken grasp of the facts.[14]

To be sure, as Malcolm Heath has pointed out, moral failings and intellectual error need not be mutually exclusive.[15] In *The Sixth Sense,* mentioned above, Malcolm is probably in error in both senses: he may be mistaken in not realizing that he has died and become a ghost: but it also may be a moral failing on his part, but one that is understandable, insofar as he is not able to come to terms with his own mortality, and pass on to the next life. Still, this does not help us answer the question of whether Aristotle has one sense primarily in mind.

In spite of the difference between the intellectual error and moral character readings of *hamartia* there is some area of common agreement. Whatever error the tragic character commits, it has to be true that:

1) the error implicates her in the causal chain that brings about her change of fortune; she does not fall to misfortune due to chance, a truly wicked character, or because of some cause that is external to her. The tragic character, in other words, is not a mere victim of bad luck at the hands of others: she must in some way contribute to her reversal of fortune; and

2) whatever error the tragic character commits, she suffers out of proportion to any mistake, moral, intellectual, or both, that she makes.

These points emerge in Aristotle's discussion of plot patterns in *Poetics* 13. After looking at the discussion there, we may be in a better position to determine if "*hamartia*" is linked to recognition and reversal or if it means a range of error from forgivable moral failing to intellectual error or range of the facts, or some third alternative.

POETICS 13: THE BEST TRAGIC PLOTS

Aristotle starts his argument in *Poetics* 13 reminding the reader of two points: first, the best tragedies must have plots that are complex, not simple (1452b30); second, tragedy must imitate fearful and pitiable events, for this is a defining feature of tragic *mimēsis*, as noted in the definition of tragedy in *Poetics* 6. The plot patterns considered in *Poetics* 13 are, therefore, ranked, according to how well they accomplish the goal of evoking pity and fear in the audience. The plots he considers involve different combinations of (1) types of moral character and (2) a change (either from bad to good or from good to bad fortune) the character experiences. There are three combinations of character and change of fortune he first discusses (1452b32f.):

13-1) A person superior (to the audience) in virtue undergoes a change from good to bad fortune.
13-2) A wicked person changes from bad to good fortune.
13-3) A wicked person falls from good to bad fortune.

Aristotle eliminates plot patterns (13-1)–(13-3) because they do not produce the right emotional response in the audience. It is easier to grasp Aristotle's reasons for eliminating plot patterns (13-2) and (13-3). Pity is inspired when someone suffers undeservedly. Moreover, the person we pity should experience a painful destruction or evil of the sort that we could expect could befall our friends or ourselves. Fear is felt for one like us (13.1453a3–4). Pity and fear cannot be aroused when a very wicked person goes from bad to good fortune (13-2). For such a person is not like the audience (and so does not inspire fear), and does not experience any undeserved suffering, and a good outcome does not inspire fear, no matter the moral standing of the character.

On the other hand, plot pattern (13-3) that imitates the action in which a wicked person goes from good to bad fortune also prompts the wrong response: it evokes "fellow-feeling" (*philanthrōpia*), a term that has variously been explained as meaning in this context, either a sympathetic sense of justice served ("poetic justice") or a completely different meaning: a sympathetic feeling that a fellow human being is suffering (what we might call "compassion").[16] But there is nothing fearful or pitiable in the action.

It is harder to understand why Aristotle eliminates pattern (13-1). This pattern imitates the actions of a person of superior virtue (*epieikēs*) who goes from good fortune to bad, owing to no fault or mistake of her own.[17] Aristotle says that this plot pattern does not inspire pity or fear, but is repugnant or disgusting (*miaros*). It is not that Aristotle holds that a good person's virtue is a buffer against the winds of misfortune. Indeed Aristotle's ethics discusses how a happy life can be derailed by great misfortunes, as happened to King Priam of Troy.[18] Aristotle also holds that while natural things and processes have a regularity and purposiveness, these processes will reach the determined end provided that there is no impediment, either in the environment or in the organism.[19] Aristotle is aware, then, that there are a variety of factors that can impede an exceptionally virtuous person's striving towards happiness. It is not, then, that pattern (13-1) is eliminated as showing an outcome that is outside the scope of how natural processes, including those involving the actions of human beings, operate.

Instead (13-1) is eliminated because, like the other two plot patterns (13-2) and (13-3), it produces the wrong emotional response in the audience. It is shocking (*miaros*) (1452b36). Why does Aristotle think that this is so? The answer is not so clear. The logic of how pity works would suggest that the greater degree of moral virtue that someone has, the greater the pity that is inspired when such a person falls to misfortune due to no fault of his own. T. C. W. Stinton proposes a plausible explanation. The sense of outrage and shock that is felt when a very virtuous person undergoes a change from good to bad fortune prompts a sense of moral outrage in the audience, and this outrage predominates and shuts out pity and fear.[20]

In *Poetics* 13.1452b35 Aristotle says that the fall to bad fortune of an exceptionally virtuous person is *not* fearful or pitiable, but repugnant (*miaros*). For Stinton's explanation to work, we need to suppose that the sense of moral outrage at the good person's fall predominates so that outrage drives out the pity and fear for the character. As Nancy Sherman notes, Aristotle thinks that intense fear is capable of driving out pity.[21] So Stinton's explanation of why the fall of the very virtuous person is shocking, not pitiable or fearful, is plausible.

An alternative explanation of why (13-1) is eliminated is also possible. Perhaps this plot structure is eliminated because pity and fear cannot be felt for a person who is vastly superior in virtue to the audience.[22] This has nothing to do with the fact that such a person's suffering is not deserved. Aristotle holds that it is someone like us that inspires pity and fear. Recall that fear is felt for one like ourselves (*Poetics* 13.1453a3; *Rhetoric* 2.5.1386a27–28) and pity is likewise felt when we come to believe that we are vulnerable to the same sort of destructive evil as the sort the person we pity (*Rhetoric* 2.8.1385b15–16). Aristotle may, then, eliminate (13-1) because the audience is simply not able to relate to the circumstance of the very virtuous person's suffering, even though they experience outrage when such a person falls to misfortune.

Now within the parameters of (1) exceptionally virtuous or wicked; and (2) change to good fortune or bad, there is one plot pattern that Aristotle does not consider. This is:

13-1-b) An exceptionally virtuous person goes from bad to good fortune—no pity and fear.

We can see why Aristotle would rank this as inferior tragedy. It does not inspire pity because there is no undeserved suffering. It also would not evoke fear, for this is felt for someone "like us" and the exceptionally virtuous person is too far above the average audience member to inspire fear. In addition, a good outcome would not inspire fear.

After eliminating (13-1)–(13-3), Aristotle turns to the plot pattern that he favors as the best combination of character and change of fortune. Aristotle's view is that tragedy is to imitate actions in which bad things happen to good people, but in a way that makes the character's change of fortune understandable and causally explicable. This brings us to Aristotle's preferred plot pattern, (13-4), which makes up for the defects in the first plot pattern and meets the requirements of poetic unity that is central to the effective plot.

13-4) A person "intermediate in virtue and justice" undergoes a change from good to bad fortune not because of vice and wickedness, but due to some error (*hamartia*).

Here Aristotle introduces the tragic character's error or *hamartia* as a way of explaining the tragic character's change from good fortune to bad. The tragic character is deserving of the audience's pity, but nevertheless commits an error or *hamartia* that explains the character's change of fortune. If the tragic character is not exceptional in virtue, but merely a good or decent person who errs but is not wicked, then her misfortune, which is out of proportion to any mistake she makes, evokes the audience's pity and fear. It is, nonetheless, understandable in light of her error. Sophocles' *Oedipus the King* is a prime example of this plot.

Aristotle's ranking of plot patterns in *Poetics* 13 is as follows:

13-1) An exceptionally good person goes from good fortune to bad—disgust, not pity and fear.
13-2) A wicked person goes from bad to good fortune—disgust, not pity and fear.
13-3) A wicked person goes from good to bad fortune—sympathy or a feeling of poetic justice (fellow-feeling), not pity and fear.

13-4) A person "intermediate in virtue and justice" undergoes a change from good to bad fortune not because of vice and wickedness, but due to some error (*hamartia*)—pity and fear.

For example, *The Passion of Joan of Arc* (*La passion de Jeanne d'Arc*) (Carl Theodor Dreyer, 1928) is an illustration of plot pattern (13-1), for it shows the courageous Joan (Maria Falconetti) trying to drive the English from France, only to be burned at the stake after she is captured and tried by French clergy loyal to the British.

There Will Be Blood (Paul Thomas Anderson, 2007), an example of pattern (13-2), shows the rise and financial success of the greedy and unscrupulous oilman Daniel Plainview (Daniel Day-Lewis) in early twentieth-century California.

The Godfather (Francis Ford Coppola, 1972) may be said to be an example of pattern (13-3). The film starts with the joyful wedding of Vito Corleone's (Marlon Brando) daughter, but the mafia head ends up losing his son, Sonny, when warfare breaks out between mafia rivals, and then dies from a heart attack.

The Sixth Sense (M. Night Shyamalan, 1999) features a plot that conforms to (13-4), with the protagonist, a caring child psychologist Malcolm Crowe (Bruce Willis) making the mistake of not realizing that he has died and become a ghost, a truth he painfully must come to terms with at the end of the film.

There is another plot pattern that Aristotle does not consider in *Poetics* 13. This is the one in which a person "intermediate in virtue and justice" goes from bad fortune to good:

13-5) A person "intermediate in virtue and justice" goes from bad fortune to good.

From what Aristotle says in *Poetics* 13, (13-4) and not (13-5) is the best plot pattern. Yet, when we turn to *Poetics* 14, Aristotle says that this plot pattern, which is exemplified in Euripides' *Iphigenia in Tauris*, is the best. This is one factor that, as noted earlier, has made the two chapters appear to be inconsistent.

POETICS 14: ACTING IN IGNORANCE WITH A FORTUNATE OUTCOME

In spite of the apparent tensions between *Poetics* 13 and 14, in *Poetics* 14 we see Aristotle doing something that is consistent with *Poetics* 13. He is arguing that the best plot patterns provide a mechanism for understanding how the tragic character's reversal of fortune could come about or threaten to come about. The relevant extenuating circumstance is the tragic character's lack of *knowledge* of what he or she is doing.

Given that Aristotle is going to talk about how the incidents of tragedy concern great harm or violence inflicted between loved ones and family members, *Poetics* 14 starts with a reminder that it is the structure of the plot that is the best tool the poet has for inspiring pity and fear, not the use of spectacle (*opsis*). While spectacle has an emotional power (14.1453b1–3), there is no place for a play that works simply on the level of the visual, with no regard for the plot as the primary vehicle for arousing emotion in the audience (14.1453b3–10).

Tragedy shows actions between persons dear to one another—relatives (*philia*) or close friends, where one person brings harm (or is about to bring harm) to kin (13.1453b15–22). It should imitate actions that "strike us as terrible or pitiable," specifically suffering (*pathos*) that occurs within relationships, such as "brother and brother, son and father, mother and son, son and mother—when the one kills (or is about to kill) the other, or commits some other such deed." He considers four possible combinations of plot patterns in which this central tragic act is: (1) either done or not done; (2) either knowingly or unknowingly.

14-1) The agent knows what he does (or is about to do); the act does not end up being done.
14-2) The agent knows what he does (or is about to do); the act is done.

14-3) The agent does not know what he is doing, the act is done (then followed by recognition).

14-4) The agent does not know what he is doing, the act is threatened but at the last minute averted.

The case in which one family member harms (or threatens to harm) another family member while acting in ignorance is a frequent theme in ancient Greek tragedy: Iphigenia almost sacrifices her long lost brother because she does not recognize Orestes. Oedipus, without knowledge of who he is and what he is doing, unintentionally kills his father at the crossroads; and Deianira, thinking that she can win back Heracles' love with a potion the Centaur gave her, unintentionally ends up poisoning him.

The worst plot pattern is (14-1), where the agent has knowledge of what she is doing, and the act is not done or carried out. Aristotle says this is "repugnant" or "disgusting" (*miaros*; 14.1453b33; cf. 1453b36) and is "not tragic," for since there is no suffering (*pathos*) it does not evoke pity and fear.

The second-worst pattern is (14-2), where the character knows what she is doing and completes the action. Aristotle does not say why this is second-worst. He must at least think that it is better than (14-1) because at least with (14-2) there is some suffering. Aristotle's explanation of why (14-2) is not desirable comes with his explanation of why (14-3) is better: "Better is the act done in ignorance, and followed by recognition; there is nothing repugnant (*miaros*) here, and the recognition is thrilling" (14.1454a2–3).

Finally, (14-4), the plot pattern where the character acts in ignorance of what she is doing, but at the last minute the act is averted, is the best. Euripides' *Iphigenia in Tauris* is an example of this: Iphigenia is about to sacrifice her long lost brother Orestes; she recognizes him as he does her, and the terrible deed is at the last minute averted. As with (14-3) Aristotle does not say why this plot is the best.

How does this discussion bear on the meaning of "*hamartia*" or error? Recall there is a dispute as to whether "*hamartia*" or tragic error should be given a wide interpretation including mistakes ranging from moral errors (but nothing truly reprehensible), to an intellectual miscalculation, to a mistake of fact or a narrow interpretation (a mistake of fact or miscalculation only). T. C. W. Stinton, an ardent defender of the wide interpretation of *hamartia*, argues that Aristotle "passes no judgment" on plots that meet (14-2). These are plot structures such as the one found in Euripides' *Medea*, in which the title character kills her children to avenge her husband's infidelity, knowing what she is doing (1453b26–27). Rather, on Stinton's reading, Aristotle is leaving it open that the error in question is a moral failing that is nevertheless excusable, allowing the audience to feel pity and fear for the character.[23]

This is not, in my understanding of the passage, quite accurate.[24] We can infer Aristotle's reasons for ranking (14-2), where the agent does the horrible deed with knowledge, below (14-3), where the agent acts in ignorance of what she is doing. He says that having a character commit the terrible act without knowledge is preferable to having a character knowingly do the deed, for in the former case there is nothing disgusting (14.1454a2–3).

The implication is that where a character acts with knowledge of what she is doing, as Medea does when she kills her children, this is "disgusting." Note this is the same term (*miaros*) that Aristotle used when he gave his reasons for eliminating the fall of the exceptionally virtuous person and the rise of the wicked person in *Poetics* 13. Aristotle's choice of words here suggests that even if there is some excusing condition, for example passion or anger, that prompts Medea to kill her children, the audience's overall emotional response to such a character is compromised.

This makes me inclined to think that by "*hamartia*" Aristotle means an error that is done out of ignorance, but nevertheless has repercussions that bear on the sense of responsibility that the agent feels for the chain of events. The agent, such as Oedipus, who acts in ignorance of what he does performs an involuntary action, and is therefore not blameworthy. Oedipus' action is involuntary, because it fails to meet both of the two conditions for voluntary action: (1) the action has its origin in the agent;[25] and (2) it is performed with knowledge.[26] To be performed with knowledge, the agent must be aware of a number of factors pertaining to the circumstances in which he acts. When the agent acts in ignorance of certain conditions in which he acts, the action is involuntary and he is not held responsible. The agent acts in ignorance when the agent is ignorant of: (1) who he is; (2) what he is doing; (3) what thing or person is affected; and sometimes also (4) the means he is using, for example some tool; (5) the result intended by his action; and (6) the manner in which he acts, for example gently or violently.[27]

The action of Oedipus killing his father satisfies the origin condition, for this action originates in Oedipus' bodily movements. There is no one forcing him to kill the man at the crossroads, so the action is not done under compulsion or constraint that comes from outside, as is the case with involuntary actions.[28] Yet it fails to satisfy the knowledge condition, for Oedipus is ignorant of the condition spelled out in (3) above: Oedipus does not realize that the person he is striking at the crossroads is his father. Therefore, Oedipus acts involuntarily, as does Deianira, who tries to win back Heracles' love with a potion the Centaur gave her, unintentionally poisoning him. Here the result intended by Deianira's action is the opposite of what she aims for (case 5 above).

Only voluntary actions are subject to punishment and blame. Therefore, Oedipus is not blameworthy for what he did. In one way this makes sense, since what the agent does (in Oedipus' case, kill his father) is not the action that the tragic agent aims to accomplish, due to the larger chain of events in which the action gets caught up. Still, Oedipus brings about the death of his father and Deianira kills Heracles, and because of these actions they are causally implicated in actions that bring about their change of fortune. Oedipus is not technically, we might say, responsible for what he did, but his action implicates him in the causal chain that leads to his change of fortune, and indeed at the end of the play, Oedipus expresses deep regret and shame for what he did, making his response to his situation even more pitiable. Aristotle seems to be saying, this kind of error, where the action is done without knowledge, but nevertheless implicates the agent in the change of fortune, is especially apt at inciting pity and fear in the audience.

In reply Stinton is likely to say that in his ethics, Aristotle is willing to allow that there are situations where someone merits pity and forgiveness, even though she acts with knowledge of what she does and chooses the morally wrong thing to do.[29] The conditions of pity and pardon would depend on the individual's moral psychology at the time that she acted. For example, Medea, the title character in Euripides' play of the same name, acts out of passion when she kills her children to avenge her husband's infidelity. Even though her act is done deliberately with knowledge of what she is doing, this is a case where her better judgment is dislodged by her anger at her husband. It is possible for a character that commits such an action to inspire pity in the audience because there are mitigating circumstances that make the action pardonable.

While in his ethics Aristotle allows that a wide range of actions merit pity and forgiveness, in *Poetics* 14 Aristotle is ranking plots based on their maximal ability to inspire pity and fear. In this regard, actions that are done knowingly cannot inspire the same degree of pity and fear as ones that are done in ignorance of what is being done. Tragedy, on Aristotle's view, is not about simply mirroring the sorts of situations we find pitiable and fearful in real life. It is about taking those natural emotional responses to fellow humans and heightening them through a plot that provides the maximal degree of pity and fear.

At the same time, those who have argued that *hamartia* is a purely intellectual error or mistake of fact seem to miss an important point. Oedipus is not blameworthy for what he did. Still, he is causally implicated in his action, and this forces him, and the audience, to see him in a different light, due to the moral gravity of the act that he has committed. Even characters that act in ignorance can be implicated in actions with grave moral consequences, thus making them occupy a middle ground between characters who are mere victims of bad luck, on the one hand, and characters who knowingly and deliberately carry out terrible deeds of violence against their kin and loved ones. This is indeed what a character such as Oedipus has to come to terms with when he recognizes just what it is he has unknowingly done.

This brings us to the ideal plot pattern in *Poetics* 14, (14-4) in which a good or morally decent character acts in ignorance of what she is doing, with the terrible deed of violence threatening but at the last minute averted. This is a happy ending, we would say, in contrast to the ideal plot pattern of *Poetics* 13, where the terrible deed is done, bringing about a change of fortune from good to bad for the character.

Why does Aristotle prefer the happy ending? As we have noted in discussing *Poetics* 13, it cannot be that he thinks that this is what will make the audience happy or pleased. Aristotle does not give his reasoning, so here we are left to speculate. Given that pity and fear are inspired the most by events that happen "contrary to expectations but on account of one another" (9.1452a1–3), he must think that a plot in which a character acts in ignorance of what she is doing, with the act of violence threatening but at the last minute averted, is the ideal way to prompt the experience of pity and fear at which tragedy aims. Why he thinks this is less clear. It may be connected to the idea that a plot in which terrible violence is threatened but at the end is averted provides a kind of sobering relief of pity and fear, showing misfortune that threatens to occur to a basically good and decent person, but is at the last minute avoided.

Aristotle's ranking of plot patterns in *Poetics* 14 is then as follows, from best to worst:

14-1) The agent knows what he does (or is about to do); the act does not end up being done. Example: Haimon's attack on Creon in Sophocles' *Antigone.*

14-2) The agent knows what she does (or is about to do); the act is done. Example: Euripides' *Medea.*

14-3) The agent does not know what he is doing; the act is done (then followed by recognition). Example: Sophocles' *Oedipus the King.*

14-4) The agent does not know what he is doing; the act is threatened but at the last minute averted. Example: Euripedes' *Iphigenia in Tauris.*

RECONCILING *POETICS* 13 AND *POETICS* 14

By looking at the rankings above, we can see there is a conflict between the recommendation in *Poetics* 13 and *Poetics* 14. For *Oedipus* comes out as second-best in *Poetics* 14, while in *Poetics* 13 it comes out as best. The solutions for addressing this conflict are too numerous to mention. There are several trends that have emerged. First, perhaps Aristotle simply changed his mind after writing *Poetics* 13.[30] Second, *Poetics* 13 is Aristotle's ranking of the best *overall* plot, while *Poetics* 14 is the ranking of the best *incidents* or scenes.[31] Third, *Poetics* 13 gives the ranking of the plots that are "most tragic," while *Poetics* 14 gives his ranking of "most powerful."[32] Fourth, *Poetics* 13 is a preliminary discussion of best plot patterns, and Aristotle's final word on what the very best plots are comes in *Poetics* 14.[33]

Of these options, I favor the fourth, but not simply because it explains the central role that recognition and reversal play in the ideally complex plots. *Poetics* 13's contribution is to argue that the best plots should include an error or *hamartia* that explains the character's change of fortune. This error is distinguished from vice and true wickedness. The tragic character is implicated in his own misfortune, due to some error that provides a causal link between his actions and subsequent change of fortune. The ideal tragic character is causally implicated in his turn of fortune, but in such a way that his error is excusable and he retains his good character.

Poetics 14 follows these points up by stipulating that the best *hamartia* involves harm to kin done in ignorance. By the end of *Poetics* 14 Aristotle concludes that the very best plot pattern is one that provides a sobering relief of pity and fear, through a disastrous deed that threatens to happen due to the character's ignorance, but is in the end averted.

NOTES

1 Reading for this chapter is *Poetics* 10–16.
2 Two scholars have been influential in shaping the consensus that it is useful to look outside the *Poetics* to understand the nature of the tragic emotions: William W. Fortenbaugh 1970 and 1975; and Alexander Nehamas 1992.
3 Aristotle's view that tragedy accomplishes a *catharsis* of pity and fear (6.1449b26) is discussed in Chapter 9, and the idea that the poet should create "the pleasure that comes from pity and fear through *mimēsis*" (6.1453b11) is examined in Chapter 11.
4 For a recent discussion of the debate around what the cognitive component of emotions is on Aristotle's view, see Jamie Dow 2009.
5 Cf. Jesse Prinz 2004: 10–11 who presents Aristotle's theory of emotions as a hybrid between cognitive and bodily reaction accounts of the emotions. I think Aristotle's account should fall on the cognitive side of this divide because he thinks that the cognitive component of the emotion (a belief, perception, or thought) is the *cause* of the bodily reaction.
6 In the former camp are Alexander Nehamas 1992; David Konstan 1999 and 2005. In the latter camp is Stephen Halliwell 1998: 175–178, especially 176. Dana LaCourse Munteanu 2012: 72 and 92–95 mostly agrees that fear is felt for oneself, but also thinks that the spectator also feels some fear for the character as well.
7 Alexander Nehamas 1992: 302.
8 See Nehamas 1992: 303.
9 See also the discussion in Chapter 7, 162–163.
10 Reading for this section is *Poetics* 11–12 and 16.
11 For an extended discussion of this film in relation to Aristotelian tragedy see Angela Curran 2003.

12 Nancy Sherman 1992 and T. C. W. Stinton 1975 favor the wide reading of "*hamartia*," where it refers to a range of errors, while J. M. Bremer 1969 favors the narrow reading of "*hamartia*" as intellectual error.

13 Cf. the discussion of Richard Sorabji 1979: 295–298, who argues that Oedipus' killing of his father at the crossroads turns out to be an unlucky mishap (*atuchēma*) rather than an error or mistake (*hamartēma*) according to *Nicomachean Ethics* 5.8. For a different reading of the relevance of *NE* 5.8 to tragic error see Dorothea Frede 1992: 212.

14 Michael Tierno 2002: 65.

15 Malcolm Heath 1996: xxxiii.

16 For the dispute about this notion in the *Poetics* see C. Carey 1988.

17 Aristotle uses the term *epieikēs* to describe the exceptionally virtuous person. The literal translation of this is "good" or "decent." A bit further in the text (1453a5–10) Aristotle says that when the three cases he discusses are eliminated there remain plots that show a tragic character who is "intermediate" in virtue between the person "superior (to us) in virtue" and the wicked person. This makes the translation of *epieikēs* at line 1452b33 as "person of exceptional virtue" rather than merely a "good or decent person" the more reasonable one.

18 *Nicomachean Ethics* 1.8.1099a6–9.

19 *Physics* 2.8.199b15–18; *Physics* 1.1.641b23–26.

20 T. C. W. Stinton 1975: 238–239.

21 *Rhetoric* 3.8.1385b34–5; N. Sherman 1992: 194 note 27.

22 See note 13, above.

23 T. C. W. Stinton 1975: 234.

24 Stinton's argument for the "wide" interpretation of "*hamartia*" is extensive and my brief comments do not do it justice. The reader is urged to consult his essay as well as N. Sherman 1992 for further arguments favoring the wide view.

25 "The agent acts voluntarily, because the initiative in moving the parts of the body which act as instruments rests with the agent himself; and where the source of motion is within oneself, it is in one's power to act or not to act" (*Nicomachean Ethics* 3.1.1110a14–18; Martin Ostwald translation 1962).

26 *NE* 3.1.111a1–3.

27 *NE* 3.1.111a3–7.

28 *NE* 3.1.111b35–36.

29 *NE* 7.3.1147a15–19.

30 See I. Bywater 1909: 224–225.

31 See Gerald Else 1957: 450–452 and D. W. Lucas 1968: 155.

32 Stephen A. White 1992: 236.

33 Elizabeth Belfiore 1992: 174–175.

WORKS CITED

Barnes, Jonathan (ed.) 1984. *The Complete Works of Aristotle. The Revised Oxford Translation* Volume Two. Princeton, NJ: Princeton University Press.

Belfiore, Elizabeth 1992. *Tragic Pleasures: Aristotle on Plot and Emotion*. Princeton, NJ: Princeton University Press.

Bremer, J. M. 1969. *Hamartia: Tragic Error in the Poetics of Aristotle and Greek Tragedy*. Amsterdam: Adolf M. Hakkert.

Bywater, I. 1909. *Aristotle on the Art of Poetry*. Oxford: Oxford University Press.

Carey, C. 1988. "'Philanthropy' in Aristotle's *Poetics*." *Eranos* 86: 131–139.

Curran, Angela 2003. "Aristotelian Reflections on Horror and Tragedy in *American Werewolf in London* and *Sixth Sense*," in Steven Jay Schneider and Daniel Shaw (eds.), *Dark Thoughts: Philosophic Reflections on Cinematic Horror*. Lanham, MD: Scarecrow Press: 47–64.

Dow, Jamie 2009. "Feeling Fantastic? Emotions and Appearances in Aristotle." *Oxford Studies in Ancient Philosophy* 37: 143–175.

Else, Gerald 1957. *Aristotle's Poetics: The Argument*. Cambridge, MA: Harvard University Press.

Fortenbaugh, William W. 1970. "Aristotle's *Rhetoric* on Emotions." *Archiv für Geschichte der Philosophie* 52: 40–70.

_____ 1975. *Aristotle on Emotion: A Contribution to Philosophical Psychology, Rhetoric, Poetics Politics and Ethics*. London: Duckworth.

Frede, Dorothea 1992. "Necessity, Chance and 'What Happens for the Most Part' in Aristotle's *Poetics*," in Amélie Oskenberg Rorty (ed.), *Essays on Aristotle's Poetics*. Princeton, NJ: Princeton University Press: 197–220.

Halliwell, Stephen 1998. *Aristotle's Poetics: With a New Introduction by the Author*. Chicago: University of Chicago Press.

Heath, Malcolm 1996. *Aristotle: Poetics*, translated with Notes and an Introduction. New York and London: Penguin Press.

Konstan, David 1999. "The Tragic Emotions," in L. R. Gámez (ed.), *Tragedy's Insights: Identity, Polity, Theodicy*. West Cornwall, CT: Locust Hill Press: 1–21.

_____ 2005. "Aristotle on the Tragic Emotions," in V. Pedrick and S. M. Oberhelman (eds.), *The Soul of Tragedy. Essays on Athenian Drama*. Chicago: University of Chicago Press: 13–26.

Lucas, D. W. (ed.) 1968. *Poetics: Introduction, Commentary and Appendixes*. Oxford: Oxford University Press.

Munteanu, Dana LaCourse 2012. *Tragic Pathos. Pity and Fear in Greek Philosophy and Tragedy*. Cambridge: Cambridge University Press.

Nehamas, Alexander 1992. "Pity and Fear in the *Rhetoric* and the *Poetics*," in Amélie Oskenberg Rorty (ed.), *Essays on Aristotle's Poetics*. Princeton, NJ: Princeton University Press: 291–314.

Ostwald, Martin 1962. *Aristotle: Nicomachean Ethics*. Englewood Cliffs, NJ: Prentice Hall.

Prinz, Jesse J. 2004. *Gut Reactions. A Perceptual Theory of Emotions*. Oxford: Oxford University Press.

Rorty, Amélie O. 1992. *Essays on Aristotle's Poetics*. Princeton, NJ: Princeton University Press.

Sherman, Nancy 1992. "*Hamartia* and Virtue," in Amélie O. Rorty (ed.), *Essays on Aristotle's Poetics*. Princeton, NJ: Princeton University Press: 177–196.

Sorabji, Richard 1979. *Necessity, Cause and Blame*. Ithaca, NY: Cornell University Press.

Stinton, T. C. W. 1975. "*Hamartia* in Aristotle and Greek Tragedy." *Classical Quarterly* 25: 221–254. Reprinted in *Collected Papers on Greek Tragedy* (Oxford University Press 1990), 143–185. Citations are to the 1975 version.

Tierno, Michael 2002. *Aristotle's Poetics for Screenwriters: Storytelling Secrets from the Greatest Mind in Western Civilization*. New York: Hyperion.

White, Stephen A. 1992. "Aristotle's Favorite Tragedies," in Amélie Oskenberg Rorty (ed.), *Essays on Aristotle's Poetics*. Princeton, NJ: Princeton University Press: 221–240.

9

CATHARSIS

INTRODUCTION: THE PROBLEM OF INTERPRETATION

It is often thought that the concept of *catharsis* is central to understanding the emotional effects of tragedy: this is because the idea that tragedy brings about a *catharsis* of pity and fear is mentioned at the end of the definition of tragedy in *Poetics* 6, a place that Aristotle sometimes reserves in the definition for the goal or final end of the thing being defined. Yet the concept of *catharsis* is not integrated into the argument of the *Poetics*: indeed it occurs in just two places in the text, once at the end of the definition of tragedy in *Poetics* 6 (1449b29) and once in *Poetics* 18 where Aristotle makes an incidental reference to a ritual of purification or *catharsis* in a play by Euripides (1455b15). The lack of an account of *catharsis* in the *Poetics* has prompted commentators to look to other works that might clarify these topics.

Scholars often turn to *Politics* 8.7 where Aristotle discusses *catharsis* in the context of ritual purification ceremonies and refers to a clearer discussion of the concept in a "treatise on poetry" (8.7.1341b38–39), something that the extant text of the *Poetics* does not provide.[1] Yet, as we will see, it is unclear how the notion of "purgation" of emotions, which is highlighted in the *Politics*' account of *catharsis*, can be made to fit with the discussion of the tragic emotion in the *Poetics*. This has inspired numerous alternative interpretations of *catharsis*, some of which have emerged as leading contenders.

With so many interpretations out there, it is tempting to back off from trying to understand what Aristotle means by *catharsis* in the *Poetics*. But this is a challenge from which the serious reader of the *Poetics* should not retreat. On the one hand, we should not think of the concept of *catharsis* as the Rosetta Stone of the *Poetics*: it is not the key to unlocking the work's true meaning.[2] On the other hand, Aristotle included the concept in the definition of tragedy for a reason, and so he must at least have thought it is, like the other components mentioned in the definition of tragedy, a necessary aspect of tragedy. Our understanding of the argument in the *Poetics* will be more complete if we can try to arrive at even a tentative conclusion about Aristotle's meaning.

A point that is often missed is that whatever *catharsis* means in the *Poetics*, it must be related not only to the specific structural requirements on the plot, such as unity and completeness, but also to the requirements on narrative structures that Aristotle lays out in *Poetics* 13–14. For Aristotle argues in these books that some patterns are better than others at eliciting the appropriate emotional response, tragic pity and fear, and the most reasonable interpretation of *catharsis* is that it essentially involves these emotions.

For reasons to be given, an account of tragic *catharsis* should also consider other works of Aristotle's that might shed light on the topic, in particular, *Politics* 8.6.1341a21–8.7.1342a20, which discusses *catharsis* in connection with music, as well as the account of the emotions offered in the *Rhetoric*. As

Paul Woodruff notes, the difficulty is in bringing these two approaches together.[3] In what follows I propose we may be able to make some headway towards resolving this challenge by building on some of the strengths found in previous accounts of *catharsis*, and attempting to address the objections these views face.

In addition to debating the meaning or nature of tragic *catharsis* in the *Poetics*, there are debates around what we will call the *objects* on which *catharsis* operates. What is it, in other words, that tragedy is a *catharsis of*? Is it the *emotions* of pity and fear in the audience, as many have maintained? Or is tragedy a *catharsis* of the pitiful and fearful incidents in the *plot*, as it has also been argued? We will track these two different variables, the nature of the *catharsis* and the object of *catharsis*, as we discuss the different options.

CATHARSIS: ROOT MEANINGS

We start by briefly considering the history of the term "*catharsis*" in ancient Greek.[4] For while not all proposals follow these root meanings of "*catharsis*," many do. One use relates to *catharsis* as medical purgation, where *catharsis* is a cleansing or purgation that removes impurities and diseases in the body, as with a laxative. *Catharsis* in this sense is therapeutic.

A second use relates to *catharsis* as purification, specifically, the ritual purification of people. *Catharsis* in this sense functioned in ritual practices to purify someone who carried a pollution of which one needs to be cleansed or to a ritual purification that participants in a ceremony must undergo.

A third sense of *catharsis* is "clarification" or clearing up, where what is clarified is some state, physical or mental, that is an impediment to a thing functioning in its proper state. This was used to refer to physical things, for example the clarification or *catharsis* of a river, as well as to the intellectual clarification of the mind or soul.[5] Clarification, as we can see, is closely connected with the idea that a *catharsis* purifies some impure state of the body or soul.

These three root meanings have historically been associated with *two* broad approaches to tragic *catharsis* in the *Poetics*.

The first general approach is associated with the sense of "*catharsis*" as purgation. The objects on which *catharsis* operates are the emotions of pity and fear and the nature of *catharsis* is purgation. The idea is that *catharsis* involves an outlet and evacuation of something that is harmful to the psyche, in the manner that a medical purgation involves a removal of something that is harmful for the body. A spectator goes to the theater to have his excess emotions drained away in the way that one might go to the doctor to have some noxious excess substance removed from one's body.

The second general approach to *catharsis* relates to the second and third sense, "purification" and "clarification." The nature of *catharsis* is to make clear, purify, or refine some condition of a thing in the way that one might remove mud or weeds from some water in a river to make it suitable for drinking.[6] Clarification accounts differ in their understanding of the *objects* on which *catharsis* operates. One sort of clarification account proposes that *catharsis* operates on the spectator's *emotions and/or cognitive attitudes*. One goes to the theater to have some condition in one (e.g. the emotions of pity and fear or an understanding of life's vicissitudes) refined, improved, or clarified, but not purged or eliminated. Other clarification accounts propose that the clearing up that occurs does not take place in the spectator, but is a resolution and tidying up of the incidents in the *plot*. This sort of clarification account is a minority approach, but it is offered due to the problems of saying just in what sense tragedy brings about a refinement or clarification of one's emotions or attitudes.

Of course, it is possible to combine both approaches, and indeed purgation and purification/clarification are closely related in that ritual purification may also be therapeutic, removing something that makes the *soul* unclean, and thereby leading to an improvement and refinement of what is left.[7] But historically, scholars have tended to align their interpretations with either the purgation or the refinement–clarification approaches to *catharsis*, for reasons we will discuss.

A BRIEF OVERVIEW OF *CATHARSIS* INTERPRETATION[8]

- Ethical education: While there are many varieties, the over-arching theme of this approach is that the experience of tragic *catharsis* brings about the habits of feeling emotions in the right way and towards the right people that are necessary for good ethical character.[9]
- Emotional release/purgation: Tragic *catharsis* involves the pleasurable release or purgation of pent-up emotions.[10]
- Intellectual clarification: Tragic *catharsis* is a clarification of the audience's understanding of the events in the plot.
- Emotional clarification: Tragic *catharsis* is a clarification of the emotions of pity and fear in the audience.[11]
- Suspense/detective novel: Tragic *catharsis* is the pleasure that the audience feels when the suspense that has been tightening throughout the play is suddenly released.[12]
- Pleasurable relief: Tragic *catharsis* is the pleasurable relief of releasing emotions in a safe environment.[13]

These proposals will be canvassed in the discussion that follows. The reader is advised, however, that some understandings of tragic *catharsis* fall into more than one category. Thus, the categories are not mutually exclusive. So, for example, one might think that *catharsis* is a clarification of the emotions of the spectator (the emotional clarification account), but also think that this clarification brings about the good habits of right emotional response that are necessary for virtuous action (ethical education).[14] Or one might think that the pleasure in tragic *catharsis* is the pleasure of having the suspense that is building through the play released (the suspense/detective model), but also hold that such release involves the pleasure in purging the emotions that the drama brings out in the spectator (purgation account).[15]

CATHARSIS AS PURGATION

The *purgation* theory, proposed by Jacob Bernays in the mid-nineteenth century, argues that *catharsis* is the purging or removal of the emotions of pity and fear analogous to a medical purgation of some noxious substance from the body.[16] Tragedy is therapeutic, for it helps the spectator rid herself of unhealthy pent-up emotions and, in doing so, provides her with a sense of enjoyable relief.

Purgation account of catharsis
The nature of *catharsis* = purgation
The object of *catharsis* = the emotions of pity and fear in the audience

The evidence for this view comes from the discussion of musical *catharsis* in *Politics* 8.7.1342a4–15, where Aristotle discusses the benefits of music, which can be used both for the purpose of education and *catharsis* (1341b39):

> For such feelings as pity and fear, or, gain, enthusiasm, exist very strongly in some souls, and have more or less influence over all. Some persons fall into a religious frenzy, and we see them restored as a result of the sacred melodies—when they have used the melodies that excite the soul to mystic frenzy—as though they had found healing and *catharsis*. Those who are influenced by pity and fear, and very emotional nature must have a like experience, and others in so far as each is susceptible to such emotions, and all are in a manner purged and their souls lightened and delighted.[17]

The medical purgation model of *catharsis* works like a homeopathic treatment, for the spectator's tendency to experience emotional excess is first excited by the music, and then restored as the release or purgation of the excess emotions helps the soul settle down (1342a7–15).[18] The point of tragic *catharsis* is then the purgation of excess emotions that threaten physical and psychological wellbeing.

While in favor for many decades, more recent commentators have tended to reject this interpretation. Aristotle does think that emotions can be felt excessively or improperly, as he says in his ethics:

> I mean moral excellence (*aretē*); for it is this that is concerned with passions and actions, and in these there is excess, defect, and the intermediate. For instance, both fear and confidence and appetite and anger and pity and in general pleasure and pain may be felt both too much and too little, and in both cases not well; but to feel them at the right times, with reference to the right objects, towards the right people, with the right aim, and in the right way, is what is both intermediate and best, and this is characteristics of excellence (*aretē*).
>
> (*Nicomachean Ethics* 2.1106b16–23; Barnes 1984)

While emotions can be experienced in excess or improperly, in the ways outlined above, Aristotle does not suggest that emotions such as pity and fear are unhealthy or harmful items that are in need of discharge. Nor is there anything false, dirty, or corrupting about pity and fear, in themselves or how a tragic audience experiences them.[19] Yet this seems to be what Bernays' model implies, for he sets up an analogy between the mind of the person who feels excess emotion and the bodily condition of someone who is afflicted with some illness.[20] The worry about the purgation account is then that there is nothing in the *Poetics* to suggest that the spectator of tragedy is in a pathological condition of emotional excess of which he needs to be healed.

There is also the objection to the purgation account raised by Jonathan Lear, which is that it is not clear what it would mean to say that an emotion is capable of being purged.[21] For emotions are not simply states of feeling: they involve a cognitive attitude (a belief, a thought, a perception) that is directed at the world.[22] Pity is directed at someone who suffers undeservedly, fear is felt for someone like us. What does it mean, Lear asks, for the person who feels emotion excessively to purge herself of the emotion, if emotions on Aristotle's view are not simply feelings or bodily states, but have a cognitive complexity that is essential to emotion? How, in other words, does one "purge" or drain off something that involves an attitude or belief directed at the world?

Lear presses several other points against the purgation account. First, the audience of tragedy is not in a neurotic condition from which they need to be relieved.[23] On the contrary, in *Poetics* 26 and elsewhere Aristotle argues that tragedy is superior to comedy because it appeals to a better audience (1461b25f.; *Poetics* 13.1453a30–36; and 6.1450b16–19). This means that any account of *catharsis* must satisfy the following condition:

> The Virtuous Spectator Constraint (VSC): A virtuous person who attends the theater can experience a *catharsis* of pity and fear.

Indeed, when we look at the passage from *Politics* 8.7 above, Aristotle suggests that the musical therapy available to those susceptible to emotional excess explains how everyone, including an audience whose emotions are just as they should be, can undergo a *catharsis* from listening to certain kinds of music.[24] Therefore, if it is right to suppose that *Politics* 8.7 bears on the meaning of tragic *catharsis*, then this is an additional reason in support of the VSC above.

The purgation theory, then, as Bernays formulated it, needs to be rejected. First, it seems to suggest that the emotions of pity and fear are impure and dirty states that need to be purged. Second, it also suggests that *catharsis* applies to one in need of healing and therapy, but there is no suggestion in the *Poetics* that this is true of the audience of tragedy. Third, *Politics* 8.7 supports the idea that every spectator is capable of experiencing the pleasure of tragic *catharsis*. Finally, Aristotle's cognitive account of the emotions poses a problem to understanding how the emotions can be purged.

CATHARSIS AS ETHICAL EDUCATION

Looking at Aristotle's account of tragedy in light of his ethics prompts what we could call the ethical education view.[25] This account has a variety of versions, but a central text that it draws on is also from *Politics* 8, where Aristotle discusses the role that imitations in music play in developing a virtuous character. Music contains imitations of states of character, such as anger, courage, or temperance. This makes listening to music effective training for developing courage, for example, because the imitations set up a response in the soul of the sort the listener would experience in real life, if she were courageous (*Politics* 8.5.1340a18–27). The person who appreciates the imitations in tragedy can get a valuable training of her ethical sensibilities, feeling the right thing at the right time towards the right person.

While linking the *Poetics* and Aristotle's ethics has its appeal, there are a number of challenges this view must answer. While the ethical education view has received wide support it also has its critics.[26] To start, in the *Poetics* Aristotle does not say that tragedy provides ethical training in learning how to recognize situations that call for pity and fear. This in itself is not a fatal flaw, however, because the *Poetics* gives us no direct clues in support of any of the proposed accounts of *catharsis*.

A more serious problem for the education account of *catharsis* is that it seems to run afoul of Lear's Virtuous Spectator Constraint. Jonathan Lear presses a point that he made against the purgation account: that the virtuous person is the target spectator for tragedy yet such a person is not in need of ethical education or improvement. It is sometimes said in reply to this objection that a moral life requires an endless training in correct feeling and judgment.[27] But Lear would insist that this reply is not accurate. The virtuous person is not in need of an ethical education, for her character has been formed and settled by the ethical training and habits that she received growing up. The good person's emotions and actions in everyday life are just as they should be, so she does not need the ethical improvement that tragic *catharsis* offers.

A further concern is that in *Politics* 8.6 Aristotle says that listening to music played on the aulos can on the right occasion bring about "*catharsis* rather than learning" (8.6.1341a23–24) and he says that the music from the aulos bears on religious ecstasy, not character (8.6.1341a21–22).[28] Here *catharsis* is contrasted with moral training and the implication is that music can bring about *catharsis* but *not* an improvement in character. There is, then, a strong challenge to the *catharsis* as moral education view, if we suppose that the Virtuous Spectator Constraint is appropriate.

CATHARSIS AS CLARIFICATION

Another main trend in the debate around *catharsis* follows the sense of "*catharsis*" according to which it means "clarification," a "clearing up" and removal of some obstacle that makes something less clear than it is in its proper natural state.[29] One variation of the clarification view is that catharsis is an intellectual clarification of the incidents in the plot.[30] This view is motivated by, among other things, the problems in understanding the broader emotional benefits of tragedy.

Intellectual clarification account of catharsis
The nature of *catharsis* = clarification
The object of *catharsis* = the structure of the incidents in the play

Proponents of this view argue that in the *catharsis* clause—"the *catharsis* of such passions (*toiauta pathēmata*)"—"*pathēmata*" refers not to the emotions of pity and fear, but to the events in the plot.

One advantage of the clarification account is that it can explain Aristotle's remark that the definition of tragedy in *Poetics* 6 is a summing up of his earlier discussion in *Poetics* 1–5. *Catharsis* appears to be the one item that does not correspond to anything in the previous discussion. On the clarification account offered *catharsis* picks up the discussion in *Poetics* 4 about the pleasure of learning that poetry offers. In addition this view explains why Aristotle says that the events and the plot are the goal of tragedy (6.1450a20–23). As Alexander Nehamas maintains, a coherent plot that resolves all the narrative questions raised earlier in the play is the goal of tragedy and the point of *catharsis*.

However, as many commentators have replied, the clarification of tragic action that a well-formed tragic plot provides must occur not only within the plot, but also in the audience. In addition, the clarification view ignores the discussion of *catharsis* in the *Politics*, and does not explain the relationship between tragic *catharsis* and pity and fear, which it is tragedy's job to arouse.[31]

Martha Nussbaum and Stephen Halliwell have independently proposed clarification accounts that rectify this neglect of the emotions of pity and fear in *catharsis*.[32] According to this approach, *catharsis* brings about a clarification of the emotions of pity and fear in the audience:

Emotional clarification account of catharsis
The nature of *catharsis* = clarification
The object of *catharsis* = the emotions of pity and fear in the audience

Nussbaum's view links *catharsis* with ethical improvement, so her clarification account is also an account of how tragic catharsis is a form of ethical education.[33] By responding to worthy tragic characters and their predicaments, the audience clarifies what sorts of things they might expect could possibly occur in their own lives. For it is the nature of pity and fear, as Aristotle understands them, that they require some kind of identification with the individual for whom pity and fear are felt. One pities another for things "which one could expect to suffer oneself" (*Rhetoric* 2.8.1385b14–15) and one feels fear for someone "like ourselves" (*Poetics* 13.1453a4).[34] Further, as we noted before, pity and fear are inspired when the spectator comes to believe that what happens to the tragic character *could* happen to oneself.[35] Responding to the characters in tragedy, therefore, gives a clarification of who and what matters to us.

The emotional clarification view of *catharsis* has been enormously influential, and some might say that it is currently the dominant approach to the topic. However, Jonathan Lear, G. R. F. Ferrari, and Pierre Destrée have independently posed strong challenges that we should consider.[36] Their over-riding objection to the clarification account is that it assumes that the pleasure the spectator takes in tragic *catharsis* is a species of the pleasure in learning and understanding, but this is not supported by the text of the *Poetics*.[37] Here I focus briefly on several arguments Ferrari poses that contest the conclusion that tragic pleasure is a species of cognitive pleasure, or the pleasure in learning.[38]

Ferrari doubts that the requirement that the tragic character be someone "like us" (13.1453a3) is in the service of promoting the spectator's awareness of her own vulnerabilities to misfortune. Instead such a character simply functions as someone who marshals the audience's sympathies.[39] Bad characters are eliminated because such an individual does not evoke the audience's sympathetic concern. If the concern of the poet was to awaken the audience to the sense of their own vulnerability to reversals of fortune, then why couldn't the plot that shows a wicked person going from bad to good fortune do the trick? As Ferrari puts it, "In a world where villains can find success, let the decent citizen quake in his bed!"[40] He concludes that Aristotle's requirements on plot and characters in *Poetics* 13 are not explained by the view that the character's function is to model and bring home the spectator's sense of vulnerability to reversals of fortune. Instead these requirements are best explained by another account of how pity and fear function in the plot of tragedy.

On Ferrrari's view pity and fear are the focus of Aristotle's analysis in the *Poetics* because they are the emotions that are engaged by tragic suspense.[41] This goes along with what I am calling the "suspense/detective novel" approach to *catharsis*. The point of the plot is to heighten tension in the audience through a sympathetic concern for the tragic protagonist and then provide the pleasure of releasing that tension with a dramatic reversal of fortune for the character.[42] This is why the events of the plot should take place, "contrary to expectations yet on account of one another" (9.1452a1–3). With the plot so configured, "The reversal crashes in; the pieces fit not as they had seemed to be, but with a new and unexpected configuration, one that only in retrospect can we see had been falling into place all along."[43] The requirement that the character be "like us" is then a way to pull the audience into an excited state of concern for him, then provide the pleasure of relief from the uncertainty of suspense by resolving how the dramatic character's reversal of fortune comes about.[44]

Towards what goal does the poet induce suspense and sympathetic pity and fear in the audience? Ferrari answers that the point is to stimulate these emotions in the audience, then to provide the pleasure that comes from purging and releasing them. "In this sense tragedy resembles a purging drug."[45] So, Ferrari is proposing, along with the suspense/detective novel account, a purgation account of tragic *catharsis*. But Ferrari disagrees with Bernays' assumption that the spectator of tragedy is in a pre-pathological condition which needs to be alleviated. Instead tragedy induces the need for the spectator to be relieved from the tension of the plot, and then provides a "cure" for the very condition that it has provoked in the spectator when it brings the plot to narrative closure.

Ferrari provides a very interesting challenge to the view that tragic *catharsis* is the pleasure taken in clarifying one's emotions. To summarize, his two main points are that: (1) the requirements on plot and character in the *Poetics* are best explained by the need to evoke suspense through sympathetic fear and pity for the character; and (2) the pleasure that tragedy provides is the purgation of these emotions through the resolution of the plot. But I am not convinced of his argument for (1), and his argument for (2) leaves unanswered the question as to why spectators would want to attend a tragedy in the first place.

With respect to (1), Ferrari speaks as if the point of tragedy is to induce an anxious sense of vulnerability in the audience. If so, then it is inexplicable why the plot in which the virtuous person goes from good to bad fortune gets eliminated. This plot is enough to put the fear of God, so to speak, in any law-abiding citizen. A proponent of the emotional clarification view could disagree that the point of tragedy, on Aristotle's view, is to make the spectator anxious or frightened, in the way Ferrari describes. They would say the point of tragedy is to evoke a complex emotional and cognitive response in the audience: the clarification, through feeling pity and fear, of what life might offer and what matters to them. Tragedy does not just make one anxious about one's own prospects; it edifies and enlightens, and this learning is a source of pleasure that compensates for the pain that comes with feeling pity and fear.

While it makes sense, in regard to argument (2), that the spectator would take pleasure in having the plot resolved after a suspenseful buildup, this raises the question, which Ferrari does not answer, as to why spectators would seek out this kind of pleasure in the first place. They are not in need of a cure from some pre-existing emotional affliction. Spectators go to the theater, he says, to have the experience of having suspense and sympathetic pity and fear built up, only to get it released. Granted that when one is on the edge of one's chair, wondering what will happen to the tragic hero, it perhaps feels good to have the tension that is built up released. Yet why would a spectator want to put herself in that situation in the first place? Doesn't life outside the theater offer its fair share of uncertainty, narrow escapes, and confrontations with undesirable outcomes?

The problem, then, with the suspense account of *catharsis* is that it is in need of a further explanation of why the pleasure of releasing tension compensates and makes up for the pain of feeling pity and fear for the characters. For some explanation of this is needed to explain why the spectator seeks out tragic drama in the first place. The emotional clarification view has an answer to this: there is the pleasure of fulfilling the desire to understand and learn, which characterizes all human beings as such, that tragedy provides.[46]

There is a line of reply available to the objection, which is to say that there is also a cognitive pleasure in following the twists and turns of the plot, and this is something that suspenseful drama provides.[47] Ferrari denies quite strenuously that tragedy offers a species of cognitive pleasure or pleasure in learning, so this explanation, which seems to be a natural account of why people read detective novels or watch suspenseful dramas, is not available to him.[48]

Does this mean that emotional clarification is a good candidate for the meaning of tragic *catharsis*? As the attentive reader has surmised, this is a view that I think has considerable appeal. My problem with this as an interpretation of *catharsis* is two-fold.

First, the idea that tragedy offers emotional clarification is often presented as going hand in hand with the idea that tragedy offers ethical education. Emotional clarification, in other words, provides a moral benefit, but the sense in which tragedy educates the emotions of the virtuous person needs to be carefully specified. For Lear is right that the good, educated audience at which tragedy aims comes to tragedy with a well-developed sense of when pity and fear are appropriate, and perhaps this means that tragedy draws on the virtuous spectator's understanding, rather than corrects or refines it.

This objection is not, I think, impossible to answer. A theme throughout the book has been that poetry not only draws on a prior capacity to think and feel a certain way, but also deepens it.[49] While the virtuous person's emotions and way of thinking about life do not need "correcting," her ways of thinking and feeling about the world and her own situation are always in need of more depth and a greater degree of understanding.[50]

Those who are sympathetic to the view that tragedy offers a kind of emotional clarification or understanding might be well advised to separate clarification from education, in the sense of correction, for this might imply the pleasure of tragic *catharsis* is not available to everyone, when Aristotle suggests that it should be.

Second, the emotional clarification account of *catharsis* struggles to account for the passages in the *Politics* where *catharsis* is linked with healing (8.7.1342a10–11) and with relief (8.7.1342a11–15). It may not be possible, as some have worried, to reconcile the discussion in *Politics* 8 with what Aristotle says about the emotional experience of tragedy in the *Poetics*.[51] Since in *Politics* 8 Aristotle discusses *catharsis* and says that an explanation of the concept will be taken up in the discourse on poetry (8.5.1341b40f.), this suggests that unless Aristotle changed his mind, the discussion in *Politics* 8.7 might give a clue to what he is thinking about tragic *catharsis*.

CATHARSIS: A REVISED PURGATION ACCOUNT

This provides some motivation to go back to the purgation account, but its faults will need to be addressed. The sticking points with the purgation account are that it conflicts with the way Aristotle thinks of the emotions as necessary aspects of a fully human life, and it suggests that the audience members are in need of some kind of psychological therapy, when there is no suggestion of this in the *Poetics*.

A central idea in the *Politics* 8.7 discussion of *catharsis* as purgation is something that we can work with: this is the point that *catharsis* lightens or relieves in some way the emotional state of everyone, including the virtuous person, whose emotions are not in excess and felt just as they should be:

> The same experience then must come also to the compassionate and the timid and the other emotional people generally in such degree as befalls each individual of these classes; and all must undergo purgation (*catharsis*) and a pleasant feeling of relief (*kouphizesthai*).
>
> (8.1342a13–16)[52]

This passage appears to suggest that: (1) *catharsis* provides some kind of pleasurable relief; and (2) that it applies to everyone, to those who feel emotions excessively and to others who feel emotions to the right degree and manner.[53] If this is right, Aristotle is thinking in this passage that *catharsis* applies to everyone, the virtuous and non-virtuous alike, because it provides a sense of relief and a lightening of some kind of burden.

If this is correct, then to apply this notion of *catharsis* in *Politics* 8.7 to the *Poetics*' account of tragic *catharsis* we should look at the distinctive way in which tragedy produces the emotions of pity and fear. Richard Kraut has made the suggestion that *catharsis* in the *Politics* passage above applies to everyone, and it involves a purging, not of the emotions of pity and fear, but of some of their painfulness as they are experienced in ordinary life.[54] This suggestion is useful for understanding tragic *catharsis*, with certain modifications.

Pity and fear are painful emotions, on Aristotle's view, yet the emotional experience of tragedy is an overall pleasurable one. Pierre Destrée has helpfully distinguished two different ways of understanding the pleasure in tragedy, which is of a paradoxical nature: transformation or compensatory.[55] Does the pain the spectator feels as she experiences pity and fear get transformed or does it remain but somehow get compensated for?

According to the transformation view, the pain of feeling pity and fear gets transformed in the context of experiencing the pleasure of relief that tragedy offers. Yet this cannot be

Aristotle's view, for he gives no indication that he thinks that the normally painful emotions of pity and fear somehow get "converted" by tragic *mimēsis* into pleasant feelings, as David Hume proposed when he considered the paradox of tragedy: how can we take pleasure in feeling pity and fear at the theater, when we find such emotions unpleasant to experience in real life?[56]

Aristotle does think that one emotion has the potential to diminish another emotion, as is evidenced by his discussion of how intense fear can drive out pity.[57] We also saw this point brought out in the discussion of why Aristotle eliminates the plot pattern that shows a very virtuous person going from good to bad fortune (*Poetics* 13.1452b33).[58] We can and do feel pity and fear for the virtuous person in such a situation, but the moral outrage we feel predominates, so that the response to such a plot pattern is one of repugnance and not the proper response of pity and fear for the character. This suggests that while the painfulness of pity and fear is not converted, eliminated, or transformed, it is possible for the pain to be diminished as well as compensated for by some other emotion that is also elicited in the spectator's experience.

What is the other emotion be that compensates for the pain? In keeping with the interpretation favored throughout the book, it is the pleasure in a kind of understanding that the tragic plot provides. A well-formed plot, with causal connections between the events, puts the pitiful and fearful events of everyday life into some kind of a coherent whole, and thereby gives the spectator a pleasurable understanding that is not available when we experience these emotions in ordinary life. The grasp of the universals concerning human action that are embedded in the plot makes the overall experience of these emotions pleasant in the context of tragedy. It is in this sense that the audience's experience of these emotions becomes less painful, and the burden of our experience of the emotions is lightened.

If this is right, then the tragic *catharsis* involves a purgation or diminishment of the painful aspect of experiencing the emotions of pity and fear in real life. Through providing a plot that clarifies the connections between actions, the plot makes it understandable how a good and decent person can experience a change of fortune that calls forth pity for suffering that is not deserved and fear for someone "like us." The pleasure of understanding in some sense compensates for the pain that the audience feels when they feel pity and fear, but this pain is not eliminated.

This fits well with what Aristotle says in *Poetics* 4, where there is pleasure in looking at a precise image of an unpleasant-looking animal owing to the pleasure in understanding (*manthanein*) that the picture makes possible as the viewer reasons out the similarities between the image and the object imitated. Grasping that the plot has also been formed into a well-constructed whole also gives the pleasure in form that Aristotle speaks of in *Parts of Animals* 2.5.645a7–15.[59]

Perhaps, then, tragic *catharsis* is a kind of purgation, but not in the way that Bernays described. It does not remove a pathological tendency to feel excessive emotion, though it is possible that it can help spectators who feel emotions excessively or incorrectly. *Catharsis*, nevertheless, has a therapeutic aspect, something that is available to all spectators, because it can lighten the burden of the painfulness of their experience of pity and fear, providing a pleasurable relief.

NOTES

1 Aristotle 1932. Some scholars think that the discussion of *catharsis* to which *Politics* 8.7 refers is either in the lost second book of the *Poetics*, which also discussed comedy, or to a lost section of the *Politics*. See Carnes Lord 1982: 146–150 and Stephen Halliwell 1998: 190–191.

2 Paul Woodruff 2009: 623.

3 Paul Woodruff 2009: 619. See also Stephen Halliwell 2009: 404.

4 See Stephen Halliwell 1998: 85–88.

5 Martha Nussbaum 1986: 389–390; and Stephen Halliwell 1998: 188.

6 Nussbaum 1986: 389 tracks this uses of "*catharsis*" in pre-Platonic texts, for example Aristophanes' *Wasps* 631 and 1046.

7 That the two senses, purgation and refinement, are not mutually exclusive is suggested by Stephen Halliwell 1998: 198, and more recently by Christopher Shields 2013: 458.

8 This list is an adaptation of the classification systems found in Paul Woodruff 2009: 622–623 and in Stephen Halliwell 1998: 350–356, which also contains a very useful survey of the main historical trends in *catharsis* interpretation. I have added in some categories to account for more recent interpretations.

9 See Martha Nussbaum 1986; Stephen Halliwell 1998 and 2009; Richard Janko 1992; and Christopher Shields 2014: 459. For the relation between the emotions and ethical character, see *Nicomachean Ethics* 2.6.1106b15–29; and 2.6.1107a1–7.

10 Jacob Bernays 2004 (reprint of his 1857 essay) is an influential interpreter in this category.

11 Nussbaum 1986: 389–390; Halliwell 1998: 193–196; Shields 2014: 258–259.

12 G. R. F. Ferrari 1999; and Dorothy Sayers 1995 (reprint of 1935 essay, originally given as a lecture).

13 Jonathan Lear 1992.

14 Along these lines see Nussbaum 1986; Halliwell 1998; and Shields 2014.

15 Ferrari 1999: 196.

16 Bernays 2004.

17 Aristotle 1984.

18 A homeopathic treatment (derived from two Greek words that mean "like disease") is based on the idea that a cure from some disease can be effected when the subject is given dilute quantities of the very substance that is causing the illness. Allopathy ("different than disease"), the traditional approach in Western medicine, brings about a cure with medicine that counteracts or opposes the condition being treated. Elizabeth Belfiore 1992: Chs. 8 and 9 proposes an allopathic interpretation of *catharsis*.

19 For this objection see Paul Woodruff 2009: 618.

20 See Bernays 2004: 327.

21 Lear 1992: 317.

22 See the discussion of Aristotle's account of emotion in Chapter 8, pp. 184–186.

23 Lear 1992: 327.

24 For a helpful discussion of this passage, and its difficulties of interpretation, see Malcolm Heath 2014: 117–118f.

25 Humphrey House 1956: 109–111; Richard Janko 1992; Stephen Halliwell 1998: 193–196; Christopher Shields 2014: 258–259. These accounts should be carefully distinguished from the more didactic "moral lessons from tragedy" approach that flourished in the neo-classical period of literary criticism. See Halliwell 1998: 351.

26 Shields 2013: 458–459.

27 See for example Nicholas Pappas 2005: 18.

28 See the excellent commentary on this section in Richard Kraut 1997: 193.

29 See Nussbaum 1986: 389–390; and Halliwell 1998: 185–186.

30 Gerald Else 1957: 224–232; Alexander Nehamas 1992: 307.

31 For these criticisms see Stephen Halliwell 1998: 356.

32 Nussbaum 1986: 388–390; Halliwell 1992: 254; Halliwell 1998: 76.

33 See also Christopher Shields 2014: 459.

34 See the discussion of pity and fear in Chapter 8, pp. 186–189.

35 See Chapter 7, p. 170.

36 Jonathan Lear 1992: G. R. F. Ferrari 1999; Pierre Destrée 2009 and 2013.

37 See Chapter 4, pp. 85–90, where the argument presented has both points of agreement and disagreement with Lear's and Ferrari's interpretation of *Poetics* 4.

38 In Chapter 11 we consider Lear's and Destrée's objections in more detail.

39 Ferrari 1999:196.

40 Ferrari 1999: 196.

41 Ferrari 1999: 194.

42 Ferrari 1999: 193.

43 Ferrari 1999: 193.

44 Ferrari (199: 195) says that it comes with the genre expectations for tragedy that the audience knows *that* something bad will happen to the character. The uncertainty lies in just *how* and *when* that bad thing will come about.

45 Ferrari 1999: 196.

46 *Metaphysics* 1.1 "All human beings by nature desire to know."

47 Noël Carroll 1984 offers this sort of "cognitive" or intellectual pleasure account of suspense in film.

48 Since Ferrari opts for a purgation account of *catharsis*, there is a further question which is: how does he reply to Lear's argument that Aristotelian emotions are not the sort of thing that are susceptible to a purge, in the way the purgation account describes?

49 See Chapter 2, pp. 39–43, Chapter 4, pp. 95–98, and Chapter 7, pp. 172–173.

50 Indeed Lear's account of the tragic pleasure as connected to the realization that we can, in tragic drama, face our worst fears and come through the experience suggests the same point. See Lear 1992: 335.

51 Woodruff 2009: 619.

52 Kraut 1997.

53 For a useful commentary on this section, see Kraut 1997: 210–211.

54 Kraut 1997: 211.

55 Destrée 2014: 6–7.

56 For a discussion of this paradox, see Chapter 11, pp. 269–270, 289–291 and Chapter 12, pp. 300–303.

57 *Rhetoric* 2.8.1386a23; and 2.9.1387a1–5.

58 See Chapter 8, pp. 198–200.

59 See the discussion of these points in Chapter 4, pp. 87–90.

WORKS CITED

Aristotle 1932. *Politics*, translated by H. Rackham. Cambridge, MA: Harvard University Press.

——— 1984. *Politics*, translated by B. Jowett, in Jonathan Barnes (ed.), *The Complete Works of Aristotle. The Revised Oxford Translation* Volume Two. Princeton, NJ: Princeton University Press.

Barnes, Jonathan (ed.) 1984. *The Complete Works of Aristotle. The Revised Oxford Translation* Volume Two. Princeton, NJ: Princeton University Press.

Belfiore, Elizabeth S. 1992. *Tragic Pleasures: Aristotle on Plot and Emotion*. Princeton, NJ: Princeton University Press.

Bernays, Jacob. 2004. "On Catharsis: From Fundamentals of Aristotle's Lost Essay on the 'Effect of Tragedy'" (first published 1857). *American Imago* 61 (3): 391–341.

Carroll, Noël 1984. "Toward a Theory of Film Suspense." *Persistence of Vision: The Journal of the Film Faculty of the City University of New York* 1: 65–89.

Destrée, Pierre 2009. "Aristote et le plaisir 'propre' de la tragédie." *Aisthe* 4: 1–17.

_____ 2013. "Aristotle on the Paradox of Tragic Pleasure," in J. Levinson (ed.), *Suffering Art Gladly: The Paradox of Negative Emotion in Art*. Basingstoke: Palgrave Macmillan: 3–27.

Ferrari, G. R. F. 1999. "Aristotle's Literary Aesthetics." *Phronesis* 44 (3): 181–198.

Halliwell, Stephen 1998. *Aristotle's Poetics: With a New Introduction by the Author*. Chicago: University of Chicago Press.

_____ 2009 "Learning From Suffering: Ancient Responses to Tragedy," in Justina Gregory (ed.), *A Companion to Greek Tragedy*. Oxford: Blackwell: 394–412.

Heath, Malcolm 2014. "Aristotle and the Value of Tragedy." *British Journal of Aesthetics* 54 (2): 111–123.

House, Humphrey 1956. *Aristotle's Poetics. Course of Eight Lectures*. London: Rupert Hart-Davis.

Janko, Richard 1992. "From *Catharsis* to the Aristotelian Mean," in Amélie Oskenberg Rorty (ed.), *Essays on Aristotle's Poetics*. Princeton, NJ: Princeton University Press: 341–358.

Kraut, Richard 1997. *Aristotle: Politics Books VII and VIII*. Translated with a Commentary by Richard Kraut. Oxford: Clarendon Press.

Lear, Jonathan 1992. "Katharsis," in Amélie Oskenberg Rorty (ed.), *Essays on Aristotle's Poetics*. Princeton, NJ: Princeton University Press: 315–340 (Originally published in 1988, in *Phronesis* 33: 297–326.)

Lord, Carnes 1982. *Education and Culture in the Political Thought of Aristotle*. Ithaca, NY: Cornell University Press.

Nehamas, Alexander 1992. "Pity and Fear in the *Rhetoric* and the *Poetics*," in Amélie Oskenberg Rorty (ed.) *Essays on Aristotle's Poetics*. Princeton, NJ: Princeton University Press: 291–314.

Nussbaum, Martha 1986. *The Fragility of Goodness: Luck and Ethics in Greek Tragedy and Philosophy*. Cambridge: Cambridge University Press.

Pappas, Nicholas 2005. "Aristotle," in Berys Gaut and Dominic McIver Lopes (eds.), *The Routledge Companion to Aesthetics*. New York and London: Routledge: 15–28.

Rorty, Amélie Oskenberg (ed.) 1992. *Essays on Aristotle's Poetics*. Princeton, NJ: Princeton University Press.

Sayers, Dorothy 1995. "Aristotle on Detective Fiction." *Interpretation* 22 (3): 405–415. Reprint of 1935 essay.

Shields, Christopher 2013. *Aristotle* Second Edition. London and New York: Routledge.

Woodruff, Paul 2009. "Aristotle's *Poetics*: The Aim of Tragedy," in Georgios Anagnostopoulos (ed.), *A Companion to Aristotle*. Chichester, England: Blackwell Publishing: 612–627.

10

COMEDY AND EPIC

INTRODUCTION: THE FINAL CHAPTERS OF THE *POETICS*

The *Poetics* open with the announcement that the treatise will discuss, "both poetry in general and the capacities of each of its genres" but its central books are a discussion of tragedy.[1] At the end of *Poetics* 22 Aristotle announces that his discussion of tragedy is complete, and he shifts his focus to a discussion of epic, analyzing the genre in terms of some of the key points he has made about tragedy (*Poetics* 23–24) as well as addressing the question in the final chapter of the work, *Poetics* 26, "Which is better, tragedy or comedy?" Along the way, in *Poetics* 25, he discusses the standards of correctness that should be applied to poetry, arguing that poetry's norms are unique to its specific goals and, following on this point, examining the different categories of faults that it is fair for critics to raise regarding poetic composition.

One genre that is not discussed in any great detail is comedy. Internal and external evidence suggests that there was a second book of the *Poetics* devoted to comedy, so scholars think this work, like many of Aristotle's other writings, was lost.[2] This chapter will be devoted to Aristotle's views on comedy, epic, and the difference between epic and comedy. We will also look at Aristotle's comments in *Poetics* 25 on the right way to be a critic of poetry, and at *Poetics* 26, in which Aristotle defends tragedy by saying that it is superior to epic. While Aristotle's comments in the *Poetics* about comedy are limited in number, we will start by briefly reviewing his key ideas. We will try to amplify them, place them in context to Plato's negative view of comedy, discuss two very different approaches to understanding Aristotle's views on comic theater, as well as see how the *Poetics*' remarks on comedy have influenced the theories of comedy that followed it. Our attention then will turn to epic and other topics that are taken up in the last several chapters of the *Poetics*.

COMEDY: EVOLUTION, STRUCTURE, AND COMEDIC IMITATION

Comedy's evolution. Recall that in *Poetics* 4, Aristotle says that there were several lines of influence for the development of poetry.[3] One stream involved a more serious form of poetry that includes hymns and encomia in praise of gods and outstanding human beings. This strand imitated the actions of noble characters (4.1448b25f.). A second stream involved invectives or satires of individuals aimed at morally base and inferior characters (4.1448b27). This strand of poetry imitated the actions of characters that are morally and socially inferior. Poets developed the serious or lighter form of poetry according to their characters, with the more serious strand of poetry leading to the development of tragedy, and the less serious side leading to the development of comedy (4.1449a1–5).

Homer, with his great epic poems, contributed to the more serious side that leads to tragedy, but he also contributed to the development of comedy, in terms of its form and content. The comedy-epic *The Margites*, which Aristotle attributes to Homer, is lost. Just as Homer's epic poems anticipated the developments to come in tragedy, so also Aristotle says his *Margites* anticipated how comedy developed as well. In this work Homer shifted the emphasis away from invective, the expression of verbal assaults on individuals, to the use of direct speech of characters, anticipating the mode of imitation used by comedy and tragedy (*Poetics* 4.1449a1). Homer also anticipated comedy's focus on characters whose faults are shameful, but not painful or destructive, prompting a response of laughter (*to geloiov*) (*Poetics* 5.1449a31–38).[4]

Aristotle comments that the earliest stages of comedy are lost because the genre was not taken as seriously as tragedy (4.1448b38–1449b5). Different local traditions lay claim to having originated comedy. The Sicilians cite the name as evidence. They call their villages *kōmai* and the early comic performers got their name (*komōidia*) by wandering through villages when banned from the cities (4.1448a36–37).

Comedy's structure. Comedy, like tragedy and epic, centers on a unified and coherent plot structure (5.1448b8). This means the episodes of the story constitute a well-defined whole, with a beginning, middle, and end, and the events are connected by necessity or probability. Like tragedy and epic, its plots also aim for and "speak of" something more general, the universal, that is, the kind of thing that a certain sort of character says or does, in accordance with probability or necessity (9.1451b5–7). In *Poetics* 9 Aristotle commends the comic poets for recognizing that poetry should focus on *possible* events that conform to a pattern of necessity and probability, rather than rely on characters whose names the audience would associate with historical events, as some of the tragic poets did (1451b10–12). It follows that like other forms of poetry with plots that embed more general patterns of significant human experience, comedy is a form of poetry that gives the pleasure of reasoning and understanding (*manthanein*).

Comedic imitation. The objects of imitation are divided into two main groups: superior or admirable (*spoudaios*) action and inferior (*phaulos*) action (2.1448a2–5, 16–18; and 4.1448b24–26). Comedy is an imitation of inferior action, but Aristotle specifies that the proper object of comic imitation (*mimēsis*) is not every sort of fault or inferiority. Rather, what comedy imitates is a fault (*hamartēma*) or mark of the shameful or the ridiculous (*aischros*; also translated as "ugly"), but one that involves no pain or destruction:

> Comedy, as we said, is mimesis of baser but not wholly vicious characters: rather, the laughable is one category of the shameful (*aischros*). For the laughable comprises any fault or mark of shame which involves no pain or destruction: most obviously, the laughable mask is something ugly and twisted but not painfully.

(5.1449a31–35)

The proper object of comic imitation is, therefore, the "ridiculous," which is understood to be a kind of error (*hamartēma*) not involving pain or destruction. This contrasts with the tragic error (*hamartia*) of *Poetics* 13, where a great error or mistake is crucial, in the ideal tragic plot, to bringing about (or threatening to bring about) the suffering (*pathos*) that is essential to tragedy (12.1452b9–10). The errors of characters in comedy differ by bringing on nothing that is painful or destructive. It follows that tragedy and comedy elicit distinct emotional responses. The plot of tragedy inspires pity and fear in the audience, ideally because of the tragic error of the protagonist (13.1452b5–6). The plot in comedy evokes laughter (*to geloiov*) (*Poetics* 5.1449a31–38).

PLATO'S VIEWS ON COMEDY

It is useful, perhaps, to consider Plato's views on comedy. While Aristotle does not mention Plato's ideas on comedy in the text of the *Poetics* that we have, some scholars think that Aristotle's account of comedy builds upon Plato's.[5] Whether or not this is true, Plato presents a strong attack on comedy and it is of interest to know of his concerns so we can understand how they compare with Aristotle's view of comedy.

Plato's critical comments on comedy, shown in a number of works, reflect a view on comedy that is still present today. In places in his dialogues he has the character of Socrates raise concerns about the harmful effects of laughter and comedy. In *Republic* 3 comedy is discussed alongside of tragedy as forms of poetry that are invitations to be irrational and not self-controlled. Comedy weakens the rule of reason in the soul, for "ordinarily when one abandons himself to violent laughter his condition provokes a violent reaction" (388e). This objection is further developed by Socrates in *Republic* 10.606c–d, where his criticisms of comedy follow on the heels of his concern that tragedy, another form of poetry, waters the emotion of pity, making it hard for even the virtuous person to exercise self-restraint and emotional composure when it comes to facing their sufferings in real life (606b–c).

> Does not the same principle apply to the laughable, namely, that if in comic representations, or for that matter in private talk, you take intense pleasure in buffooneries that you would blush to practice yourself, and do not detest them as base, you are doing the same thing as in the case of the pathetic? For here again what your reason, for fear of the reputation of buffoonery, restrained in yourself when it fain would play the clown, you release in turn, and so, fostering its youthful impudence, let yourself go so far that often ere you are aware you become yourself a comedian in private.
>
> (606c–d; Hamilton and Cairns 1961)

The concern that Socrates raises about comedy in this passage is the same sort of problem he has with tragedy. Comedy prompts behavior, such as laughing at the buffoons in the comedic play, that once released in the context of the comic theater, are hard to clamp down on when the spectator exits the theater and continues with his daily life.

This concern about the detrimental emotional effects of comedy on the soul is also elaborated on in several other works. In the *Philebus* 48a–50b, Socrates argues that malice is pain in the soul (50a), and that laughter at what is ridiculous is a form of malice. Laughter is morally problematic because it involves taking pleasure in our friends' misfortunes (4950a). Further, comedy is a mixture of pleasure with pain (50b): for what we enjoy is seeing not only our enemies, but also our friends, suffer. There is pleasure in the laughter, but pain in the feeling of envy we have towards our friends (50a). With regard to comedy in the theater, Socrates says that the audience takes pleasure in laughing at characters in comedy that imagine themselves to be stronger, wiser, and more beautiful than they are. These characters are ridiculous and the object of the audience's scorn. The conditions of these comedic characters are not a laughing matter—for they are in a state of self-ignorance, which is an evil (49d). In Plato's *Laws* 11.934d–936a, Socrates discusses the dangers of laughter that is mixed with anger. Angry people are apt to turn laughter against their fellow citizens (935d), which undermines civic harmony. Therefore, Socrates concludes that no composer of comedic verse will be allowed to satirize a fellow citizen under any circumstance (935e).

Through the character of Socrates, Plato then raises several central concerns about comedy: first, there is a concern about the basic emotions that comedy inspires in a person who jokes: comedy prompts scorn, disdain, malice, envy, and an excess of bad temper. Second, comedic theater has a harmful effect that spills over to the conduct of daily life; for the person who takes delight in laughing at the faults of others in the comedic theater finds pleasure in doing so, and continues this behavior in daily life. This undermines the sense of civic unity and stability that is essential for life in the ideal state.

Plato's negative assessment of the value of comedy is reminiscent of the harsh criticism of comedy that is raised by a central character in Umberto Eco's wonderful murder mystery novel,

The Name of the Rose (1983; Jean-Jacques Annaud directed a wonderful film adaptation in 1986). The story presents a fictional scenario in which a Sherlock-like monk-detective, Brother William of Baskerville (played by Sean Connery in the film), investigates a series of murders in an Italian abbey during the year 1327. It turns out that at the center of the murder plot is the lost second book of the *Poetics*. The worry on the part of the murderer (he who shall not be named!) is that in writing about comedy, Aristotle has dignified a genre devoted to laughter, which is a mockery to God and the religious state of mind.

In the *Poetics* Aristotle does not reply to Plato's criticisms of comedy. Yet we have good reason to think that he would disagree with it. For one thing, Aristotle does not share Plato's negative view of the emotions. It is natural for human beings to feel emotions, and indeed emotions that are felt in the right way, towards the right objects and in the appropriate circumstances are an expression of a person's virtue.[6] Second, while leisure and play are not the ultimate goal of human life, they nevertheless are necessary to it, and Aristotle holds that comedy contributes to the human need for leisure and amusement. Hence, comedy has a place to play in a fully human life.[7]

What, more exactly, is this role? How does the comic theater contribute to a fully human life?

COMEDY'S ROLE IN A HUMAN LIFE: TWO CONTRASTING READINGS OF THE *POETICS*

We can try to ascertain Aristotle's views on these topics by considering the contrasting interpretations offered by two influential interpreters of Aristotle's account of comedy, Stephen Halliwell and Malcolm Heath.[8]

In a chapter that forms part of a comprehensive and tour de force book on ancient Greek laughter, Halliwell argues that Aristotle made a virtue out of laughter. While the seventeenth-century philosopher, Thomas Hobbes, proposed that laughter is an expression of contempt, and suggested it was an expression of a person's sense of superiority over another,[9] Halliwell makes the case that, in contrast, Aristotle thinks that laughter has a role in a virtuous life. To make his interpretation, Halliwell appeals to the discussion of virtuous laughter (*eutrapelia*, which Halliwell translates as "good humor" or "urbane wittiness") found in *Nicomachean Ethics* 4.8.[10]

In Aristotle' ethics, virtue or human excellence (*aretē*) is a mean in feeling and action. The key to being virtuous is to feel the appropriate feeling and perform the action that is a mean between two extremes, a deficiency and an excess. On the excessive side is the person who Aristotle calls the "vulgar buffoon" (*NE* 4.8.1128a6): this is the person who "is the slave of his sense of humor, and spares neither himself nor others if he can raise a laugh, and says things none of which a man of refinement would say" (4.8.1128a32, 1128a6). On the deficiency side is the "boorish and unpolished" person who, "can neither make a joke themselves nor put up with those who do" (4.8.1128a9–10).

The virtuous state, or the mean, is what should be aimed for: this is embodied in the person who is "ready-witted" (*eutrapelia*). This individual is versatile, is able to see the incongruities in a situation ("turn this way and that"), he says what is becoming, and also avoids pain to the object of his fun (4.8.1128a11–12). The ready-witted person will make jokes that involve innuendo rather than crude and explicit jests. While play is not the goal of life, according to Aristotle, this virtuous form of joking has its place in life because it provides the pleasures of play and relaxation.[11]

This virtuous laughter cannot have anything in common with hubris, which involves a sense of superiority over others, for the ready-witted person will avoid causing pain to the object of his fun.[12] This means that the satire of the buffoonish portrayals found in certain forms of comedy would have nothing in common with *eutrapelia* or virtuous comedy.[13]

With this characterization Aristotle is trying to set up the idea that there is a morally appropriate and a morally inappropriate way to engage in laughter and humor. On the other hand, while appropriate and restrained laughter belongs to a life that includes leisure and amusement, jesting is nevertheless "a sort of abuse, and there are things that lawmakers forbid us to abuse, and they should, perhaps, have forbidden us even to make a jest of such" (*Nicomachean Ethics* 4.8.1128a29–31).

How does Aristotle's discussion of the playful and virtuous laughter between friends and associates relate to the discussion of comedy in the *Poetics*? As Halliwell notes, when comedy is said to imitate the actions of people worse than normal (*Poetics* 2.1448a3), this takes the appropriate subject matter of comedy outside the realm of a virtuous laughter between friends, who are presumed to be equals.

Yet Halliwell argues that in *Nicomachean Ethics* 4.8.1128a22–24, Aristotle expresses a preference for the more ethically acceptable humor found in comedic theater that avoids contempt and ridicule. Hence, the ideal of virtuous laughter that Aristotle says is the right way for friends to engage with one another has application to the *Poetics*. For Aristotle makes clear that comedy evolved to its proper form when it left behind the invectives of earlier forms of comedy (*Poetics* 4.1449a3–4). In addition, Halliwell suggests that Aristotle must have also thought that because the audience's laughter is directed towards characters that are fictional, the problem with laughing at people who are inferior to you is to a certain extent lessened, even if there may also be some hostile laughter expressed by the characters *within* the drama.[14] Finally, an important point that Halliwell makes is that Aristotle regarded playful and virtuous laughter as a refinement and channeling of the hostile form of laughter.[15]

There are several key claims, then, that form part of Halliwell's interpretation of Aristotle on comedy.

First, even though comedy is a form of play, ethical standards still apply.[16] This means that Aristotle's account of comedy should be understood in light of his ethics. There is a right and a wrong way to engage in laughter, the characteristic response to comedy. The wrong ways are either to take joking to an excess by causing pain to the object of one's laughter or to not be able to take a joke or make a joke at one's own expense. The right way to engage in laughter is *eutrapelia*: this is laughter that is not an expression of contempt or scorn based on a sense of superiority to others, as Hobbes thought, but is instead a way of using humor to engage in leisurely play with others.

Second, Aristotle's comments about how comedy should be conducted in everyday life carry over, with certain limitations, to what is said about comedy in the *Poetics*. Both treatments of laughter share a concern that what is laughable should not involve pain to the objects of laughter.[17] The account of comedy in Aristotle's ethics explains and reinforces the recommendations for the proper objects of comic imitation in the *Poetics*. Even though comedy imitates the actions of inferior people whose ridiculous faults prompt laughter, the characters of comedy should not be the butt of the most hostile forms of laughter, scorn or contempt.[18] If this is so of fictional characters in comedy, it applies even more to the people we laugh at in our daily lives.

According to Halliwell then, the ethical standards that Aristotle says regulate the right use of laughter in everyday life also apply, within certain constraints, to the imitations of the comic theater.[19]

In complete distinction to Halliwell's ethical treatment of Aristotelian comedy is the interpretation argued for by Malcolm Heath.[20] Heath does not think that it is valid to extrapolate Aristotle's views on what is ethically acceptable in everyday socializing to what is acceptable in poetry. Heath draws on *Poetics* 25 to support this claim. In that chapter Aristotle seeks to defend poetry against its detractors.[21] He argues that poetry does not have the same standard of correctness as politics (*politikē*, Aristotle's term for ethics in public and private life, 25.1460b3–15) and he suggests that faithfulness to historical or scientific fact is not as important to poetry as is internal coherence and plausibility ("It is less serious not to know that a female deer has no horns than to depict one unconvincingly" (25.1460b30–32; see also 25.1460b15–20).

To illustrate, while it might be inappropriate to laugh in real life at the errors of people who embody the foibles of Laurel and Hardy, this would be the appropriate response to the antics of the comic duo in film. Poetry, like any other art, follows its own standards of correctness, and from this Heath infers that Aristotle holds that the norms for virtuous behavior in our everyday lives do not apply to poetry.

In addition, Aristotle does think that exposure to indecent language needs to be regulated by the state. For in *Politics* 7.17.1336b12–23, Aristotle discusses how youth that are exposed to obscene and abusive language could acquire a "taint of meanness from what they hear and see" (1336b4–5). But Heath observes that Aristotle expresses no such concern that obscenity and abuse in comedy for adults needs to be regulated. Aristotle says:

> But the legislator should not allow youth to be spectators of iambi or of comedy until they are of an age to sit at the public tables and to drink strong wine; by that time education will have armed them against the evil influences of such representations.

> (7.17.1336b20–22)[22]

This passage does not express admiration for the content in comic poetry, but neither does it suggest that there should be a state prohibition banning adults from exposure to it. Aristotle implies that it is enough that well-bred youth not come into contact with obscenity in comedy until after they are grown and have been formed by a proper upbringing.

Heath also offers a different reading of *Nicomachean Ethics* 4.8.1128a30–31 than the one Halliwell offers. Aristotle is willing to consider that there should be state restraints on abuse and mockery in social life (*NE* 5.8.1128a30f.), but he does not propose a reform of the content of comedy. Where Halliwell sees in this passage a preference for the more recent style of comedy, Heath thinks that Aristotle is making a different point. The newer forms of comedy are not preferable, it is rather that they simply comport better with the standards of behavior in everyday life, and reflect a shift in sensibilities of the public.[23]

In response to this last point, Halliwell would no doubt point to Aristotle's discussion in the passage of how the well-bred person will not make jokes that involve abuse (4.8.1128a30). This seems to be a correct observation, but this does not settle the central dispute between the two authors, which is: do the standards of behavior that apply in ethics, and to the well-bred person, also apply in forms of poetry, such as comedy?[24]

I will leave the reader to ponder the relevant texts and decide which interpretation makes the most sense. Here are a few points to keep in mind: first, in *Politics* 8.5, Aristotle points to a parallel between our emotional responses to imitations in music and to the objects that are imitated: "Someone who is accustomed to feeling pain and pleasure in things that are likenesses is close to someone who reacts in the same manner to true things" (8.5.1340a23–25; Kraut 1997).

In this text Aristotle is not saying that it *should* be the case that we react to things and their likenesses in the same way. Instead he is observing that our reactions to reality and to imitations are, as a matter of fact, similar with respect to feeling pleasure and pain, which are the basis for all emotions.

This point of a similarity in reaction to real things and their imitations also finds support in the discussion of how the audience responds to tragic characters in *Poetics* 13. The plot that shows a highly virtuous person going from good fortune to bad is eliminated because it gives the wrong emotional response: it does not evoke pity and fear, but disgust (13.1452b35). Aristotle is not saying that one *should* not feel pity and fear for the fall into misfortune of such a virtuous person. Instead he is likely observing that, *as a matter of fact*, the plot that shows a very virtuous person falling into misfortune produces the wrong emotional response in the audience, because of the moral outrage that it evokes.[25] Aristotle seems to recognize that due to the fact that tragedy is an imitation of human life and action (*Poetics* 6.1449b23–24; 2.1448b29), the audience will respond to the characters and their situations in tragedy in the way they will in real life, by bringing moral evaluations to bear on the tragedy.

This suggests that the ethical evaluations we make in daily life are relevant to how we respond to characters in fiction, due to the similarity between mimetic art and real life. Indeed mimetic art succeeds in moving the audience by imitating an action that is realistic and true to life, so it makes sense that the moral evaluations that the audience apply in everyday life will also come into play when we watch tragic or comedic theater.

Pity and fear for Aristotle clearly have an evaluative dimension, because the former is felt for the one who suffers undeservedly (*Rhetoric* 2.8.1385b12–19) and the latter is felt due to imagining some destructive or painful evil in the future (*Rhetoric* 2.5.1386 a27–28). It is clear that to respond with these emotions to characters, the spectator must make certain assessments about value that is lost or threatens to be lost for the characters. It is not clear how Aristotle would spell out the state of mind of someone who responds with laughter at the ridiculous fault of a character.[26] It is likely he would think that the spectator of comic theater also makes an evaluation of the moral seriousness of the character's error. Indeed, this would seem to be necessary if the laughter of comedy is prompted by a fault or error that does not involve pain or destruction (5.1449a31–35).

How does all of this bear on the question whether the virtue that people should display in their everyday lives applies as well to comedy? These points suggest that Aristotle thinks the audience's response to the characters in poetry has an ethical dimension in that it is grounded in their assessment of the moral worth of the characters. Yet if comedy is an imitation of the actions of people inferior to most, the *characters* in comedy cannot be expected to behave in ways that conform to the standards for virtue that Aristotle sets out in his ethics. Perhaps then

Heath is right that it would make no sense to require that the characters in comedy live up to the standard for ethical action that Aristotle sets out in his ethics.

Still, it is logical to maintain that Aristotle supposes that the audience of comedy will bring whatever ethical sensibility they have developed in daily life to their response to the characters and their predicaments in comedy. If, as in tragedy, the characters in comedy were to fall too much outside of how the audience expects that people worse than most behave, then is it also reasonable to think that the audience could not find pleasure in watching such characters in action?

While Heath is right to note that the standards for correctness in poetry are not the same as in politics and ethics, it is likely that Aristotle also holds that the psychology of the viewer's response to poetry is very much connected with the habits of mind and the aspects of moral decision making that viewers employ in their everyday lives. This suggests that to be successful, comedy should draw on and develop a response to the characters that it is in some sense natural for the audience to experience in their everyday lives. For if the behavior of the characters is too much of an affront to the audience's sense of propriety, their response will not be the pleasure in laughter at the failings of the characters. It will be a sense of moral condemnation at the characters' behavior that will interfere with the audience's pleasure in the comic performance.

Perhaps this suggests, then, a way of addressing the dispute between Halliwell and Heath. The standards for virtuous laughter that guide us in everyday life are relevant for how the poets should construct their plots and characters. For if the comic poets stray too far from the audience's sense of propriety there is a possibility of backlash from the audience, producing moral outrage and not pleasure. This means that poetry is in some sense constrained by considerations of ethics, but not because it is unseemly for the poet to promote plots with unethical characters. Clearly if comedy imitates the actions of those inferior to most, then less than virtuous behavior is the stuff on which comedy is based. The right way to present comic characters is to have them stay within a range of behavior that makes it possible for the audience to experience the pleasure of laughter, rather than the pain of moral condemnation.

THE PROPER PLEASURE OF COMEDY

Throughout the *Poetics* Aristotle refers to the idea that each genre of poetry has its proper pleasure (*oikeia hēdonē*). In *Poetics* 14, Aristotle refers to the idea that tragedy and comedy have their own distinct pleasures. This remark occurs in the context of a discussion of the tragic plot with a double structure, which has opposite outcomes, for example, the good tragic protagonist in the end confronts but ultimately avoids disaster while the bad character ends up seeing his or her demise (1453a30–32). Aristotle comments that it is thought that the double-plot structure is the best, but this point is mistaken:

> It is thought to be best because of the weakness of audiences: the poets follow, and pander to the taste of the spectators. Yet this is not the pleasure to expect from tragedy, but is more appropriate to comedy, where those who are deadliest enemies in the plot, such as Orestes and Aegisthus, exit at the end as new friends, and no one dies at anyone's hands.

> (14.1453a32–36)

Aristotle does not tell us specifically what emotions it is appropriate for comedy to elicit. Contemporary psychologists think that laughter is a larger grouping of distinct sorts of emotional responses with different profiles.[27] Based on the text we do have we can speculate as to what the pleasure proper to comedy would involve.

First, comedy is an imitation or *mimēsis* of actions of individuals that are inferior to most. As a *mimēsis* it involves the completion or perfection of an effect that is natural for the audience to have in response to real life events and people.[28] Now in real life it would not be appropriate to laugh at someone who slips on a banana peel and gets hurt. Someone who laughed in this way would not be displaying a good sense of propriety or human decency. Still, some (perhaps the "weaker" audience to which Aristotle refers) might have the impulse to do so. There is something comical about seeing someone slip on a banana peel in a comic play, provided that the person does not sustain any serious injury!

We might think of Aristotelian comedy as a form of imitation that takes a natural response, laughter at some mistake or misstep, and completes or perfects it. For it provides a circumstance in which it is fine to laugh at the foibles of others, provided that this error does not result in pain or destruction, and the circumstance in which the audience takes pleasure does not involve a person who is truly vicious. The proper pleasure involved in comedy may have to do with taking a natural human response, found in people who are less than completely virtuous, of laughing at others' foibles and mistakes and channeling this impulse into a source of laughter (*to geloiov*) that provides an opportunity for leisure (*Poetics* 5.1449a31–38; see also *Politics* 8.3.1337b36–1338a1).

Second, the virtue of having a plot where the events happen "contrary to expectations" and yet "on account of one another," which is a desirable feature in the tragic plot (*Poetics* 10.1452a1–3) also holds in comedy. We would not expect that mortal enemies would, by the play's end, exit as new friends, without hurting one another, but this is what happens in the comic plot. It follows that as in tragedy, there is a (retrospective) cognitive pleasure that comedy provides: the audience might not have expected the reversal in the plot where Orestes and Aegisthus emerge as friends; but when it happens, this is a source of delight. Because the events in the comic plot are linked by probability or necessity, the audience has the cognitive or intellectual pleasure of understanding how the outcome was intelligible even if it is not something that they could have predicted in advance.

It is interesting to consider how this idea of laughter at an unlikely outcome has been taking up even by some dramaturges, such as the great twentieth-century German playwright, Bertolt Brecht, who was critical of Aristotle's prescriptions for drama. Brecht rejected the idea that drama should be based on a plot with events that are linked by probable or necessary connection. But he often made use of the notion that laughter is provoked at an unlikely outcome. In the finale of Brecht's comedy *The Threepenny Opera* (*Die Dreigroschenoper*, 1928), the central character, a notorious London criminal, MacHeath ("Mack the Knife") is in jail and things look dire for the thug as he is due to be executed for his crimes. The play ends with a comic reversal, when a messenger arrives on horseback to announce that the Queen has pardoned Mack, and that she has awarded him a title, a castle, and a pension. The entire cast, including MacHeath's jailers, breaks out in song and good celebration.

EPIC'S PROPER FOCUS ON UNIFIED ACTION

In *Poetics* 23 Aristotle turns his attention to epic. Earlier, in *Poetics* 4, Aristotle argues that tragedy evolved from epic by building upon and improving the genre (1449a2). It follows that epic and tragedy have some components in common, but tragedy advances epic by adding additional components and features that enable it to surpass epic in terms of the quality of the pleasure that epic provides to the audience. The natural question to investigate in our discussion of epic is then: what is it that tragedy does better than epic, and how does it accomplish this superior pleasure?

Epic and tragedy, of course, both are forms of imitation (*mimēsis*), imitations of people in action (4.1448b27). Earlier, in *Poetics* 2, Aristotle argued that both epic and tragedy share the same *objects* of imitation, people who are superior to most, in both a moral and social sense (1448a3), but the two genres differ in their *mode* or manner of imitation: epic employs narration; tragedy uses the dramatic mode with characters acting out the story.[29]

Epic and tragedy also differ in their spatial and temporal dimensions. Along the spatial axis, because epic employs narration, it is capable of representing actions that occur simultaneously. Temporally, tragedy aims to stay within the time frame of "a single revolution of the sun, or close to it," while epic has no such constraints in time span (*Poetics* 6.1449b11–12). These distinctive features enable epic to have greater variety and diversity of episodes (1455a28–30). In *Poetics* 23, Aristotle argues that in spite of these differences, the epic plot needs to meet certain of the same fundamental constraints that are true of the plots of tragedy (1449a15f.). Epic should concern a single, unified action. Unity concerns the requirement that the episodes be connected by probability and necessity, and that the action be structured into a well-formed whole that has a beginning, middle, and end.[30]

That is, like tragedy, epic is contrasted with history, which is not concerned with an action that centers on a central, unified goal, but chronicles or records actions over a period of time that are coincidentally related to one another, for example two battles that occur on the same day, but have nothing else in common (*Poetics* 23.1459a24–25). In contrast, epic is like tragedy: the plot must construct a series of actions that form a unified whole, with the episodes centered around a central goal, and the events of the plot must not be contingently related to one another, but instead follow from the preceding events in a way that keeps the action integral to the central plot. Aristotle illustrates this idea of poetic unity, as he did when discussing tragedy, in terms of the analogy with a living thing in which all the parts of the animal are there to serve the creatures' characteristic life functions (23.1459a20; 24.1450b33–35).

Homer comes in for praise, as he did earlier in *Poetics* 8, for recognizing above all other epic poets that the plot must concern a single unified action. Rather than try to have a plot that concerned the entirety of the Trojan War from beginning to end, Homer focused on a certain time period and added other episodes in to achieve diversity without distracting from the central plot line. While most epic poets do not achieve this goal of unified action, Homer does and this gives support for Aristotle's view that tragedy's proper form was "glimpsed" in the way in which Homer composed plots with a coherent and unified structure (*Poetics* 4.1449a3).

DIFFERENCES BETWEEN EPIC AND TRAGEDY

Poetics 24 focuses on the differences between epic and tragedy. In *Poetics* 6 Aristotle commented that epic and tragedy "have some components in common" (1449b17–20), and in this section Aristotle states the parts that are common to both. Epic has four of the six qualitative parts of tragedy: plot, character, reasoning, and diction, but because tragedy is read or recited, not performed, it lacks spectacle, the aspect of the play that relates to performance, such as stage appearance and visual effects.[31] In addition, tragedy lacks song or music with lyrics. Epic shares with tragedy four basic plot structures: simple, complex, character-based, and suffering (*pathos*) focused.[32] Tragedy and epic both involve reversals, recognition, and scenes of suffering.[33] It seems to follow that the goal of epic is to evoke the same emotions as does tragedy, pity and fear. Aristotle does not talk about the "*catharsis*" of pity and fear that epic produces, but given the structural similarities between epic and tragedy, and the fact that it involves actions that prompt pity and fear, some commentators have speculated that epic, also, must produce a *catharsis* of these emotions.[34]

Epic possesses three virtues that issue from its narrative mode of imitation and from its greater length: grandeur, variety, and diversity of episodes (24.1459b29f.). Epic lacks the requirement that the action takes place within twenty-four hours and this permits it to have a greater length that can add to its scale or weight. Tragedy must have magnitude: the action must be long enough to allow for the comprehension of the reversal of fortune for the tragic character, but epic's larger time frame allows for a more sweeping scale of events, and this can add to its overall impact, provided the events are integrated into the plot, as they are in Homer's poems. The greater length also allows for a diversity and variety of episodes, as does the mode of imitation: narration. For example, Peter Jackson's *The Lord of the Rings* trilogy and the *Hobbit* trilogy (based on the novels of Tolkien) take the form of epic dramas, with the action spanning over a number of years in each trilogy, and the scene of the action shifting back and forth between different locations.

Narration, as previously noted, allows for the imitation of actions that are temporally simultaneous, but spatially discontinuous. The epic narrator can say things such as, "While the battle was raging in the city of Troy, outside the city limits and far, far away, another trouble, such and such, was brewing." As Aristotle's example of Homer also illustrates (24.1460a5–11), the epic narrator can also combine narration with dramatic acting of the characters as a way to tell the story. But as Gerald Else notes, the overarching framework of narration allows for the possibility to move forward and backward in time, to dissolve from narration into dramatization and back, and this also creates the variety and diversity of episodes in epic.[35]

EPIC PLEASURE, THE IRRATIONAL, AND DECEPTION

Poetics 23 speaks of the pleasure that is proper to epic (1459a20), without saying what exactly this is. It is of interest to try to identify the broader nature of this pleasure, both for understanding Aristotle's views on epic and also for what it might imply about the proper pleasure of tragedy. *Poetics* 24 may be helpful in this regard because it highlights some important differences between epic and tragedy that bear on the question whether epic is aiming for the same effect as tragedy or something different.

Both tragedy and epic aim at the astonishing or awesome (*to thaumaston*) (24.1460a12–13). We saw this aspect of tragedy in the discussion of *Poetics* 9 where Aristotle argued that events that prompt pity and fear are those that occur "contrary to expectation yet on account of one another" (9.1452a3). When, in particular, a plot features an unexpected reversal of fortune (*peripeteia*), this evokes a sense of awe in the audience. Yet Aristotle also thinks that the unexpected events must be integral to the plot and follow previous events according to probability or necessity, showing how one event happens *because* of the other.

Tragedy, in other words, has events that may appear to be irrational to the audience in that the character's reversal of fortune is not something that is predicted in advance. This is just the *appearance* of irrationality, however, because the unexpected in tragedy is not what is causally undetermined or random. In *Poetics* 24 Aristotle argues that epic has more room for the truly irrational, which he says is the chief cause of awe or wonder (1460a14), because it is read or recited, not performed. A sign that the awesome is a source of pleasure is that no one can resist exaggerating when telling a story, to give pleasure (1460a18).

Because epic is read or recited, not dramatized in front of the audience on stage, discrepancies and irrationalities in the plot of the epic can more easily escape the audience's notice.[36] A skillful poet can also disguise irrationalities in the story line, as Homer does, perhaps, in the way that Odysseus, disguised when he returns home, is able to convince Penelope of his improbable account of how he got there (1460a19–25).[37]

THE PROPER PLEASURE OF EPIC

Epic's proper or characteristic pleasure is referred to in several places, but never explained (23.1459a21; 26.1462b13f.). It is difficult to say with certainty anything on this topic, since Aristotle does not offer a definition of epic, nor does he say what he thinks is epic's goal or purpose. Given that epic has different resources, and works within different parameters, we might expect him to think that epic's distinctive pleasure is something that exploits something unique to it, such as the lack of strict time constraints or its use of the narrative mode of *mimēsis*, which enables it to have a greater diversity of episodes. However, in *Poetics* 23, he says that the plot of epic should concern a single, unified action, with the episodes connected by probability and necessity, and the action structured into a well-formed whole that has a beginning, middle, and end so that it may "produce the pleasure proper to it" (23.1459a18–20). Here the proper pleasure of epic relates to its sharing tragedy's emphasis on a complete and unified plot that maintains and does not violate the causal connections between events.

In spite of the similarities between epic and tragedy, there is an uncertainty as to whether epic and tragedy inspire the same emotional response in the audience. Tragedy prompts pity, fear, and amazement through a plot in which things occur "contrary to expectations but on account of one another" (10.1452a2–3). Epic evokes these same emotions in the audience, but *Poetics* 24 maintains that there is a greater scope in epic for the irrational, which is the chief cause of awe (24.1460a13–14). Irrational events should ideally not be included in the events that are dramatized in tragedy, for they will be noticed when they are enacted on the stage. Irrational events are more easily able to go undetected in epic, since the events in the drama are reported rather than acted out on the stage.

This means there is an uncertainty as to the nature of the proper pleasure of epic. If, as Aristotle sometimes suggests (*Poetics* 4.1448b35), epic is a prototype for tragedy, then we would expect that epic does not have its own distinctive pleasure, and it aims for the same emotional effect as tragedy, but is less successful at this. This is what Aristotle seems to say in *Poetics* 26 when he argues that tragedy is superior to epic in its artistic effect (1462b12). Yet we would expect that the distinct mode of storytelling that epic employs (narrative not dramatic enactment) and its different time frame might imply that there are unique emotional experiences that epic can make available to the audience that tragedy cannot provide. For while both epic and tragedy mandate that the audience imagine a fictional world, the ways in which the audiences of each genre come to imagine the world represented in the fiction are unique to each type of drama.

POETICS 25: THE RIGHT WAY TO BE A CRITIC OF POETRY

Poetics 25 is a rather difficult and confusing chapter in which Aristotle discusses the standards of correctness and effectiveness in poetry. His concern is with "problems" (*problēmata*) and their solutions (1460b6). A problem is an apparent flaw in the work that can be solved if we keep in mind such factors as how poets use language and the fact that the poet is an imitator. Many of his replies to problems involve keeping in mind poetry's goal of being a work that is an imitation of some reality.

Aristotle stresses that poetry does not have the same standards of correctness as politics (*politikē*, Aristotle's term for ethics in public and private life) or any other art (25.1460b14). He expands on this point by suggesting that faithfulness to historical or scientific fact is not a failing that need imply a defect in the work as a whole: "It is less serious not to know that a female deer has not horns than to depict one unconvincingly" (1460b30–32). Aristotle's approach is to divide faults that pertain to the art of poetry, ones that impair the work as a whole, and incidental or less serious faults. Imitating a deer with horns when she does not have them is annoying and distracting, but not as serious as committing an error that pertains to the poetic art. The book goes on to discuss five general types of criticisms: that things are impossible, irrational, harmful, contradictory, or contrary to artistic standards.

To prepare the way for this discussion, Aristotle reminds his reader that poetry is a mimetic art, and he categorizes the sort of things that the poet imitates: (1) the kinds of things that are or were the case; (2) the kinds of things that people say and think; (3) the kind of thing that ought to be the case. These are all appropriate uses of imitation and referring to them can help address some of the problems that pertain to the five general types of criticisms.

In the first category are the characters in Euripides' plays, in which people are imitated as they really are (1460b34). The second category, what people say and think, includes stories about the gods (1460b36), which Xenophanes charged involved the mistake of anthropomorphizing the gods, that is, making them in the image of humans. If it is objected that a poet uses them in a play, the reply to make is that people, in fact, said and thought like this. The third category, imitations of what ought to be the case, are useful when someone objects that an action or situation the poet imitates is false. The poet can reply that may well be, but still, perhaps this is how things ought to be (1460b33).

Impossibility. Aristotle argues that in general, there should be no impossibilities (1460b27). He says that impossibilities may be accepted if they support "the goal of poetry" (1460b24), presumably meaning the goal of eliciting pity and fear in the audience and the plot. Aristotle's example is Homer's portrayal of the pursuit of Hector. This scene was said before to evoke awe because it contains irrational elements (1460a14–16). Because these impossibilities are in epic, and so not represented on the stage, Homer can get away with it and it has a great emotional impact.

Some impossibilities, such as the representation of a female deer with horns or the imitation of a horse throwing out both right hoofs, are "incidental" flaws rather than essential faults that transgress the art of poetry (1460b16). While a hind with horns or a horse moving both right legs at once infringes the science of zoology, it is a less serious error in poetry (1460b30).

Irrationalities. Aristotle illustrates the irrational with examples from classical myths, including the myths told about the gods. He says, "Refer irrationalities to what people say; and there is also the defense that they are sometimes *not* irrational since it is probable that improbable things occur" (1461b13–14).

The first point is that irrationalities may not be contained in the plot as a whole, but rather pertain to received opinion. The second point he makes, that it is probable that improbable things occur, is harder to understand, because it sounds contradictory.

Probabilities have to do with what holds usually or for the most part. The probable (*eikos*) is what happens for the most part, but not always (*Rhetoric* 1.2.1357a35; 2.25.1402a22). Aristotle's defense to the charge of irrationality that, "it is probable that improbable things occur" echoes a phrase that he uses in *Rhetoric* 2.24.1402a10–25, where he considers that a certain event that goes against a general rule for what is probable, can be made to appear probable in a specific case. He associates the tactic of making what is absolutely improbable appear probable with the sophist Protagoras, and says that spurious or apparent probability has no place except in rhetoric, the art of speech making, or eristic, the art of fallacious reasoning in which one attempts to make the weaker argument appear to be stronger.

Why, then, does Aristotle bring in the "improbable can be probable" in a particular case as a defense of the use of irrational action? It is difficult to say with certainty. Some scholars have concluded that his comment shows that Aristotle is accepting that just *apparent* and not genuine probability is sufficient to inspire pity and fear in the audience.[38] I am inclined to interpret Aristotle's comment as in line with his earlier point in *Poetics* 24 that "Things probable though impossible should be preferred to the possible but implausible." Aristotle is not advocating the use of impossibilities, improbabilities, or irrationalities. As an account of a particular *scene* that is irrational, the poet can defend herself by saying that the action made sense in that particular context, even if it was just an apparent probability. Still, Aristotle is not advocating widespread use of irrationalities.[39]

If Aristotle was thinking that the poet could just make use of what appears to be probable in a particular case, as the Sophists did in their speeches, there would be no point in his repeatedly stressing the formula that the events in the plot occur according to "probability or necessity," where what is necessary refers to a class of action that occurs without exception, according to causal laws.

At the same time he recognizes that a series of events that does not happen by probability or necessity can have the *appearance* of purpose and causal order. This is a point he noted earlier, in *Poetics* 10, when he says that when Mitys' statue randomly kills Mitys' murderer, this sort of thing does not *seem* random; instead it feels like the working out of what we now call poetic justice (10.1452a8–10). These plots are finer, he says, than plots that give no semblance of purpose or order. But plots in which episodes do not follow one another by probability or necessity are composed by bad poets through their own fault or by good poets who wish to include incidents in a plot when doing so breaks up the causal continuity of the episodes (10.1451b35–1452a1). While some specific uses of irrationalities can work, impossible and irrational episodes should be minimized or ideally not used at all.

When it comes to errors that are apparent contradictions, Aristotle takes to task critics who assume a passage is contradicting something else said elsewhere, without considering if the words in question have a different meaning in the passage in question. It is better to give the poet credit by considering all possible meanings and picking the one that is most probable that the poet, and an intelligent person, would give to the context (25.1461a32–35).

Another category of problems refers to errors that relate to artistic standards. Errors in diction must be examined to determine if in the context in question, inept diction suits the character that delivers it or involves non-literal use of language, as in metaphor, or is intentionally ambiguous or has some other function that serves the imitation of action (1461a9–32).

In answering the charge of immorality, whether an action or speech, Aristotle says that it is necessary to consider the action or speech in context: the identity of the agent should be considered, to whom he acts or speaks, and for what end, for example whether the action was the occasion of "greater good" or to "avert greater evil" (1461a5–7). So, to illustrate with a contemporary example, lying is immoral, but if a character lies in order to avert some great evil or because it promotes some great good, this should be taken into consideration by a critic.

While *Poetics* 25 is useful for seeing Aristotle's advice to critics, his guiding theme that poetry has its own standards of correctness is of special interest. Some have taken his comments that poetry does not have the same norms for correctness as politics and other arts to suggest what has been called art autonomism: this is the view that came to prominence in the mid-eighteenth century that art is for "art's sake" and that aesthetics forms its own realm, separate from ethics and standards of historical or scientific truthfulness. Art autonomism is often coupled with aesthetic formalism: this is the view that the aesthetic value of a work of art does not derive from anything external to the work, but is instead a function of the work's formal structure.

Aristotle is saying that poetry has its own standards. Still, this does not mean that he accepts either art autonomism or aesthetic formalism. These views would be inconsistent with the ideas that Aristotle develops throughout the *Poetics*. Aristotle traces the success of tragedy as a work of art to its emotional impact on the audience. This emotional response is directly related to the audience's ability to recognize that the action is an instance of an intelligible pattern of human life and behavior: the kind of thing that could take place, according to probability or necessity (9.1451b6–8). Tragedy is an imitation of possible human life and action, and to have its proper impact, the audience must be able to recognize the similarities between the action in the play and situations that they could find themselves in.

Aristotle holds, in other words, that to the extent that this is possible, tragedy should be a realistic imitation of how human life and action could go. Tragedy is not, then, off in its own separate realm, even if it need not adhere to the same standards as politics, zoology, or other arts. As an imitation of human action and life, it and other mimetic arts directly call for the audience to make a comparison between the work and life. Things in the world happen, for the most part, according to cause and effect. Tragedy takes this basic premise and tries to build a plot that is even more unified and coherent in terms of causal connections than the way events appear in ordinary life.

POETICS 26: TRAGEDY AS SUPERIOR TO EPIC

The *Poetics* concludes with Aristotle reflecting on the question whether epic or tragic *mimēsis* is better. Given the extensive concentration on epic and tragedy, it is natural that Aristotle should raise this question. While critics of tragedy have argued that it is inferior to epic (it is the "vulgar" art form), Aristotle sets out to establish that the opposite is the case.

Aristotle first sums up the argument as to why critics have found that tragedy comes up short in comparison with epic. The assumption the critics make is that the better form of poetry appeals to a better *social* class, those who are decent or noble (*epieikēs*) (26.1461b27f.). Tragedy is thought to be inferior to tragedy because it appeals to a vulgar (*phaulos*) class of people, perhaps meaning uneducated or base.[40] Why would this be thought be the case?

Epic is read or recited, while tragedy is performed (1461b28–30). As a form of poetry that is performed on stage, tragedy relies on visually appealing sets, dance, and the chorus to achieve its impact on the audience. In addition, Aristotle adds, the actors in tragedy assume that the spectators are not sophisticated enough to notice things without their overacting, so they engage in profuse movement and antics to get the attention of the audience (1461b28–32).

This means that epic "is addressed to decent spectators who have no need of gestures, but tragedy to crude spectators" (26.1462a1–3). Tragedy is, to these critics, the ancient Greek equivalent of the Hollywood film, with special effects and the acting of big-name stars commanding the attention of a mass audience, while epic is like art-house cinema: appealing to a smaller and more socially select class of people.[41]

Aristotle's first reply to these critics is that the objection does not concern the art of tragedy, but the actor's art, and overacting can occur in epic recital as well as in the performance of a tragedy. He does not discount the use of gesture and movement, and indeed in *Poetics* 17 he advises the poet to work out the plot as he composes in gestures since this will get the poet in the grip of the emotions he is trying to inspire with the plot, making it more likely that the audience will also feel inspired with genuine emotion (17.1455a28–32). The critics miss the mark because tragedy achieves its effects even without the movement and gestures of the actors: as Aristotle argues in *Poetics* 6, "tragedy's capacity is independent of performance and actors" (1450b18–19); and this point is made again in *Poetics* 14 where it is said that even without seeing a play performed, a person hearing the events read out loud experiences horror and pity (1453b3–6). This means that performance is not an essential aspect of how tragedy achieves its emotional impact. Aristotle's second reply is that the critics place too much emphasis on the performances of individual actors. Not all actors try to use overacting and antics to play to the crowd.

Aristotle proceeds to give his positive argument as to why tragedy is superior to epic. First, tragedy contains all the same parts as epic, but also contains spectacle (*opsis*) and song (*mousikē*). While song is the "greatest embellishment" of tragedy (6.1450b15), spectacle (*opsis*) is least integral to tragedy (6.1450b15–19); these are nevertheless two parts that can heighten the emotional impact of tragedy.

A second argument relates to magnitude: because tragedy achieves its effect in a shorter span of time, it allows for a more intense effect. This point is illustrated with the thought experiment where a poet draws out Sophocles' *Oedipus* to have the same length in hexameters as Homer's *Iliad*. The impact would be diluted (26.1462b1–3).

Third, tragedy is not only more concentrated, its plot is more unified. An epic poem yields material for several tragedies. Yet the best epic poems, such as Homer's *Iliad* and *Odyssey*, are like the complete and whole plots of tragedy. While they are composed of many episodes, Homer essentially imitates a single, unified action (1462b9–10).

Because tragedy is superior to epic in having more parts, its smaller magnitude allows for a more concentrated pleasure, and it has greater unity, this means that tragedy is superior to epic on these points. Aristotle also says that tragedy is superior in its artistic effect, and this is related to the fact that it gives no ordinary pleasure, but "the one specified" (26.1462b14). It is commonly supposed that the pleasure to which Aristotle refers is the pleasure the poet should create that, "comes from pity and fear through *mimēsis*" (1453b10–13).[42] Because tragedy is more effective at achieving its goal, the pleasure that comes from pity and fear through the use of imitation, tragedy is superior to epic. What proper pleasure, then, is it that tragedy succeeds in delivering? The answer to this question is discussed in the chapter that follows.

NOTES

1 Reading for this chapter is *Poetics* 5, 18, 24, 25 and 26.
2 See Richard Janko 1987: 43–46 for his reconstruction of the outline of topics that were addressed in this lost second book and Janko 1984 for a discussion of Janko's reconstruction of *Poetics* 2. However, the reader should be aware of the highly speculative nature of Janko's reconstructions of *Poetics* 2. See Malcolm Heath 2013 for a critical evaluation of Janko's edition of the fragments.
3 See Chapter 3, pp. 65–66.
4 See Gerald Else 1957: 196–201 for a discussion of the historical figures that Aristotle might have in mind in his examination of the development of comedy.
5 See Else 1957: 186. "Aristotle's theory of the comic, i.e. the laughable, rests on Platonic foundations but goes beyond them." But it should be noted that this view of the relationship between Aristotle's and Plato's views on comedy is not shared by everyone, including Malcolm Heath, whose views I discuss in the next section.
6 *Nicomachean Ethics* 2.1106b15–23.
7 For his views on the importance of leisure and play in a human life, see *Politics* 8.3.1337b33–1338a1.

8 Stephen Halliwell 2008; Malcolm Heath 1989.

9 The relevant passages in Hobbes' writing on comedy are discussed in Quentin Skinner 2004. For a discussion of the contemporary form of Hobbes' theory, the superiority theory, and other major philosophical accounts of comedy, see John Morreall 2013.

10 *NE* 4.8.1127b33–1128b9, citations are to Barnes 1984.

11 Halliwell 2008: 308. See *Politics* 8.3.1337b33–1338a21, where Aristotle discusses play as a form of "restorative" medicine.

12 *NE* 4.8.1128a8.

13 *NE* 4.8.1128a23–25.

14 Halliwell 2008: 327. See also *Poetics* 9.1451b12–14, where Aristotle commends the comic poets for recognizing that they can make up fictional characters to construct a plot, in contrast to the tragic poets, who tend to base their plots around characters that are known from traditional stories.

15 Halliwell 2008: 328.

16 Halliwell 2008: 310.

17 Halliwell 2008: 327. See *Poetics* 5.1449a and *NE* 4.8.1128a8.

18 Halliwell 2008: 327.

19 Halliwell observes (2008: 327) that hostile laughter is nevertheless permitted between the characters in the comic theater, even if it is not appropriately directed *towards* the characters in comedy.

20 Heath 1989. Note that Heath's essay was written before Halliwell's book, so what follows is my reconstruction of several lines of difference between the two authors.

21 See the discussion later in the chapter on pages 258–263.

22 Jonathan Barnes 1984.

23 It is not entirely clear which are the new comedies to which Aristotle refers, but it is likely that some of them must belong to the period in comedy that is now called "Middle Comedy," comedy that was written and performed in the fourth century BCE. Albrecht Dihle (1994: 225) describes this period as follows: "There was a general disappearance of the ribaldry once probably sanctioned by rural fertility cults and later the exclusive province of comedy in the fifth century BC. This ribaldry was now obliged to give way to urban respectability."

24 This is an important and highly debated topic that has received widespread attention in contemporary aesthetics. For an accessible discussion about the contemporary debate see Elisabeth Schellekens 2007: 63–92.

25 See the discussion of this plot pattern in Chapter 8, pp. 199–200.

26 See W. W. Fortenbaugh 2002: 120–126 for the suggestion that Aristotle would find laughter a pleasant emotion and for useful comparisons between Aristotle's views and contemporary superiority and incongruity accounts of comedy. For a helpful discussion of these contemporary accounts see John Morreall 2013.

27 D. P. Szameitat et al. 2009.

28 See the account of *mimēsis* in Chapter 2, pp. 34–43.

29 For a discussion of the differences between the narrative and dramatic modes, see Chapter 3, pp. 54–62.

30 See *Poetics* 6.1450b22–22.

31 See Chapter 6, pp. 133–138, for a discussion of these qualitative parts.
32 See *Poetics* 18.1455b32f.
33 See Chapter 8, pp. 189–194, for a discussion of reversal, recognition, and suffering.
34 See Stephen Halliwell 1998: 200 and 263.
35 Else 1957: 610. For a discussion of what Aristotle means in *Poetics* 24 in prais-
    ing Homer for speaking as little as possible in his own voice (1460a5–6) see
    Chapter 3.
36 Irrationalities such as the improbabilities in Achilles' pursuit of Hector (*Iliad*
    22.131–144; *Poetics* 24 1460a14–17) or the irrational aspects of Odysseus' setting
    ashore (*Odyssey* 13.116ff.; *Poetics* 25 1460a35–b2).
37 For a discussion of Aristotle's comments on the introduction of irrational and
    improbable events into the plot, see Chapter 5, pp. 118–122.
38 For this point see Paul Woodruff 2009: 624, note 9.
39 See Chapter 7, pp. 175–176, for the argument for this claim and replies to objec-
    tions to it.
40 Aristotle uses the term "*phaulos*" to refer to the characters in comedy, and he uses
    the term *epieikēs* to refer to a highly virtuous sort of character in tragedy, whose
    supreme virtue makes her not suitable for the appropriate tragic plot. The com-
    parison is not exact, but these critics would in effect be saying that tragedy stands
    to epic as Aristotle thinks comedy stands to tragedy!
41 This might seem like an incongruous comparison to us today, given that perfor-
    mances of ancient Greek tragedy today are much less widely seen than Hollywood
    films. For an argument that ancient Greek tragedy functioned as a popular "mass
    medium" see Alexander Nehamas 1988.
42 But as we noted in the previous section, it is unclear whether Aristotle thinks that
    epic and tragedy indeed aim at the same proper pleasure.

WORKS CITED

Barnes, Jonathan (ed.) 1984. *The Complete Works of Aristotle. The Revised Oxford Translation* Volume Two. Princeton, NJ: Princeton University Press.
Dihle, Albrecht 1994. *A History of Greek Literature from Homer to the Hellenistic Period*. London and New York: Routledge.
Else, Gerald 1957. *Aristotle's Poetics: The Argument*. Cambridge, MA: Harvard University Press.
Fortenbaugh, W. W. 2002. *Aristotle on Emotion* Second Edition. London: Duckworth.
Halliwell, Stephen 1998. *Aristotle's Poetics: With a New Introduction by the Author*. Chicago: University of Chicago Press.
—— 2008. *Greek Laughter: A Study of Cultural Psychology from Homer to Early Christianity*. Cambridge: Cambridge University Press.
Hamilton, Edith and Huntington Cairns (eds.) 1961. *The Collected Dialogues of Plato Including the Letters*, with Introduction and Prefatory Notes. Princeton, NJ: Princeton University Press.
Heath, Malcolm 1989. "Aristotelian Comedy." *Classical Quarterly* 39 (2): 344–354.

——— 2013. "Aristotle *On Poets*: A Critical Evaluation of Richard Janko's Edition of the Fragments." *Studia Humaniora Tartuensia* 14.A.1 (Open Access Journal).

Janko, Richard 1984. *Aristotle on Comedy. Towards a Reconstruction of Poetics II.* London: Duckworth.

——— 1987. *Aristotle, Poetics: With the Tractatus Coislinianus, Reconstruction of Poetics II, and the Fragments of the On Poets.* Indianapolis, IN and Cambridge: Hackett Publishing Company.

Kraut, Richard 1997. *Aristotle: Politics Books VII and VIII.* Translated with a Commentary by Richard Kraut. Oxford: Clarendon Press.

Morreall, John 2013. "The Philosophy of Humor." *Stanford Encyclopedia of Philosophy* http://plato.stanford.edu/archives/spr2013/entires/humor/.

Nehamas, Alexander 1988. "Plato and the Mass Media." *The Monist* 71 (2): 214–234.

Schellekens, Elisabeth 2007. *Aesthetics and Morality.* New York and London: Continuum Press.

Skinner, Quentin 2004. "Hobbes and the Classical Theory of Laughter," in Tom Sorrell and Luc Foisneau (eds.), *Leviathan After 350 Years.* Oxford: Oxford University Press: 139–166.

Szameitat, D. P., K. Alter, A. J. Szameitat, C. J. Darwin, D. Wildgruber, S. Dietrich, and A. Sterr 2009. "Differentiation of Emotions in Laughter at the Behavioral Level." *Emotion* (June) 9 (3): 397–405.

Woodruff, Paul 2009. "Aristotle's *Poetics*: The Aim of Tragedy," in Georgios Anagnostopoulos (ed.), *A Companion to Aristotle.* Chichester, England: Blackwell Publishing: 612–627.

RECOMMENDED READING

Belfiore, Elizabeth 1987. "Aristotle on Comedy." *Ancient Philosophy* 7: 236–239.

Golden, Leon 1984. "Aristotle on Comedy." *The Journal of Art and Art Criticism* 42 (3): 283–290.

11

THE DISTINCTIVE
PLEASURE OF TRAGEDY

THE PROPER PLEASURE OF TRAGEDY:
SOME PRELIMINARIES

Aristotle mentions the proper or characteristic pleasure of tragedy (*oikeia hēdonē*) at several places throughout the *Poetics*. In *Poetics* 14 he describes it as a pleasure that comes from pity and fear and is produced through *mimēsis* (imitation). The proper tragic pleasure, Aristotle tells us, should be "built into the events," meaning, based on the structure of the plot (14.1453b13). Aristotle's formulation, "the poet should create the pleasure that comes from (*apo*) pity and fear through (*dia*) *mimēsis* (*mimēseōs*)" calls attention to a puzzle that many have noticed: that the pleasure spectators take in tragedy is paradoxical.[1]

What is the problem? On the one hand, it is true that:

1) Pity and fear are painful emotions that involve the expectation or remembering of critical harms.

Pity and fear are painful emotions. Aristotle defines pity as "a feeling of pain at an apparent evil, destructive or painful, which befalls one who does not deserve it" (*Rhetoric* 2.8.1385b11–12). Fear is a pain or disturbance due to imagining some destructive or painful evil in the future (*Rhetoric* 2.5.1382a22–23). Pity and fear, then, both involve pain.

On the other hand:

2) The poet should create the pleasure that comes from pity and fear through *mimēsis*.

The problem is that there is an apparent contradiction between: (a) feeling pity and fear in response to the characters and their situations; and (b) taking pleasure in the work of tragedy. How do pain and pleasure co-exist in the experience of tragedy?

So Aristotle's formulation, "the pleasure from pity and fear through *mimēsis*" raises the question: how does the experience of pity and fear in the special circumstances of watching a tragedy produce the proper pleasure of tragedy? If we can address that question, we have an answer to the question of just what the proper pleasure of tragedy is.

We should call to mind Aristotle's notion of pleasure (*hēdonē*). Aristotle discusses pleasure in two different books of the *Nicomachean Ethics*. According to Book 7, pleasure is an unimpeded activity (*energeia*) of our natural state (7.12.1153a13–15). This account makes a central connection between what a thing is, its basic nature or essence, and what it does or its activity (*energeia*). To be a human being is to be involved in activity that characterizes the kind, human being. Characteristic activities for human beings include sense perception and understanding. So the idea with the account of pleasure in Book 7 is that pleasure for a human being is an unimpeded activity of our natural condition.

According to Book 10 pleasure is something that accompanies and completes such a natural activity (*NE* 10.4.1153a13–15). Here he makes the point that an activity that is an expression of a natural state is complete and perfect, in itself. Pleasure does not need to be added to make the activity more perfect. In this second account, then, pleasure supervenes or rides piggyback on the unimpeded activity of a natural state. Aristotle also adds that pleasure occurs when some natural disposition in us is brought into good condition.

Aristotle sometimes uses the notion of "completion" or "perfection" (*telos*) to refer to the specific pleasure that comes from the distinctive emotional experience of tragedy.[2] In *Physics* 2 Aristotle says that art (*technē*) completes nature (*physis*) by bringing about that which nature is unable to finish (199a15). Nature, for example, is not able to take the wood from the tree to make a house, so instead the art (*technē*) of house building accomplishes what nature is not able to complete. Applying this idea to understand the function of the art (*technē*) of tragedy, recall that tragedy is an imitation (*mimēsis*) of human action and emotion. We can say that tragedy is the art (*technē*) of producing an object that calls forth and completes a certain potential found in the materials of human life and action.

More formally, we can say that poetry is the art (*technē*) of making an imitation (*mimēsis*) that: (1) reproduces some of the features of a human action; (2) produces some of the natural effects of the sort that could be produced by experiencing the action in real life; (3) completes or perfects these effects in a way that makes the overall experience pleasurable.

If we can determine which natural capacities Aristotle thinks that tragedy's imitations perfect or complete, and in what way tragedy is the perfect object for eliciting these natural dispositions, then we can make some headway in understanding the proper pleasure of tragedy.

Finally, we should note three requirements for a solution to the problem of the proper pleasure of tragedy:

1) Show why the pleasure is unique or distinctive to tragedy in contrast to other forms of poetry (e.g. comedy).

The proper pleasure should be something that characterizes tragedy, in contrast to other forms of poetry and mimetic arts.

2) Give an account that explains the role that imitation (*mimēsis*) plays in producing the tragic pleasure.

Since Aristotle makes clear that the proper pleasure of tragedy comes about through or by means of (*dia*) *mimēsis*, any solution should explain the role that imitation (*mimēsis*) plays in producing the proper pleasure of tragedy. In particular, *mimēsis* in relation to tragedy includes the plot, since plot is the imitation (*mimēsis*) of action and is the construction of events (6.1450a3).

3) A correct account should show how the emotions of pity and fear are integral to the proper pleasure of tragedy.

With these preliminaries in mind, we are ready to consider some solutions to the problem of what makes possible the proper pleasure of tragedy.

PLEASURE IN ONE'S VIRTUOUS RESPONSE TO TRAGEDY

Malcolm Heath offers an influential proposal, which operates from the assumption, based in *Poetics* 26, that Aristotle holds that tragedy appeals to a morally better and more educated audience.[3] He distinguishes between two things:

1) the audience's response to the imitations in tragedy, which prompt the painful emotions of pity and fear; and
2) the audience's correct, virtuous response to tragic imitations, which involves an exercise of the capacity to feel the right emotion, towards the right object, in the right circumstances, which is a sign of virtue.

The first response, the feeling of pity and fear for the characters, is a source of pain, while the second reaction, which is a "meta-response" (a response to a response), is a source of pleasure to the virtuous members of the audience. For they have the perception that they are exercising well their capacity for virtuous action, and pleasure involves the perception that one has come into the realization of one's nature.

Aristotle's view is that happiness (*eudaimonia*) is activity in accordance with virtue or human excellence (*Nicomachean Ethics* 1.1098a15–16). The activity of responding in the right way, with the right emotion, to the right person, in the right condition is an expression of our natural state (2.1106b35–1107a3). On Heath's view, the proper pleasure of tragedy comes when the spectator believes and grasps that her response of pity and fear, while painful, is as it should be, for the situations that tragedy imitates call for such emotions: for these are characters that suffer misfortune that is not deserved and because the audiences see the characters as "like them," the audience believes they are subject to the same reversal of fortune.

While Heath presents an ingenious argument, there are several questions about it. First, the proper pleasure the audience feels in response to tragedy is something that should be distinctive to tragedy and to the experience in the theater. It should not be something that is typically available in real life. This is because the pleasure comes from pity and fear *through* imitation. But in real life, virtuous people typically and routinely have the correct responses to the sufferings of others, feeling the right emotion, to the right degree, in the right way, as is the mark of a virtuous person (*Nicomachean Ethics* 2). This means that real life events afford the same opportunity of satisfaction in one's sympathetic response as do events in the theater. Why is it then necessary to go to the theater to experience this pleasure in one's correct moral reaction?

Perhaps Heath can explain how tragedy exercises or places some special sort of demand on the spectator's capacity for virtue in a way that it does not in real life, and then he can answer this concern.[4] Heath wants to stress, however, that tragedy appeals to a morally better audience,[5] meaning that the spectator's capacity for responding appropriately is already just as it should be and is not in need of correcting. Interpreted in this way, tragic plots might make certain *intellectual* demands on the audience, but tragedy would not make any moral demands on the audience that were not available in real life.

For example, by having the events of a plot proceed "contrary to expectations, yet on account of one another," the character's change to misfortune might come about in an unexpected way, for example, as with Sophocles' *Oedipus*, in which his desire to obtain knowledge comes back to bite him when it leads to the discovery that he is the cause of the plague on his city. This turnaround might place demands on the spectator's ability to comprehend just how such a reversal came about. Her wonder and amazement at the change in fortune could prompt her to go back and revisit the causal connections in the plot that make the change intelligible. But this would be an intellectual demand that tragedy makes on the spectator, not one that exercises or calls forth her capacity for virtue in a way that is not available in real life.

Perhaps one other line of reply is possible for Heath. He could say that in real life it would be inappropriate to take pleasure in one's correct response of pity and fear for people who suffer misfortunes. For it is morally inappropriate to take pleasure in one's good virtue while the objects of one's pity and fear suffer! On the other hand, in tragedy, no one is *really* suffering. So tragedy provides an opportunity to take pleasure in the correctness of one's virtuous response, without giving the appearance that another's pain and suffering is the opportunity to pat oneself on the back, as it were, for being a virtuous person.

If this line of reply is successful, this leaves a final remaining concern about Heath's proposal: what role, if any, do the structural requirements on the plot, such as unity and causal structure, play in making possible the proper pleasure? Aristotle says that the proper pleasure of tragedy must arise from the plot and the structure of the events. If so, we need an account that explains the key role that the plot plays in making the proper pleasure possible.

THE MERRY-GO-ROUND ACCOUNT

In several recent papers, Pierre Destrée offers an original account of the proper pleasure of tragedy that we can consider.[6] Destrée shares with Heath the overall idea that the characteristic pleasure in tragedy is not an intellectual or cognitive pleasure (a view we will discuss next). According to his view, the pleasure that the audience members feel in response to tragedy is akin to the pleasure that a person feels on a merry-go-round ride.

For example, when a child rides a merry-go-round, he knows that the little horse he is riding is safe, and that he is not in danger, and this enables him to feel pleasure in the ride. If suddenly the child had the feeling of no longer being secure or safe, his feeling of pleasure would stop. Destrée argues that the merry-go-round provides a model of why adults can enjoy feeling pity and fear in the context of the tragic theater. The proper pleasure of tragedy is based on the fact that the spectator knows that what is happening on stage is not real, and so she can enjoy "the activity of pitying and fearing without any painful involvement in the real world."[7]

Like Heath's proposal, Destrée's account has some very interesting connections with contemporary aesthetics. But it also raises some questions. First, what activity (*energeia*) of a natural state of human beings would be exercised on Destrée's view of the proper pleasure? Pity and fear are passions (*pathē*), not activities. So feeling the emotions of pity and fear would not be an activity in which we exercise our natural state. On the other hand, virtue is a fixed disposition (*hexis*), the exercise of which is an expression of our natural state. If Destrée is suggesting that the proper pleasure is the *correct* or appropriate feeling of pity and fear, then this is virtuous activity, and the proper pleasure in tragedy would then be the pleasure that Heath describes: feeling pity and fear correctly, towards the right person at the right time in the right way.[8] This is not the idea at which Destrée aims. Instead it is the idea that we "experience the emotions in a safe environment."

Destrée explains that when we experience these emotions in a secure environment, we can enjoy the experience of these emotions "without any painful involvement in the real world."[9] The point he is making here is intuitively plausible when applied to the merry-go-round. You do not feel truly terrified when spinning around on a merry-go-round, for you feel secure in thinking you are in a controlled environment where nothing bad would happen.

So many remarks in the *Poetics* suggest that the point of tragedy is to make a vivid and convincing experience that brings the action to life before the spectator's eyes.[10] In this sense the merry-go-round is not a good analogy for the pleasure in tragedy, since the point of tragedy *is* to evoke genuine pity and fear in the audience, and this is painful.

Of course, Destrée is making an important point that the spectator must recognize that the suffering on the stage is not really happening or she cannot take the proper pleasure in tragedy. If the spectator loses her grip, for example, on the fact that what she is seeing is an imitation of suffering, rather than real life sorrow, her experience of tragedy will not be pleasurable. Instead it will be just like her experience of real life tragedies. Thus, the merry-go-round may not be a good analogy for the experience of tragedy, precisely because people on the merry-go-round are not really scared that something will happen, while the spectator of tragedy does, Aristotle thinks, feel genuine pity and fear, and these emotions are painful.

Here it is worth noting a point that Destrée himself makes: everything that Aristotle says in the *Poetics* speaks to the idea that the emotions of pity and fear for the characters are genuine.[11] In addition, although this point is controversial, it can be argued that what Aristotle says in his discussions of emotion in his treatises on philosophical psychology is compatible with thinking we can feel genuine pity and fear in response to tragic characters. Sometimes it is maintained, to the contrary, that a text in *De Anima* 3.3 says that the mere imagining of something threatening cannot cause genuine emotion, only the *belief* that something is actually threatening can:

> Again, when we form an opinion (*doxasōmen*) that something is threatening or frightening, we are immediately affected by it, and the same is true of our opinion of something that inspires courage; but in imagination (*phantasia*) we are like spectators looking at something dreadful or encouraging in a picture.

(De Anima 3.3.427b2–4)

As Ian McCready-Flora has rightly noted, in this text all Aristotle is saying is that the mere imagining (*phantasia*) of some terrible event is not sufficient to produce emotion *immediately*, yet the belief that there is something threatening or frightening is sufficient.[12] As Destrée notes, there is another passage in the *Movement of Animals* in which Aristotle says that imagination and thinking have the power to move us to shudder and be frightened as do actual objects (7.701b18–22). The *De Anima* passage, then, does not show that the spectator of tragedy cannot experience genuine emotion towards events that are merely imagined.

Aristotle stresses, both in *Rhetoric* 2.5 and 2.8 and in the *Poetics*, the point that listeners and spectators can be made to feel emotion when the speaker and the poet use techniques that "place things before the eyes" (*pro hommatōv*), that is to bring them to life.[13] If all of the preceding points are correct, then the upshot is that Aristotle's philosophical psychology allows for the *possibility* that in some cases, imagination can generate genuine emotion, provided that the things imagined are brought to life and made vivid.

Destrée's reading of Aristotle bears some interesting similarities to the "control" theory solution to the paradox of tragedy.[14] This is the idea that the spectator of tragedy is "in control" of her emotions in a way that she is not when she responds to real life tragedies and it is this aspect of control that makes tragic pleasure possible. The important point about control, suggests Marcia Eaton, is that "we are excused from certain general demands placed upon us and we are able to react in appropriate aesthetic ways."[15]

For example, because the action on stage is not real, no practical action is demanded of the spectator. She cannot help Oedipus, for example, when he gouges out his eyes, nor can she shout out to Iphigenia that she is about to kill her long lost brother! The spectator is free to enjoy watching the action unfold, without feeling the need to intercede and help. And if we are feeling too overwhelmed watching a tragedy, whether in a play or in a film, we can leave the theater and refuse to listen to the story. This gives us a control in the theater that we are missing in response to real life tragedy.

Still, feeling in control does not, by itself, explain how we can take pleasure in the imitations of the tragic theater, when we do not in real life. The fact that I *could* put an end to the pain of feeling pity and fear for the characters by leaving the theater does not explain, in itself, how the pain can co-exist with pleasure in the experience of tragedy. The vast majority of viewers do not leave the theater; they remain. These spectators feel pity and fear, which are painful, yet they also take pleasure from "pity and fear through *mimēsis*." How is this possible?[16]

The focus on control and the safety of the experience of tragedy raises the question of in what sense, on Destrée's view, the spectator is to have some sense of distance from the action. If, to illustrate, a spectator at a performance of Shakespeare's *Othello* were to keep thinking of his own marital problems while watching the play, he could not be properly appreciating the events unfolding on the stage. Some might say that aesthetic appreciation, therefore, involves some kind of psychic distance from the action.[17] But there is so much stress in the *Poetics* on the idea that tragedy is a convincing and believable imitation of human action and life, such as, when, for example, Aristotle says that just hearing the event of *Oedipus* is enough to cause the listener to be "filled with horror and pity at the incidents" (14.1453b4–6). This does not sound like someone who is at some sort of emotional distance from the events that are taking place in the drama.

Finally, we need some explanation of the role that the plot plays in producing the proper pleasure of tragedy. For the pleasure in tragedy, on Destrée's view, is traced to the fact that the experience is not real, rather than to the particular way that tragedy imitates an action, and this seems to be a problem with this account.

COGNITIVE PLEASURE AS THE PROPER PLEASURE OF TRAGEDY

One proposal for how to understand the proper pleasure of tragedy is that it is a cognitive pleasure: it involves the pleasure of learning and understanding.[18] On this view, tragedy involves the completion or perfection of the human capacity for learning and knowledge. The plot of tragedy is based on the universal, that is, the sort of thing that it suits a certain sort of person to say or do, by necessity or probability (9.1451b7–8). When the audience grasps the universal pattern concerning human action that is embedded in the plot, they gain the pleasure of learning. On this view, then, the pleasure of learning is the proper pleasure of tragedy.

The argument is made in *Poetics* 4 that contemplating the precise images of things such as vile looking animals or corpses can be pleasurable and the explanation he gives is that contemplating these images affords the pleasure of "inferring (*sullogismos*) and understanding (*manthanein*)" in which the viewer matches up elements in the image with some features of a person that she has previously encountered (4.1448b10–18). There is a process of recognition involved in grasping the likeness in even a simple portrait of an individual, and this involves the viewer in reasoning out the similarities and differences between the subject in the portrait and her recollections of like objects. Such a process of reasoning and understanding affords pleasure to the viewer, for all humans by nature desire to learn.[19] Further, in *Rhetoric* 1.11.1371b5–12 Aristotle says that all acts of imitation, including painting, sculpture, and poetry, give delight to the viewer because they engage the spectator in a process of reasoning and understanding. These two texts secure the general point that the pleasure we take in a work of mimetic art *as* an imitation is based in some kind of pleasurable understanding the work provides to the viewer or spectator.

How does it then come about, on the cognitive pleasure view, that the pain of pity and fear can co-exist with the overall pleasure of tragedy? *Poetics* 4 is helpful on this point. There and in *Parts of Animals* 2.5.6445a5–25 there is the suggestion that the pleasure in recognizing the figure in the image can somehow *compensate* for any negative response that the spectator feels in response to looking at objects that produce distressing emotions.[20] So, for example, in the *Parts of Animals* passage Aristotle suggests animals whose sensory appearance is repulsive can still, when viewed through the idea of the philosophy student, be a source of pleasure for the student who can see how even the most humble animal's parts serve the animal's end or characteristic activity.

In the *Parts of Animals* passage it is particularly clear that Aristotle is saying that the pleasure the student takes in learning about the causes and functioning of the animal's parts can somehow co-exist and compensate for the pain and revulsion felt in response to the sensory presentation of the animal. Here the animal is viewed in two different ways: on the one hand, from a sensory point of view that is repelling; and on the other hand, from the point of view of the viewer as a student of nature, who understands how the parts of the animal work together to serve the life functions of the animal.

Cognitivist interpreters suggest that this same model of learning-compensating-for-pain can also account for the characteristic pleasure of tragedy. Imitations in tragedy inspire the painful emotions of pity and fear, but the pain can in some sense be balanced out by the pleasure the spectator takes in understanding the larger causal process, which the plot makes clear, that brings about a character's reversal of fortune. Through feeling pity and fear we come to be made more aware of what circumstances truly merit our pity and fear.[21]

There are several problems with the account of the proper pleasure as cognitive pleasure.[22] First, cognitive pleasure is not unique to tragedy. Other forms of poetry, such as comedy and epic also are structured around plots that embed universal patterns of human action, and other forms of mimetic art, more generally, are sources of pleasurable learning. So cognitive pleasure cannot explain the distinctive or characteristic pleasure of tragedy.

Second, the proper pleasure comes "from pity and fear through *mimēsis*." The cognitive account does not explain the crucial role the emotions play in producing the characteristic pleasure. On the cognitive view, the pleasure is taken in tragic imitations, in spite of, but not because of, the emotions of pity and fear. Any account of the proper pleasure of tragedy must explain the role these emotions play in producing tragedy's characteristic pleasure. Third, there is an unanswered question, which is, why should spectators seek out the pleasure of learning from tragedy when there are other, pain-free means of pleasurable learning, for example, from the imitations of happy events that nevertheless are a source of learning and understanding?

Of these three objections, the third is the easiest for the cognitive theorist to answer. As Aristotle's discussion of the pleasure of learning from vile or nasty looking animals suggests, things that prompt uncomfortable emotions may be the source of great understanding. If the payoff of learning from tragedy is great enough, as its proponents often maintain, the overall pleasure that the audience gets from learning might outweigh or cancel out the pain from feeling pity and fear.[23] This would provide an experience that is overall greater in total pleasure than that found in works of mimetic art with imitations of happy things only. The first two objections, however, seem to be decisive, motivating us to look for another account of the proper pleasure.

This cognitive pleasure account also bears some interesting similarities with discussions in contemporary aesthetics. For example, there is the paradox of horror: horror evokes fear and disgust of the monster; yet viewers and readers of horror fiction enjoy watching or reading horror fiction. How can that be? Both the paradox of horror and the paradox of tragedy are related to the broader paradox of negative emotion: how can viewers and readers take pleasure in works of art that evoke negative emotions?[24]

Noël Carroll proposes a solution to the paradox of horror that he suggests is indebted to Aristotle's *Poetics*.[25] Carroll argues that the pleasure spectators and readers take in horror has to do with the plot structures in the work of horror, which turn on tracking the monster, a creature that piques our curiosity because it violates the categories of science, for example the zombie that is both living and dead, or the wolf-man.[26] While horror inspires the pain of fear and disgust and revulsion at the monster, it also piques the viewer's or reader's curiosity. While fear and revulsion are painful, there is intellectual pleasure in discovering, tracking, and confirming the existence of the monster, and the pain from fear and revulsion is the "price one has to pay" for getting the intellectual pleasure of the monster.

Alex Neill has made an objection to Carroll's solution to the paradox that parallels one of the concerns about the cognitive pleasure solution to the pleasure of tragedy. Neill argues that

Carroll has failed to explain how the feelings of fear and disgust towards the monster are integral to the experience of horror.[27] There is, in other words, in horror a pleasure that comes *from* fear and disgust, not *in spite* of feeling these emotions. Carroll's account does not work, in other words, because it does not explain how the emotions of fear and disgust are integrated into the experience of horror, rather than existing as some independent player that sits alongside curiosity in the monster. In this sense, Carroll's solution, Neill maintains, fails to explain the particular attraction of horror.[28]

PROPER PLEASURE IN TRAGEDY AS EMOTIONAL UNDERSTANDING

It is possible to rectify the defects in the cognitive account by: (i) addressing the central role that the emotions of pity and fear play in facilitating the pleasure in learning and understanding; and by (ii) explaining the central role that the plot plays in facilitating the distinctive emotional experience of tragedy. According to this fourth proposal the proper pleasure in tragedy is the pleasure of understanding, which involves an altered comprehension of the human condition that the feeling of pity and fear provides. I will call this for short the "emotional understanding" account.

The idea that the distinctive pleasure of tragedy is some kind of emotional understanding is not a new proposal. It is found, for example, in the works of Martha Nussbaum and Stephen Halliwell.[29] Yet this view needs to be given new life, because in spite of its influence, and while Nussbaum's and Halliwell's remarks are very suggestive, it is not clear what exact role the twin items of the tragic emotions, pity and fear, as well as the plot, play in producing the proper pleasure of tragedy.

In *Poetics* 4 Aristotle suggests that even the delight one takes in an elementary recognition of a figure in a picture involves the same faculties of recognition, reasoning, and at a very elementary level, the grasp of the "why" that is called for by more sophisticated forms of understanding, such as philosophy.[30] The argument of *Poetics* 4, while focusing on an elementary portrait of someone, lays the groundwork for the *possibility* that more sophisticated forms of mimetic art will call forth more complex forms of understanding. This idea is followed up in *Poetics* 9, where Aristotle says poetry is "more philosophical" (*philosophōteron*) than history because the plot constructs the actions and interactions of the character in terms of a larger pattern of what a certain kind of person will say or do in a specific situation, according to probability or necessity (9.1451b8). The poet orders events into a coherent and unified whole so that the audience grasps a universal pattern of human experience that is exemplified in the structure of the plot. It is this interest in revealing a universal pattern of action that makes poetry closer to philosophy than history, which is more concerned with the particular rather than the universal.

We can give these universals in the plot more content by noting the plots of tragedy are by their nature built around situations that by their nature dispose people to feel pity and fear for the dramatic agents.[31] The themes of ancient Greek tragedy are built on scenarios—such as family ties and the conflict between loved ones, the inevitability of death, and acting without full knowledge of the consequences of one's actions—that by their very nature appeal to the interests of human beings. Because tragedy features incidents, such as the harm that one family member inflicts on another that speak to the basic features of the human situation, just hearing the events that occur is enough to make the listener experience horror and pity, even without seeing the drama performed (14.1453b3–5).

Why does tragedy aspire to universality, the sort of thing that a certain person might say or do, by necessity or probability (9.1451b6–7)? If we read *Poetics* 9 in conjunction with *Poetics* 14, where Aristotle says that the point of tragedy is to provide the pleasure from pity and fear through *mimēsis*, the answer is that the point of the universals in the tragic plot is to provide this distinctive emotional experience. This also makes sense in light of Aristotle's discussion in *Poetics* 13 and 14 where he ranks tragic plots on the basis of how well they prompt pity and fear in the audience.

In addition, the connection between the structure of the plot and pity and fear is also raised in *Poetics* 10 where Aristotle says that tragic pity and fear are especially aroused when events happen "contrary to expectations yet on account of one another" (10.1452a3–4). Pity and fear, as well as wonder or amazement are especially aroused by a reversal of fortune that is contrary to the audience's expectations, yet in retrospect is understood as a necessary or probable result of the events that preceded it.

Understood in this way, tragedy aims at universality, a necessary and probable connection between events, because it is the best way to achieve the proper emotional response in the audience. The link between tragic pity and fear and the structure of the plot, which *Poetics* 9 says makes poetry more philosophical (*philosophōteron*) and more serious (*spoudaisteron)*, also points to the idea that the specific emotional response that tragedy offers is somehow linked with understanding of some kind.

Further, if, as argued, the generic pleasure in all mimetic arts *as* an imitation is pleasure of learning and recognition, it makes sense that the distinctive pleasure of tragedy would be a species of the generic sort of pleasure, only one in which the emotions of pity and fear play a central and inextricable role.[32] If we can say more about how pity and fear facilitate some kind of understanding, this will make it plausible that the distinctive pleasure of tragedy is a kind of understanding that pity and fear make possible.

GETTING TO EMOTIONAL UNDERSTANDING: FROM SYMPATHY TO EMPATHY

I suggest that there are different stages that the spectator goes through as she follows the plot.[33]

1) The spectator grasps that there is a similarity between the events imitated in the tragedy and her retained past experiences of similar events.
2) She grasps the universal in the plot that shows why the character's change of fortune is necessary or probable.

Note that in stages (1)–(2), there is the possibility that tragedy will reveal some truth about human nature and action that was previously not recognized by the spectator. This is the implication of Aristotle's remarks in *Poetics* 10 that a plot should proceed in a way where events occur "contrary to expectations but on account of one another" (10.1452a1–3).[34] For example, Amélie Rorty suggests the idea that in Greek tragedy, "everything that is best in the protagonists makes them vulnerable to reversals."[35]

For example, Oedipus is a curious person with a desire for knowledge, a trait one normally thinks of as a virtue or excellence. When he presses to find the cause of the plague on his kingdom this leads him to discover something unexpected: knowledge of his real identity. It is this very desire for knowledge, to uncover the truth, that leads to his reversal of fortune.

3) The spectator feels pity and fear for the character.

What moves the spectator to feel pity and fear for the character is coming to understand how the character's reversal or change of fortune is unexpected, but nevertheless follows from the actions that went before it. Pity and fear occur when events happen "contrary to expectation but on account of one another" (10.1452a1–3). The universals concerning character and actions that are embedded in the plot help the spectator to understand how the character's change of fortune is understandable, yet not deserved. Because the character's suffering (or threat of such suffering) is not merited, and because the character suffers a loss of the kind that she, the spectator, fears for herself, the audience feels pity and fear for the character.

We can, with some caution, use some contemporary terms to describe this sort of emotional response to the characters. Sympathy is an "other-focused" emotional response in which one feels *for* another.[36] You feel pity *for* Oedipus and fear *for* Iphigenia when she is just about to unknowingly kill her long lost brother.

4) The spectator comes to understand that the suffering and loss the character feels is something that she, the spectator, could experience as well.

Aristotle says that we pity another for that which we might expect to befall ourselves or some friend of ours, and to befall us soon (*Rhetoric* 2.8.1385b15–16). In this phase the spectator comes to understand that *she*, the viewer, is like the character in that what Oedipus or Antigone suffers could happen to her as well—she could suffer the losses on which the themes of tragedy are based—the bonds between family and loved ones broken, the trials of love and the prospect of death. If a king such as Oedipus can undergo a reversal of fortune, all the more is this true of the spectator, because fear occurs when people can be made to feel that someone who is stronger than they are suffer an unexpected misfortune (*Rhetoric* 2.5.1383a10).

5) The spectator comes to feel fear and concern for herself.

Here the spectator comes to feel what philosophers of emotion call empathy with the tragic character, a state in which she imagines what it is like to be *in* the character's shoes and facing the loss that the character faces or experiences. For the spectator feels vulnerable to the same sort of loss that the character faces or experiences.

One interesting debate around empathy concerns whether it is possible, through empathizing with someone, to gain knowledge of feelings and experiences we have not previously experienced.[37] One central concern is that when we try to imaginatively put ourselves in another's shoes, we only succeed in imagining what it would be like for *ourselves* to be in Medea's situation, for example. Given the different psychologies, social standing, gender, race, and so on between people, the concern is that the insights that we think we gain from trying to take up another's perspective may be an inaccurate understanding of how someone different from us experiences the world.

Aristotle's view that tragedy focuses on certain universal themes that concern all human beings may help to mitigate this concern. Tragedy concerns certain universal themes, such as the loss of family, the struggles of love, the breaking of civic bonds, and the facing of death, which speak to the core of what concerns all of us as human beings. To use a contemporary example, consider the film *Twelve Years a Slave* (2013, Steve McQueen), based on the true-life autobiography of Solomon Northrup, a free black man from upstate New York who was sold into slavery in the years before the civil war. Solomon may be so different from us in the time at which he lived, his race, social class, gender, and so forth that it may be hard to imagine what it is like to be a free man and then be enslaved as he was.

Aristotle would say that the loss Solomon experiences, of his family, his community, and his ability to deliberate and pursue his life as he decides he wants it to be, are harms that all human beings could, *qua* human beings, understand. In this sense we *can* use our understanding of what we would feel like to be in his shoes, for as human beings we share his concern with things such as love, death, and family and civic bonds.

6) In virtue of these feelings, the spectator comes to understand how the universal embedded in the plot applies to her own situation as well.

Through feeling pity and fear for the character and then for herself, the spectator comes to an altered understanding of the universals concerning action that are embedded in the plot. The spectator's response of pity and fear is then the means by which she has a changed understanding of the truth embedded in the plot, because she comes to feel that the truth is not some abstract possibility, but is something that she feels applies to her life as well as the lives of other human beings.

What, then, is the proper pleasure of tragedy? On this fourth proposal it is the pleasure of coming to an altered comprehension of both the spectator's situation and the human condition that is made possible through feeling pity and fear for the tragic characters.[38] While pity and fear are not pleasurable, tragic pity and fear are based on an understanding of human life and action that the plot provides. This response of pity and fear is, in turn, the means by which this understanding is deepened through the feelings of pity and fear the spectator has for the character. The pain of pity and fear is balanced by a sense of enlarged understanding that the experience of tragedy provides, enabling the spectator to think and feel differently about her place in the world and her shared connection with others.

RETURNING TO THE PARADOX OF TRAGIC PLEASURE

We should return to our opening question: how can the overall experience of tragedy be pleasurable when it necessarily involves the painful emotions of pity and fear? We might consider again the discussion in *Parts of Animals*, where Aristotle talks of how the fascination with the form and organization of an animal's parts can compensate for an unpleasant subject matter:

> For if some have no graces to charm the sense, yet nature, which fashioned them, gives amazing pleasure in their study to all who can trace links of causation, and are inclined to philosophy. Indeed, it would be strange if mimic representations of them were attractive, because they disclose the mimetic skill of the painter or sculptor, and the original

realities were not more interesting, to all at any rate who have eyes to
discern the causes. We therefore must not recoil with childish aversion
from the examination of the humbler animals. Every realm of nature is
marvelous . . . so we should venture on the study of every kind of animal without distaste; for each and all will reveal something beautiful.
Absence of hazard and conduciveness of everything to an end are to be
found in nature's works in the highest degree, and the end for which
those works are put together and produced is a form of the beautiful.

(*Parts of Animals* 1.5.645a8–25)[39]

As it turns out, if the fourth proposal for the proper pleasure
of tragedy is right, this passage is not quite the way that tragic
pleasure is produced. The philosopher takes pleasure in studying the form and organization of the animal's parts, *in spite* of
the unpleasant sensory appearance of the animal. If the proper
pleasure of tragedy takes place *from* pity and fear by means of
the plot, then the pleasure of understanding is *because of* the
feelings of pity and fear that the spectator experiences for the
character. Pity and fear are integral to the pleasure of tragedy,
while the sensory experience of the animal is an obstacle that
needs to be overcome to achieve the pleasure of understanding
that a philosophical study of the animal provides.

If there is the pleasure of an altered understanding, but the
pain from pity and fear, then what makes the overall experience
pleasurable? In the *Rhetoric* it is said that certain feelings can
"drive out" (*ekkroustikon*) other feelings, such as happens when
intense fear drives out pity (*Rhetoric* 2.8.1386a23). This point
is also noted in *Poetics* 13 where Aristotle suggests that the plot
pattern in which a supremely virtuous person falls to misfortune
is repulsive (*miaros*), not pitiable and fearful (13.1452b333).[40] It
is part of Aristotle's philosophical psychology that it is possible
for one emotion to diminish or knock out the other. What makes
it possible for the pleasure of understanding to predominate in
the overall experience of tragedy?

This takes us back to the notion of pleasure as an activity
that perfects or completes some natural state. There are many

activities that characterize what it is to be a human being, but one that Aristotle returns to again and again is the human desire for knowledge. "All human beings, by nature, desire to know" (*Metaphysics* 1.1.980a23). If the last proposal is correct, tragedy affords the pleasure of understanding, but not in the way that the study of philosophy does, for example. For it essentially involves the exercise of the emotions as a means by which the spectator brings alive the truths concerning action and life, embedded in the plot.

CONCLUSION

In this chapter we have surveyed four possible solutions to the puzzle of what the proper pleasure of tragedy is. While I favor the fourth (pleasure in emotional understanding), it is left to the reader to decide which one is most persuasive or to come up with a new proposal that improves on the defects of all of them. It is perhaps not remarkable that the *Poetics* could give rise to four distinctively different ideas as to the nature of the distinctive pleasure of tragedy. But what is remarkable is the connection between these accounts and contemporary discussions around the paradox of tragedy and the nature of the spectator's response to the character's suffering and predicament. This suggests that the central questions the *Poetics* raises regarding the nature of tragedy and the interest we take in it are still with us today.

NOTES

1 This paradox is touched on in Chapter 12, pp. 300–303.
2 See *Poetics* 26.1462a18–b1.
3 Malcolm Heath 2001. Heath notes the similarity between his interpretation of Aristotle and Susan Feagin's account (Feagin 1983) of the pleasure in tragedy as a pleasurable meta-response that the audience takes to their morally correct responses of pity and fear for the characters. See Heath 2014 for a new and slightly modified statement of his position.
4 I thank Katy Meadows for this observation.
5 See *Poetics* 25.

6 Destrée 2009 and 2013.

7 Destrée 2013: 23.

8 The idea that the proper pleasure of tragedy is the pleasure taken in the correct expression of pity and fear seems to be Dana LaCourse Munteanu's proposal for the proper pleasure of tragedy. See Munteanu 2012: 131.

9 Destrée 2013: 23.

10 See *Poetics* 17.1455a23–25 and 17.1455a28–32. Munteanu 2012: 93–96 makes a persuasive argument to the conclusion that the poet should aim to place things "before the eyes" (*pro hommatōv*), that is to bring them to life. But she also says that the emotions the spectator feels in the theater are "less intense" than those caused by real events (2012: 99). So she may agree with Destrée's point.

11 See Destrée 2013: 14–15.

12 Ian McCready-Flora 2014. For the view that belief *is* necessary for genuine emotion, see Jamie Dow 2009.

13 Munteanu 2012: 93–96.

14 See Marcia Eaton 1982 and John Morreall 1985.

15 Eaton 1982: 60. See also John Morreall 1985: 97.

16 For a discussion of the control theory and some other questions about it, see Robert J. Yanal 1999: 145–148.

17 For a classic statement of this view in the aesthetics literature see Edward Bullough 1989 (reprinted from 1912).

18 See Elizabeth Belfiore 1985: 349–360 and David Gallop 1990:160–162 for two influential statements of this view.

19 *Metaphysics* 1.1.980a22.

20 See discussion of these passages in Chapter 4, pp. 77, 78–79, 88–89.

21 Belfiore 1985: 360.

22 See Heath 2001: 10.

23 For one such proponent of the benefits of tragedy, see James Shelley 2003. He argues that the pleasure in tragedy comes about as a pleasurable relief in finally coming to terms with truths about one's life that one has tried to deny.

24 For interesting essays that engage with solutions to this problem see Jerrold Levinson (ed.) 2014.

25 Noël Carroll 1990.

26 Carroll 1990: 184–186.

27 Alex Neill 1992.

28 For Carroll's response to this objection see Carroll 1992.

29 Martha Nussbaum 1986: 388–390; Nussbaum 1992: 281–282. Stephen Halliwell 1992: 252–254, especially 253; Halliwell 2011: 232–236.

30 Chapter 4, pp. 86–88.

31 See Chapter 6, pp. 144–145.

32 For a more detailed argument to the conclusion that the pleasure in a work *as* an imitation is the pleasure of understanding, see Chapter 4, pp. 89–90, 94–95.

33 There are several other recent interpretations of the proper pleasure of tragedy as involving some kind of emotional understanding. See Gregory Michael Sifakis 2001 and Munteanu 2012: 97–99.

34 For objections to this understanding of the phrase "contrary to expectations but on account of one another" see G. Ferrari 1999, and for replies to Ferrari's concerns, see Chapter 9, pp. 226–228.

35 Amélie Rorty 1992: 11.

36 Alex Neill 1996: 175; and Carroll 2011: 173–175.

37 For the concern that we cannot, see Derek Matravers 2011: 25–30.

38 See also Paul A. Taylor 2009 for an interesting discussion of how according to the *Poetics* sympathy for the character promotes insight into the human condition. Taylor is concerned with the problem of verification, of how we know that the universals embedded in the plot are true. As I interpret him, Aristotle supposes that the spectator uses his prior understanding of human life and action to make sense of the plot, so the problem of verification does not arise for Aristotle in the way that Taylor supposes.

39 Aristotle *Parts of Animals* in Jonathan Barnes 1984.

40 For this observation about *Poetics* 13 see T. C. W. Stinton 1975: 239.

WORKS CITED

Aristotle 1984. *Parts of Animals* translated by W. Ogle, in Jonathan Barnes (ed.), *The Complete Works of Aristotle. The Revised Oxford Translation* Volume One. Princeton, NJ: Princeton University Press.

Barnes, Jonathan (ed.) 1984. *The Complete Works of Aristotle. The Revised Oxford Translation* Volume One. Princeton, NJ: Princeton University Press.

Belfiore, Elizabeth 1985. "Pleasure, Tragedy and Aristotelian Psychology." *Classical Quarterly*. New Series 35 (2): 349–361.

Bullough, Edward 1989. "'Psychical Distance' as a Factor in Art and as an Aesthetic Principle," in George Dickie, Richard Sclafani, and Ronald Roblin (eds.), *Aesthetics: A Critical Anthology*. Boston, MA: St. Martins Press: 758–782. Reprinted from *The British Journal of Psychology* 5 (1912): 87–98, 108–117.

Carroll, Noël 1990. *The Philosophy of Horror*. New York and London: Routledge.

———— 1992. "A Paradox of the Heart: A Response to Neill." in *Philosophical Studies* 65 (1/2): 67–74.

———— 2011. "On Some Affective Relations Between Audiences and the Characters in Popular Fiction," in Amy Coplan and Peter Goldie (eds.), *Empathy. Philosophical and Psychological Perspectives*. Oxford: Oxford University Press: 162–184.

Destrée, Pierre 2009. "Aristote et le plaisir 'propre' de la tragédie." *Aisthe* 4: 1–17.

———— 2013. "Aristotle on the Paradox of Tragic Pleasure," in J. Levinson (ed.), *Suffering Art Gladly: The Paradox of Negative Emotion in Art*. Basingstoke: Palgrave Macmillan: 3–27.

Dow, Jamie 2009. "Feeling Fantastic? Emotions and Appearances in Aristotle." *Oxford Studies in Ancient Philosophy* 37 (Winter): 143–175.

Eaton, Marcia 1982. "A Strange Sort of Sadness." *Journal of Aesthetics and Art Criticism* 41: 51–63.

Feagin, Susan 1983. "The Pleasures of Tragedy." *American Philosophical Quarterly* 20: 95–104.

Gallop, David 1990. "Animals in the *Poetics*." *Oxford Studies in Ancient Philosophy* 8: 145–171.

Halliwell, Stephen 1992. "Pleasure, Understanding and Emotion," in Amélie Osksenberg Rorty (ed.), *Essays on Aristotle's Poetics*. Princeton, NJ: Princeton University Press: 241–260.

_____ 2011. *Between Ecstasy and Truth. Interpretations of Greek Poetics from Homer to Longinus*. Oxford: Oxford University Press.

Heath, Malcolm 2001. "Aristotle and the Pleasures of Tragedy," in Øivind Andersen and Jon Haarberg (eds.), *Making Sense of Aristotle Essays in Poetics*. London: Duckworth: 7–24.

_____ 2002. "Aristotle on the Function of Tragic Poetry by Gregory Michael Sifakis." Review by Malcolm Heath. *Hermathena* 172 (Summer): 91–98.

_____ 2014. "Aristotle and the Value of Tragedy." *British Journal of Aesthetics* 54 (2): 111–123.

Lear, Jonathan 1992. "*Katharsis*," in Amélie Oskenberg Rorty (ed.), *Essays on Aristotle's Poetics*. Princeton, NJ: Princeton University Press: 315–340.

Levinson, Jerrold (ed.) 2014. *Suffering Art Gladly: The Paradox of Negative Emotion in Art*. Basingstoke: Palgrave Macmillan.

Matravers, Derek 2011. "Empathy as a Route to Knowledge," in Amy Coplan and Peter Goldie (eds.), *Empathy. Philosophical and Psychological Perspectives*. Oxford: Oxford University Press: 19–30.

McCready-Flora, Ian 2014. "Aristotle's Cognitive Science: Belief, Affect and Rationality." *Philosophy and Phenomenological Research* 89 (2): 394–435.

Morreall, John 1985. "Enjoying Negative Emotions in Fiction." *Philosophy and Literature* 9 (1): 95–103.

Munteanu, Dana LaCourse 2012. *Tragic Pathos Pity and Fear in Greek Philosophy and Tragedy*. Cambridge: Cambridge University Press.

Nehamas, Alexander 1992. "Pity and Fear in the *Rhetoric* and the *Poetics*," in Amélie Oskenberg Rorty (ed.), *Essays on Aristotle's Poetics*. Princeton, NJ: Princeton University Press: 291–314.

Neill, Alex 1992: "On a Paradox of the Heart." *Philosophical Studies* 65 (1/2): 53–65.

_____ 1996. "Empathy and (Film) Fiction," in David Bordwell and Noël Carroll (eds.), *Post-Theory: Reconstructing Film Studies*. Madison: University of Wisconsin Press: 175–194.

Nussbaum, Martha 1986. *The Fragility of Goodness: Luck and Ethics in Ancient Greek Tragedy and Philosophy*. Cambridge: Cambridge University Press.

_____ 1992. "Tragedy and Self-Sufficiency: Plato and Aristotle on Fear and Pity," in Amélie O. Rorty (ed.), *Essays on Aristotle's Poetics*. Princeton, NJ: Princeton University Press: 261–290.

Rorty, Amélie Oskenberg (ed.) 1992. *Essays on Aristotle's Poetics*. Princeton, NJ: Princeton University Press.

Shelley, James 2003. "Imagining the Truth," in Matthew Kieran and Dominic Lopes (eds.), *Imagination, Philosophy and the Arts*. London: Routledge. London and New York: Routledge: 177–186.

Sifakis, Gregory Michael 2001. *Aristotle on the Function of Tragic Poetry*. Heraklion, Crete: Crete University Press.

Stinton, T. C. W. 1975. "*Hamartia* in Aristotle and Greek Tragedy." *Classical Quarterly* 25: 221–254. Reprinted in *Collected Papers on Greek Tragedy* (Oxford University Press 1990), 143–185. Citations are to the 1975 version.

Taylor, Paul A. 2009. "Sympathy and Insight in Aristotle's *Poetics*." *Journal of Aesthetics and Art Criticism* 66 (3): 265–280.

Yanal, Robert J. 1999. *The Paradoxes of Emotion and Fiction*. College Park: Pennsylvania State University Press.

12

THE *POETICS* AND CONTEMPORARY AESTHETICS

INTRODUCTION: THE *POETICS* TODAY

The *Poetics* has inspired significant trends in aesthetics, and this has never been more so than today, when many of the issues and problems that are addressed in the work are receiving renewed attention by philosophers of art. Philosophers today engage in heated debates on the issues that are raised in the *Poetics*. Do we learn from art, and if so what do we learn? If we do learn from art, just how does this learning take place? Does art reveal truth? How can art reveal truth when art imitates make-believe, imagined worlds, rather than the real one?

Some paradoxes that have received a lot of attention by aestheticians also seem relevant to Aristotle's discussion in the *Poetics*, even if he does not directly discuss them. The so-called "paradox of fiction," the puzzle of explaining how it is that we can respond with genuine emotion to characters in fiction, has generated a great deal of discussion in aesthetics. So has another paradox, the "paradox of tragedy," the problem of explaining why it is that we enjoy tragedy when it inspires negative, painful emotions.

In addition there are also Aristotelian tendencies in contemporary aesthetics, including the trend in philosophy of art and film, to define certain artistic genres by reference to the intended affective response from the audience, must notably in Noël Carroll's discussion of the philosophy of horror,[1] but present in discussions of other genres, such as melodrama, as well.

This chapter explores the connection between the *Poetics* and contemporary aesthetics, noting both how the work has directly inspired discussions in philosophy of art, as well as considering how Aristotelian-inspired solutions to contemporary problems may shed a new light on these discussions.

THE PARADOX OF FICTION

Samuel Johnson, in his 1765 *Preface* to the plays of Shakespeare, may have been the first to raise a paradox that has come to be known as "the paradox of fiction." Johnson asked the question: how is it possible to respond with genuine emotion to that which we must know is not real? The "paradox of fiction" is a puzzle that has long concerned aestheticians for it suggests that there is something problematic or possibly even irrational about our emotional response to fiction. For it seems, on the one hand, that we accept that characters and events in fiction genuinely move us; but we also accept, on the other hand, that we can be genuinely moved only by what we take or believe to be actual.

More formally:

1) We are genuinely moved by fiction.
2) We know that that which is portrayed in fiction is not actual.
3) We are only genuinely moved by what we believe is actual.

This is a genuine, philosophical paradox because we have reasons to think that each one of these claims is true. But if (2) and (3) are true, then it follows that:

4) We cannot be genuinely moved by fiction.

Why is this a problem? Aristotle gives no suggestion in the *Poetics* that we do not experience genuine emotion in response to the characters in a work of fiction. Indeed he says in *Poetics* 13 that pity and fear are felt in response to the characters (1453a3). He also thinks that to take pleasure in an artistic imitation one must appreciate that the work *is* an imitation of some subject (4.1448b18–19). So he would not agree that we do not have genuine emotions in response to fiction because we think that the characters are not real.

Aristotle does not raise the paradox. But given that he evidently thinks we have genuine emotions in response to characters, we would expect that he would have some solution to the paradox. One response to the paradox is to deny premise (1) above, that we are genuinely moved by characters in fiction. A champion of this view is Kendall Walton, who argues that readers of fiction just experience quasi-emotions, not full-fledged emotions. For genuine emotions must be directed at objects that we take to exist, and we know that the characters in fiction are not real. So we cannot experience genuine emotion in response to fictions.[2]

Another solution to the paradox is the Thought Theory proposed independently by Peter Lamarque and Noël Carroll.[3] Thought Theory denies premise (3) above, that we can only be moved by what we believe to actually exist. Sometimes merely the thought of danger or suffering is sufficient to generate emotion. Even though Bob believes that it is safe to fly, for example, he might construe the situation of taking a flight as dangerous, and feel genuine fear. If this is correct, then our responses to characters in fiction are like emotions in real life contexts: they can be produced just by thoughts or imaginings.

What might Aristotle say about the paradox and these solutions? Everything that Aristotle says in the *Poetics* speaks to the idea that the emotions of pity and fear for the characters are genuine.[4] In addition, although this point is controversial, it can be argued that what Aristotle says in his discussions of emotion in his treatises on philosophical psychology is compatible with the idea that imagination, without belief, can prompt genuine emotion. Sometimes it is maintained, to the contrary, that a text in *De Anima* 3.3 says that mere imagining of something threatening cannot cause genuine emotion, only the *belief* that something is actually threatening can:

> Again, when we form an opinion (*doxasōmen*) that something is threatening or frightening, we are immediately affected by it, and the same is true of our opinion of something that inspires courage; but in imagination (*phantasia*) we are like spectators looking at something dreadful or encouraging in a picture.

> (*De Anima* 3.3.427b2–4)

As Ian McCready has rightly noted, in this text all Aristotle is saying is that the mere imagining (*phantasia*) of some terrible event is not sufficient to produce emotion *immediately*, yet the belief that there is something threatening or frightening *is* sufficient.[5] In addition, there is another passage in the *Movement of Animals* in which Aristotle says that imagination and thinking have the power to move us to shudder and be frightened as do actual objects (7.701b18–22). The *De Anima* passage, then, does not show that the spectator of tragedy cannot experience genuine emotion towards events that are merely imagined.

Aristotle stresses, both in the *Rhetoric* 2.5 and 2.8 and in the *Poetics*, the point that listeners and spectators can be made to feel emotion when the speaker and the poet use techniques that "place things before the eyes" (*pro hommatōv*), that is bring them to life.[6] If all of the preceding points are correct, then the upshot is that Aristotle's philosophical psychology allows for the *possibility* that in some cases, imagination can generate genuine emotion, provided that the things imagined are brought to life and made vivid.

Where does this leave Aristotle's likely response to the paradox of fiction? If the above interpretation of Aristotle's view of emotions is correct, he would say that in some circumstances it is possible to be genuinely moved by imagining the suffering of a tragic character. The discussion of the various techniques the poet uses to elicit pity and fear suggests that to get the proper emotional response, the poet needs to *build on* the act of imagination, with various techniques that bring the action alive, and make the spectator feel that the action is taking place in front of her eyes, and that what the character suffers is something that she, also, is liable to experience.

THE PARADOX OF TRAGEDY

The great eighteenth-century Scottish philosopher, David Hume, begins his essay, "Of Tragedy," by noting a paradox that has puzzled philosophers of art since Aristotle: tragedies produce, and are made to produce, pleasure for the audience. Yet how can we feel pleasure in response to dramatic representations of human suffering when these events are presented in a tragedy, yet take displeasure when we encounter such situations in real life? This is the paradox of tragedy. Consider, for example, the blockbuster, *Titanic* (James Cameron 1997). This film tells the story of a romance that takes place between Rose and Jack as they sail on the ill-fated maiden voyage of the *Titanic*. By the end of the film we see disaster strike as the *Titanic* sinks, with most of the passengers, including Jack, going down with the ship. How could this film be a source of pleasure when the film's ending, with its depiction of mass devastation, is sad and upsetting?

We can formulate the paradox as follows:

1) Works (film, literature, art) of tragedy produce painful feelings most people prefer to avoid in real life (e.g. pity, sorrow, fear, and disgust).

2) But, at the same time, readers and viewers of tragedy find the experience enjoyable.

As Hume notes, the paradox is only heightened by noticing the fact that spectators of tragedy are "pleased in proportion as they are afflicted." He means that the audience appears to enjoy tragedy not despite, but because of, the painful emotions that it elicits.

Hume's observation calls to mind Aristotle's statement that the poet should create the pleasure that "comes from pity and fear through *mimēsis*" (*Poetics* 14.1453b10–12). Though Aristotle does not raise the paradox, Aristotle's formulation of the proper pleasure of tragedy suggests that he has a solution to it.

Solutions to the paradox generally take one of two forms. The first line of reply is to argue, as Hume did, that the painful emotions that tragedy elicits get converted into pleasure. He argued that imagination, imitation, and artistic expression are all "naturally" pleasurable to the mind, and that when they "predominate" over the unpleasant feelings, the painful feelings are "converted" into pleasant ones:

> this extraordinary effect [occasioned by tragedy] proceeds from that very eloquence with which the melancholy scene is represented . . . By this means, the uneasiness of the melancholy passions is not only overpowered and effaced by something stronger of an opposite kind, but the whole impulse of passions is converted into pleasure, and swells the delight which the eloquence raises in us.[7]

Hume argues that we should distinguish:

- object of representation—characters and events portrayed;
- medium of representation: the imagination of the author, imitation, performance, costumes, and so on.

His idea is that in responding to tragedy the painful emotional responses are directed at what is depicted, the suffering of the character. The pleasure we experience is directed at the manner of depiction. What in ordinary life would cause sadness and pain becomes an object of delight and enjoyment in virtue of the form of the artistic presentation. Though insightful in other respects, Hume's analysis does not explain how it is that this conversion from pain to pleasure in response to tragic representations takes place, except to suggest that the pleasure in tragedy depends on our knowledge that the suffering that is represented is fictional. We need a further analysis of how it is we take pleasure in suffering when it is represented through the artistic renderings of the tragic playwright, yet experience displeasure when these same events are experienced in ordinary life.

A second line of reply is the compensation view: this is the idea that the audience does not enjoy the negative emotions that tragedy elicits, as such. Rather tragedy provides additional resources for enjoyment that compete or combine with the negative emotions. It is likely, with certain qualifications, that this is how Aristotle would approach the paradox.

First, we take pleasure in the imitation of human suffering, not the suffering itself. Second, because tragedy is a representation or imitation of human life and action, there is a close parallel between our responses to tragedy's depictions of human suffering and our responses to events in the real world. But when put together correctly, the plot of a tragedy clarifies the connections between actions that lead to the reversal of fortune and misery for the tragic protagonist. This means that tragedy makes human suffering *intelligible* or explicable by means of a plot that brings about an understanding of the tragic events that evoke our pity and fear. Because we can learn from Oedipus' situation and take pleasure in this learning, our overall response to tragedy is pleasurable, in spite of the pain we feel when experiencing pity and fear.

While the outline of this solution has an Aristotelian ring, this solution does not address Hume's point that the spectators of tragedy are, "pleased in proportion as they are afflicted." That is, we enjoy tragedy not in spite of, but because of the painful emotions that we feel in response to the characters. If the pleasure in learning competes with the pain that the audience feels when they experience pity and fear, it is not clear how it is that spectators feel pleasure through pity and fear.

Aristotle's view that tragedy produces the proper pleasure that comes from pity and fear through *imitation* provides a solution to this problem. Following along with the account offered in Chapter 11, the proper pleasure is the pleasure in the emotional understanding that tragedy affords. It is *through* feeling pity and fear for the characters that we come to a deeper understanding of the character's change of fortune, and so in the process, insofar as the characters are "like us," come to understand and know ourselves more deeply. This emotional understanding is specifically connected to the structure of the plot; embedded in the plot is a universal pattern of human action that follows by necessity or probability (*Poetics* 9 and 10). Grasping this universal pattern is then a necessary condition for feeling pity and fear. But the experience of the emotions, which are painful, is a way for the audience to bring alive the understanding of the universal pattern that is embedded in the plot.

It is then the pleasure in the emotional understanding, brought about by pity and fear, that makes the overall experience pleasurable, while the emotions of pity and fear are painful.

FILM COGNITIVISM AND THE *POETICS*

The cognitive account of art, the view that we can learn from art, not only has a long history going back to the *Poetics* but is still around and defended today. "Cognitivism" in film theory loosely describes an approach developed in the mid-1980s. Cognitivists allude to universal psychological structures that have evolved in humans as relevant to viewing films. Some of these abilities concern visual information processing; others involve more complex kinds of interpretative and emotional responses.

How this theory works can be illustrated with several examples. First, consider David Cronenberg's remake of the 1958 classic, *The Fly*. Jeff Goldblum plays Seth Brundle, a scientist working on teleportation. Just when he thinks he has ironed out the last bug (no pun intended), the intervention of a common housefly turns Seth into a six-foot insect. The transformation from man to fly is gradual but horrific, and is witnessed by Veronica, a reporter documenting Seth's story. Seth cannot prevent the transformation to a fly from taking place, and he urges Veronica to shoot him, which she eventually does. This movie has many gory scenes, especially as Seth is shown evolving into the fly creature. It also is very tragic, with the ending of Veronica shooting Seth and her intense sorrow at Seth's passing.

As a horror film, this movie raises a puzzle similar to the paradox of tragedy: with all its gore, and the fear that the fly-creature evokes, why would this movie compel audiences' interest and give them pleasure from watching it? This is the paradox of horror. Noël Carroll develops a response in *The Philosophy of Horror* that deliberately draws on Aristotle's *Poetics* (N. Carroll 1990: 159–194). He argues that Seth, as a monster who crosses species boundaries, arouses our curiosity even as he evinces our disgust. The film poses the question, will Seth turn into a fly and how will this take place? The plot proceeds to answer this question. In order to reward our interest in answering these questions, the fly-creature, as an impossible and improbable being, must be disgusting and disturbing. So, while the character of Seth is disturbing and repulsive, the film is satisfying because it engages some of our central cognitive skills.

Second, consider the film previously mentioned, *Titanic*. A cognitive account of the film would argue that in spite of the disaster that the film depicts, *Titanic* provides the audience pleasure by posing a set of questions that the plot proceeds to answer: Will Jack and Rose get together as a couple? How will they overcome the objections that Rose's mother has to the match? What will the sinking of the ship be like? Will Rose and

Jack go down with the ship? And so on. The audience can take pleasure in this film through seeing these questions resolved as the story moves along, even though the film's ending, with its depiction of mass devastation, is sad and upsetting.[8]

However, as noted in Chapter 11, Aristotle thinks that the proper pleasure of tragedy comes about *from* pity and fear and by means of the plot.[9] This means the painful emotions of pity and fear are integral to the pleasure that the spectator takes in tragedy. This brings out a major difference between Aristotle's approach to the pleasure of tragedy and Carroll's approach to the paradox of horror.

On Carroll's view, fear and revulsion are the "price that we have to pay" for having our curiosity about the monster satisfied. In contrast, for Aristotle, pity and fear are integral to the proper pleasure of tragedy. The emotions are *the means* by which the spectator comes to think and feel differently about the insights about human action that are embedded in the plot. On Aristotle's view of tragedy, then, pity and fear do not merely co-exist with the pleasure of learning from tragedy. They are essential to the spectator coming to an altered understanding of human nature and action that the plot provides.

EMPATHY, SYMPATHY, AND SIMULATION

Philosophers of art have been greatly interested in the specific responses of sympathy and empathy with characters. The word "sympathy" is used for a range of emotional responses in which one experiences emotions on behalf of others. These emotional responses include pity and compassion for someone's suffering. In sympathy we feel *for* someone. *Empathy*, in contrast, is feeling *with* someone based on an informed understanding of a person's situation. In empathy I assess or reflect on how the other person is feeling and because I recognize that he is feeling a certain way, I share his feeling.

Philosophers have been interested in sympathy and empathy as modes of engaging with fictional characters. Noël Carroll has argued that most often spectators or readers feel sympathy and not empathy with characters.[10] This is because the viewer's emotional response is not congruent with the characters, due to a discrepancy between what the character knows and what the audience knows. If the audience knows more than the character, for example, they see the monster hiding behind the door about to jump out, then they may feel fear for the character, while she is blissfully unaware that she is in any danger.

Recently, however, philosophers have focused on empathy as a mode of engaging with characters in fiction (see A. Coplan 2011). This is because it is thought that empathizing with characters is a form of experiential knowledge. For in feeling empathy with someone, I come to know and feel what it is like to be in the other person's situation. In this way, empathy with characters is linked with understanding and self-knowledge. Through empathizing with characters, I must imagine what the character's beliefs, emotions, and desires might be. This involves imaginatively projecting oneself into the character's shoes. This is useful for gaining experiential knowledge, for empathizing with the character is a way for me to understand perspectives and situations that are foreign to me. This enables me to not only broaden my horizons, but also gain self-knowledge, as I gauge my own reactions to being imaginatively in the character's shoes.

Empathy is also linked to a concept used in the philosophy of mind: simulation. It is argued by some philosophers that I overcome the "problem of other minds," the challenge of understanding what others are thinking and feeling, through simulating in my imagination how others are thinking and feeling. Simulation is a form of empathy, then, and it is useful for gaining knowledge in the same way that empathy is.

Empathy and simulation are also thought to be a way to acquire moral knowledge. Imaginatively projecting oneself into the character's shoes is a means to try on new value systems by vicariously experiencing them in fiction. By empathizing with the title character in Ralph Ellison's novel, *Invisible Man*

(1952), I can come to understand something of what it is like to have the experiences of a young African American male who faces people who misunderstand and disrespect him, as well as stereotype him. This can lead to a new moral perspective on how it is that I should treat other people, based on my taking up in my imagination a character and situation that is dramatically different than my own.

Where does Aristotle enter into the debate?[11] Would he say that we sympathize, empathize with, or simulate a character's situation? It is not hard to see how Aristotle would say that you feel sympathy for the characters. I feel pity for Oedipus' undeserved misfortune, a painful emotional state that is like what some philosophers describe as sympathy: a distressing state of concern directed towards someone. But, what about empathy? Would Aristotle say that the viewer also experiences empathy with tragic characters?

The *Poetics* says that I feel fear in response to the character who is like oneself (13.1453a5). Aristotle's comment that we feel fear for one "like ourselves" suggests that he may be talking about fear for the character being based on a kind of empathy, where a core idea is that empathy involves a taking up of the perspective of someone else that involves sharing their feelings. Although Oedipus is superior to me in social standing, he is also like me in that he suffers a misfortune that, in virtue of the plot, I believe might happen to me, as well. I can imagine being Oedipus, not because I am psychologically or socially identical to him, but because the loss and suffering that occurs within his relationships, such as the loss of his parents, his home, and his city, are the sorts of losses that I, as a human being, fear that I could be vulnerable to, as well (14.1453b19–20).

If this is right, then tragic fear is directed both towards the character and towards myself because he is walking in the shoes that I could just as easily be in myself. I feel empathy with Oedipus because the plot has brought me to the realization that I know, in a certain respect, something of what the character is feeling because the plot prompts me to imagine what I would feel like if I were to be in the tragic character's situation.

As Paul Taylor has noted, simulation theory holds that what enables simulation of another's thoughts and feelings is a common biological and psychological constitution.[12] It is because I am like another human being, biologically, cognitively, and psychologically, that I am able to go from imagining being that person in his situation to having a sense of how the other person feels. This observation is surely pertinent to understanding how I might be able to use my own reactions to a character like Oedipus to imagine what he is thinking and feeling. Tragedy depicts suffering that especially occurs within families, and this naturally evokes pity and fear in the audience. The plots of tragedy are built around certain human situations that are designed to draw out our sense of shared humanity with the character.

This means that it is easier for the audience to truly empathize with Oedipus and the other characters in tragedy, because his situation is not an idiosyncratic one that they might have a hard time comprehending. The audience can truly empathize with being Oedipus in his situation, then, based on the fact that it is the purpose of tragedy to draw out a sense of a common shared humanity with the characters. It is this sense that Oedipus suffers the same fate that I could experience that helps the audience imagine being in his situation, and come to understand what being Oedipus feels like.

THE *POETICS* AND COGNITIVISM IN THE ARTS

Cognitivism with respect to the arts is the view that art as a discipline belongs to the group of knowledge-conveying activities. Aristotle is an art cognitivist, for he holds that works of mimetic art provide the opportunity of learning and understanding. Whether art is a source of learning is the topic of one of the liveliest debates in aesthetics today. It is interesting to consider where and how the *Poetics* enters into this debate.

Now one challenge that philosophers of art face today is reconciling what seem to be two very different ways that we speak of and value art. On the one hand, many philosophers are inclined to think that works of art are to be valued for the insight that they can provide into human behavior. In this vein, works of art are described as "enlightening" or "insightful," suggesting that they have some kind of knowledge to offer. On the other hand, art is valued as a source of aesthetic pleasure. We value art because we appreciate the technique and skill with which it is made, its use of fiction and its appeal not to facts, but to our imagination, and because works of art are sometimes beautiful and the experience of them sublime. This conflict between art as a source of aesthetic pleasure and art as a source of knowledge is often not easy to reconcile.

Within the context of Aristotle's *Poetics* this tension does not explicitly arise. This may be due to the fact that Aristotle does not have a concept of aesthetic pleasure. This is an idea that came on the scene in modern eighteenth-century aesthetics, which maintained that art is a separate and autonomous realm, and that the pleasures we take in art derive from the fact that art is cut off from the concerns of everyday matters and life. In contrast, Aristotle thinks that works of mimetic art do not mobilize a special aesthetic sense, but instead call upon the viewer to use the very same emotional and cognitive capacities that she exercises in everyday life. On this view, art and our experience of art are much more continuous with daily life, and so it is not surprising that Aristotle holds that the reactions we have to works of *mimēsis* are close to those we would have to those same events, if encountered in reality. So the aesthetic pleasure versus learning conundrum is not one that arises within the *Poetics*.

One form of art cognitivism holds that the highest form of knowledge is philosophical knowledge. This is knowledge of the fundamental definitions of things, as Socrates attempted to find in Plato's early dialogues when he asks questions such as: What is virtue? What is knowledge? Socrates hoped to find answers to these questions in the form of explicit definitions, which would state the fundamental nature of, for example, virtue or knowledge. The problem with setting this sort of standard as the bar that works of art must meet is that very few artworks contain answers to these types of philosophical questions.

In this connection philosophers seeking to argue that art can be a source of philosophical knowledge have regarded *Poetics* 9 with special interest. For in that chapter Aristotle says that the poet does not imitate what has happened—she tells us what must happen or could possibly happen. So there is a way in which poetry and more specifically tragedy can give us knowledge of the world. The hope is that the universals concerning human action that are embedded in the plot can be a source of philosophical knowledge.

Aristotle does think there is some similarity between the work of the poet and the work of the philosopher. With a unified and coherent plot, the poet brings a regularity and structure to human events, enabling the viewer to understand why the characters were bound to suffer or experience good fortune. In this sense the poet shares the philosopher's interest in the why and the causes of things.

One conclusion we drew was that the poet is not a teacher, and the point of poetry is not to assert some universal generalization (e.g. "Justice is psychic harmony") as the answer to a philosophical question. The plot shows that the sequence of actions imitated is probable or necessary, and so exhibits the cause or explanation for the character's change of fortune. But the poet does not assert this universal truth through the plot. Indeed Aristotle says that the poet should not speak in his own voice, but rather the responses that tragedy elicits should be built into the structure of the events themselves (*Poetics* 6.1450b8–12; 14.1452a18–21). Certainly, Aristotle's argument finds support from the point that when works of art or literature pursue ideas too directly, as philosophers do, this is regarded as a defect in the work.

We also said that the generalizations that are embedded in the plot are guided by the purposes of the poet, which are to inspire emotion in the audience. Emotions are felt for particular individuals, so even though the characters and action exemplify some general pattern concerning human action and life, the plot cannot stray too far from the level of experience or it will not be capable of having the proper emotional impact on the audience. This means that the generalizations that are embedded in the plot will not be as precise and accurate as those that the philosopher seeks.

On the other hand, one can understand how it is that even though the universal truth concerning human action is implicit in the content of the drama, it is nevertheless possible to reflect on the plot and bring this truth to light. Indeed, Aristotle's view is that it is our emotional response to the characters and their situations that can bring about this sort of reflection. So the mechanics of the emotional response to tragedy provide the means by which the viewer can reflect on the knowledge that is implicit in the structure of the plot.

NOTES

1 Noël Carroll 1990.
2 Kendall Walton 1978.
3 Peter Lamarque 1981: 291–304. Noël Carroll 1990: 79–87. Sara Worth 2000 proposes that Aristotle would accept the Thought Theory solution.
4 See Destrée 2013: 14–15.
5 Ian McCready-Flora 2014. For the view that belief *is* necessary for genuine emotion, see Jamie Dow 2009.
6 Dana LaCourse Munteanu 2012: 93–96.
7 David Hume, 1963: 244.
8 See the discussion in Chapter 11 (pp. 279–283) of the proper pleasure in tragedy as cognitive pleasure.
9 See Chapter 11, p. 290.
10 Carroll 1990: 88–96.
11 See the discussion of empathy in Chapter 11, pp. 285–288.
12 Paul A. Taylor 2009.

WORKS CITED

Carroll, Noël 1990. *The Philosophy of Horror or Paradoxes of the Heart*. New York and London: Routledge.

Coplan, Amy 2011. "Will the Real Empathy Please Stand Up? A Case for a Narrow Conceptualization." *The Southern Journal of Philosophy* 49, Spindel Supplement: 40–65.

Destrée, Pierre 2013. "Aristotle on the Paradox of Tragic Pleasure," in J. Levinson (ed.), *Suffering Art Gladly: The Paradox of Negative Emotion in Art*. Basingstoke: Palgrave Macmillan: 3–27.

Dow, Jamie 2009. "Feeling Fantastic?—Emotions and Appearances in Aristotle." *Oxford Studies in Ancient Philosophy* 37: 143–175.

Hume, David 1963. "Of Tragedy," in Hume, *Essays: Moral, Political, and Literary*. Oxford: Oxford University Press.

Lamarque, Peter 1981. "How Can We Fear and Pity Fictions?" *The British Journal of Aesthetics* 21 (4): 291–304.

McCready-Flora, Ian 2014. "Aristotle's Cognitive Science: Belief, Affect and Rationality." *Philosophy and Phenomenological Research* 89 (2): 394–435.

Munteanu, Dana LaCourse 2012. *Tragic Pathos: Pity and Fear in Greek Philosophy and Tragedy*. Cambridge and New York: Cambridge University Press.

Taylor, Paul A. 2009. "Sympathy and Insight in Aristotle's *Poetics*." *Journal of Aesthetics and Art Criticism* 66 (3): 265–280.

Walton, Kendall 1978. "Fearing Fictions." *Journal of Philosophy* 75 (1): 5–27.

Worth, Sara 2000. "Aristotle, Thought, and *Mimesis*: Our Responses to Fiction." *Journal of Aesthetics and Art Criticism* 58 (4): 333–339.

RECOMMENDED READING

Livingston, Paisley 2009. "Narrativity and Knowledge." *Journal of Aesthetics and Art Criticism* 67: 25–36.

Matravers, Derek 2014. "The (so-called) 'Paradox of Fiction,'" in *Fiction and Narrative*. Oxford, UK: Oxford University Press.

Plantinga, Carl 2009. "Hume on the Paradox of Tragedy," in *Moving Viewers: American Film and the Spectator's Experience*. Berkeley and Los Angeles, CA: University of California Press: 174–188.

Walton, Kendall 2015. "Empathy, Imagination and Phenomenal Concepts" (Chapter 1) and "Fictionality and Imagination: Mind the Gap," in *In Other Shoes: Music, Metaphor, Empathy, Existence*. Oxford: Oxford University Press.

13

CONCLUSION

INTRODUCTION

The arguments in the *Poetics* are often compared to the extended discussion of the arts found in Plato's most famous dialogue, the *Republic*. In this work, especially in Book 10, Plato uses the character of Socrates to launch an attack against poetry (here understood to include ancient Greek tragedy and comedy, as well as the epic poems by Homer) and painting. Plato's discussion of the arts, which constitute the earliest major writing on the subject, has played a foundational role in the history of philosophy of art.

It seems fitting, then, that we might draw out the main lines of argument in the *Poetics* in light of Plato's criticisms. This is the task taken up in this concluding chapter.

THE *POETICS* AND PLATO'S CRITICISM OF THE ARTS

Many scholars assume that in the *Poetics* Aristotle was giving a rejoinder to Plato's criticisms of the arts. After delivering a battery of arguments against poetry in Book 10 of the *Republic*, Socrates closes with what appears to be a challenge to the defender of the arts. Poetry's supporters are allowed to come and argue against poetry's exclusion from the ideal city, provided they can show, "that she is not only delightful but beneficial to orderly government and all the life of man. And we shall listen benevolently, for it will be clear gain for us if it can be shown that she bestows not only pleasure but benefit" (607d–e). Many assume that in the *Poetics* Aristotle took up Plato's challenge. Yet, if Aristotle does address the problems that Plato raises, he does so indirectly, for at no point in the *Poetics* does Aristotle openly reply to Plato as is sometimes the case in his other writings.[1] So, it is clearer to proceed by asking how it is that Aristotle *could* reply, based on his arguments in the *Poetics*, rather than assuming that in the *Poetics* Aristotle is aiming to reply to some or all of Plato's criticisms. These answers still hold great philosophical interest, given that the echoes of Plato's concerns are still with us today.[2]

In his writings Plato has the character of Socrates lodge a series of arguments against poetry:

1) Poetry is not a rational activity, a *technē*, because the poet composes under the influence of divine inspiration, not reason.
2) Poetry should be censored due to its harmful psychological effects on the young.
3) The imitations of poetry are inferior kinds of objects, from a metaphysical point of view: they are far removed from truth and reality because they are imitations of sensible appearances.
4) Poetry does not convey knowledge.
5) Poetry, because it inspires pity and fear, is capable of corrupting the souls of even the "best" citizens in the city.

One challenge that Plato raises to poetry concerns its status as a "*technē*" (Objection 1 above). As explained previously, the ancient Greek term "*technē*" (pl. *-ai*) and its Latin counterpart, *ars*, are translated in different contexts as "art," "craft," or "skill." In its core meaning, *technē* refers to a practical skill that involves the rational exercise of some body of knowledge. *Technē*, therefore, is a broad category that includes many activities that can be practiced by learning a set of rules or procedures, for example, carpentry, medicine, furniture making, and shipbuilding. The key pre-Platonic assumption is that the creators of poetry are practitioners that exercise some rational skill. Plato challenges this view in his dialogue, the *Ion*, where Socrates argues that the poet composes under the influence of some kind of divine inspiration, not reason:

> And what they say is true, for a poet is true, for a poet is a light and winged thing, and holy, and never able to compose until he has become inspired, and is beside himself, and reason is no longer in him.
>
> (*Ion* 534b3–5; E. Hamilton 1961)

This charge is significant because it is suggested in the *Ion* as well as in other of Plato's works that knowledge is the result of rational inquiry alone. If the poets compose by being inspired, rather than from reason, then poets cannot, Plato concludes, use their craft to convey knowledge.

The second objection Plato raises occurs in *Republic* Books 2 and 3, which concerns the question of how to educate the young citizens, the Guardians, who will group up to be the rulers of the ideal city or *polis* that is the subject of Plato's *Republic*. In Plato's time storytelling and poetry formed a major part of a child's education. Children did not simply read, but also recited, memorized, and performed poetry, especially Homer's great epic poems, the *Iliad* and the *Odyssey*. Socrates asks whether or not in the ideal city the storytellers and poets should have the same prominent role in the young Guardians' education. It is decided they should not, and that poetry must be censored due to its harmful effects on a young person's soul.

i

It should be clarified that Plato thinks there is such a thing as the objective moral truth and that for any given situation the wise person, the philosopher-rulers of the *Republic*, should be able to adopt a single point of view from which to assess what is best for the city. In this regard, poetry and other forms of stories are problematic, for they can support popular yet mistaken views about the nature of the gods and justice (364a–b). It is especially important that the young Guardians are not exposed to these stories, for their souls are so impressionable that the opinions they take in can make an indelible and unalterable mark on them (378e3–4). Poetry needs to be censored, therefore, as stories and poetry have a significant influence on shaping a person's character and attitudes.

Socrates raises objections (3)–(5) in Plato's *Republic* 10. Objection (3), that works of imitation are metaphysically inferior objects, is raised within the context of the framework of Plato's theory of Forms. What are most real are the Forms: non-spatial, immaterial objects that are outside the temporal order and so not subject to change. Forms are contrasted with sensible particulars, which are in flux, and so constantly appear different, for example, the rose that appears to be beautiful at one moment and to one observer will decay and lose its beauty. In contrast, Forms, being outside the world of flux, are constant and have a stable nature: the form, Beauty-Itself, is beautiful, and it can never be thought to be not beautiful; and in general, for any Form, F-ness, F-ness is always F, and it is never not-F. Forms, then, are the true realities of which sensible objects are mere appearances.

The problem with poetry is that it, along with painting, imitates (or to use Plato's language, "participates in") the *appearance* of the external things they are modeled after. The painting of the bed is an imitation of the external look of the bed, which in turn is an imitation or copy of the form, Bedness-Itself. As such, painting is twice removed from the true reality, the Forms. Poetry is also said to be an imitator of "images of excellence" or virtue (600e6). Poetry can never lay claim to being able to imitate true virtue, because the calm and rational temperament, which is the true mark of a virtuous person, is not easily imitated (604e). Instead the poet imitates the mere appearance of virtue, and so is far removed from truth and reality.

The fourth argument, that poetry lacks knowledge, follows from the third. If poetry is twice removed from the true reality, it is congenitally unable to convey knowledge to the audience. Instead the poet creates distorted images or copies of virtue and vice, such as people whose actions appear to be admirable, when they are not (603d–e).

The final objection concerns Socrates' concerns about the pernicious emotional effects on the audience. Poetry is able to create an imbalance in the soul, even of the most virtuous individuals. The well-brought-up spectator feels pleasure because of being able to let his guard down, abandon himself, and let his feelings for the character hold sway (605d3–4). This is a "vicarious pleasure" (606b4) because the spectator feels pleasure through imagining what it must be like to be a tragic character such as Oedipus, and takes pleasure in giving vent to an outpouring of grief rather than working to keep his emotions in check, as the well-brought-up spectator knows that he should (605d9). Mimetic poetry, therefore, corrupts the soul by letting the emotions dominate, when the emotions need to be moderated by reason.

ARISTOTLE'S DISAGREEMENTS WITH PLATO

First, we can consider how Aristotle might respond to Plato's charge that poetry is not a *techne*, a rational procedure based on rules and procedures that can be learned. In the opening lines of the *Poetics*, Aristotle says that he will discuss the art (*techne*) of poetry in general and the entire work is devoted to reconstructing the norms and procedures that govern correct poetic composition. The entire *Poetics*, then, is Aristotle's demonstration that poetry is an art or *technē* because there are principles of poetic composition that underwrite good works of poetry.

At the same time, Aristotle leaves it open that even excellent poets such as Homer compose by means of "art (*technē*) or nature" (*Poetics* 9.1451a24), for to possess a *technē* requires, on Aristotle's view, an explicit grasp of the principles that govern the discipline and the ability to teach these rules to other (*Metaphysics* 1). Unlike Socrates, then, Aristotle finds the evidence for poetry's status as a rational, rule-governed activity in the successful works of poetry, not in the state of mind of the poet.

Second, there is no direct reply in the *Poetics* to Socrates' charge that poetry should be censored due to its harmful psychological effects on the young. However, in *Poetics* 4 Aristotle says that, as a matter of fact, it is by means of imitation or *mimēsis* that children learn their earliest lessons, so he holds that imitation in children is a source of pleasurable learning, and it is from this basic human instinct to imitate that the mimetic arts develop. In addition, in his ethics, Aristotle observes that children take their first steps towards becoming virtuous by following the example of their parents and performing just actions to the point where they are not just mimicking the adult actions: they also perform the just act *as* the just person would, with the same state of mind and intent (*Nicomachean Ethics* Book 2). His comments on *mimēsis* and children indicate that he thinks that it is educational.

Third, Aristotle inherits from Plato Socrates' view that poetry and painting are forms of *mimēsis* or imitation, but he rejects the idea that poetry is an imitation or copy of some pre-existing reality. The poet's job is not to say what in fact happened, but rather the things that might or could happen or are possible according to probability or necessity (9.1451b5–7). So while Aristotle accepts that poetry is *mimēsis*, he takes a radically different approach to the objects of imitation.

Further, Aristotle insists that universals do not exist separately from sensible particulars. While he agrees with Plato that the universal is the proper object of knowledge, he holds that universals ("human being," "zebra") are embedded in and cannot exist apart from sensible particulars. It is through having a plot that is structured according to probability and necessity that the audience comes to comprehend a universal pattern of human action that is a source of pleasurable understanding.

Poetics 4 also develops the idea that the appreciation of even the simplest work of imitation is an intellectual or cognitive process. When a viewer contemplates an image of something, such as a cat, she must recognize that the work as an imitation by reasoning out the similarities and differences between the imitation and the object that is imitated. Even the simplest form of imitation involves the pleasure of "understanding and inferring what each thing is" (4.1448b15–17).

Finally, what would Aristotle say to Plato's charge that poetry inspires the emotions of pity and fear, and this has the effect of weakening the hold of reason in the spectator? Here we can break Aristotle's response into three different aspects: (1) his general view of the emotions; (2) catharsis; (3) the proper pleasure of tragedy.

First, Aristotle's view should be considered in light of his broader account of emotions. Emotions are closely connected with sense perception, and the emotions of pity and fear, in particular, involve the imagination. Yet Aristotle also holds that while emotions belong to the non-rational part of the soul, they nevertheless are said to "in a way" (*pos*) share in reason (*Nicomachean Ethics* 1.13). Further, emotions involve the object of the emotion being represented in a way that gives the grounds for the emotions, for example the person one pities is someone who experiences underserved suffering. Experiencing emotions, on Aristotle's view, is not then an invitation to irrationality. Therefore, Aristotle has a fundamental disagreement with Plato's concern that poetry is a corrupting influence because it inspires the emotions.

What does the *Poetics* say about the benefits of feeling pity and fear in response to tragic characters? Aristotle often says that tragedy should evoke pity and fear in the audience, without telling us why this is so. Aristotle's views on the benefits of tragedy perhaps can be found in the notion of *catharsis*, although as noted, Aristotle's exact meaning is not spelled out in the *Poetics*. As I have interpreted tragic *catharsis* in the *Poetics* this involves the purging or purification of some of the pain involved in experiencing the emotions of pity and fear. A well-formed plot puts the pitiful and fearful events of everyday life into some kind of a coherent whole, and thereby gives the spectator a pleasurable understanding of these incidents that is not available when we experience these emotions in ordinary life. This does not mean that the pain involved in feeling pity and fear is eliminated or converted. What gets transformed is the overall experience of pity and fear in the context of tragedy. As a result the burden of feeling pity and fear in response to situations that merit it is relieved.

How is this a benefit? The virtuous person will feel the correct emotions at the right time towards the right person. While such an individual does not need an incentive to be virtuous, their virtuous responses to real life situations may be made easier to bear as a result of watching tragedy. In the less than fully virtuous person, feeling pity and fear in response to underserved suffering may be something that the individual avoids, because of the pain that is involved. The association of pleasurable understanding and pity and fear can help a person regard pity and fear and the real life situations that call them forth differently. This is a practical benefit of feeling pity and fear for tragic characters.

The proper pleasure of tragedy is, according to the interpretation of Chapter 11, emotional understanding. This seems like the most direct route that Aristotle has for responding to Plato's concern about tragedy inspiring pity and fear. Tragic pity and fear have a doubly cognitive aspect: as emotions, they involve responses to the import and significance of undeserved suffering. Through feeling emotions we respond to circumstances that matter to us, making an emotional response an occasion for us to deepen our understanding of what really is important to us. The tragic emotions of pity and fear are inspired by the audience's grasp of a universal pattern concerning human action that is embedded in the plot. Pity and fear for tragic characters is, therefore, based on an understanding of the situation that brought about their change of fortune, and these emotions are also the means by which the significance of this universal pattern can be brought home to us, making this knowledge come alive because it is directed towards the vivid particulars in the drama.

Plato is concerned that poetry prompts a strong emotional response from the audience that can have a spill-over effect: tragedy and works of poetry are capable of calling forth from the audience imaginative and emotional responses that may carry over to real life. This is dangerous, Plato thinks, because the audience will take the action on stage to be a model for how they should behave in their daily lives.

Aristotle is not worried about the spill-over effect. In contrast, he would regard this as a benefit of feeling for the characters in tragedy. Tragedy inspires a natural and human response to feel pity and fear for situations and characters that merit these responses. If tragedy has the capacity to affect us significantly like the ways that situations and people in the real world do, then the idea that we can learn from our emotional responses to tragedy becomes quite plausible.

NOTES

1 Richard Janko 1987: xiii argues that Aristotle wrote of his disagreement with Plato's views of poetry in his lost dialogue, *On Poets*, of which only a few fragments remain. See Janko xiii–xiv and 60–61.
2 Alexander Nehamas 1988.

WORKS CITED

Hamilton, E. and H. Cairns 1961. *The Collected Dialogues of Plato Including the Letters*, with Introduction and Prefatory Notes. Princeton, NJ: Princeton University Press.

Janko, Richard 1987 *Aristotle, Poetics: With the Tractatus Coislinianus, Reconstruction of Poetics II, and the Fragments of the On Poets*. Indianapolis, IN and Cambridge: Hackett Publishing Company.

Nehamas, Alexander 1988. "Plato and the Mass Media." *The Monist* 71 (2): 214–234.

GLOSSARY

Aesthetics from the Greek term "*aisthēsis*" meaning "sense perception." Alexandra Baumgarten coined the term in the eighteenth century to refer to the study of beauty in nature and art. It is now often used as a synonym for "the philosophy of art."

Aischros, ugly and twisted, as in the laughable mask that represents comedy (see *Poetics* 5.1449a34).

Anagnōrisis, see **recognition**.

Amazement (*to thaumaston*) is the reaction aroused when events occur contrary to expectation but in accordance with probability or necessity. The term may be synonymous with "astonishment" (*ekplēktikos*, *ekplēsis*). See *Poetics* 9 1452a1–11 and 14.1453b37–54a9).

Aretē, virtue or excellence, a mean in feeling and action (see *Nicomachean Ethics* 2).

Art (*technē*) refers to a practical skill in making something, in accordance with a knowledge of the rules and methods that produces the desired results. More specifically in Aristotle, the terms refers either to (i) a capacity to act in accordance with reasoned procedures to produce a certain result (*Nicomachean Ethics* 6.4.1140a20–23) or (ii) the knowledge of why certain generalizations that govern a discipline, such as medicine or shipbuilding, are valid (*Metaphysics* 1.1.981a23–30).

Atuchēma (mishap), acts done in ignorance, where the result could have been reasonably foreseen (see *Nicomachean Ethics* 5.8).

Aulos, a wind instrument often played at festivals in honor of the god **Dionysus**, and also used to accompany the performances of Greek tragedy.

Beauty is related to proportion and size (see *Metaphysics* 13.3.1078a31–b5; *Politics* 7.15.1248b8–10), not to what we might think of as the aesthetic appeal of its sensible properties. It is the design of a thing that enables it to carry out its natural function, and the design or organization of its parts is, in its own right, an object of beauty, even when the sensory appearance of something is unsightly (*Parts of Animals* 1.5.645a23–25).

Catharsis of pity and fear, literally, the cleansing, purification, or purgation of the emotions of pity and fear.

Change (*metabasis*) is the change (*metaballein*) of fortune for the character between the two end points of good and bad fortune (*Poetics* 7.1451a13–16). It is the basis for prompting pity and fear in the audience. It can go in either direction in tragedy (7.1451a13–14, 1455b27–28) even if the best kind (in *Poetics* 13) is from good to bad (1453a14–15).

Character (*ēthos*), the fixed and settled disposition of an individual, in virtue of which we ascribe qualities (1450a12), and that element which reveals moral purpose (1450b8).

Chorus is a part of ancient Greek tragedy and comedy. They used song to comment on the action of the play.

Cognition is often raised in connection with the pleasures of learning from poetry. Cognitive pleasures involve grasping propositions that formulate some truth about a subject.

Cognitivism, as a general theory about art, is the view that art can enhance our understanding of human experience.

Comedy (*komōidia*), a genre of poetry, employing the **dramatic** mode of imitation (***mimēsis***), with characters that are worse than most, and evoking laughter (see *Poetics* 2).

Complete, a plot that has a beginning, middle, and end and is unified by necessary or probable connections.

Complex plot, an imitation of an action, as in the plot, that has **reversal** and **recognition** (*Poetics* 10.1452a11–21 and 10.1452b31).

Complication (*desis*), a part of the plot that extends from the beginning of the imagined action to the point before there is a change to prosperity or adversity (*Poetics* 18.1455b23–25).

Denouement (*lusis*), a part of the plot that extends from the beginning of the change from prosperity or adversity to the end of the play (*Poetics* 18.1455b25–27).

Deus ex machina, from the Latin "god out of the machine," is a term used to refer to an improbable or artificial turn in the plot, as when at the end of Euripides' *Medea*, the title character is spirited away in a chariot.

Diction (*lexis*), the spoken verses in the play, excluding the lyrics in songs (*Poetics* 6.1449b35).

Dionysius is the ancient Greek god of wine and revelry.

Dithyrambic poetry is a form of poetry out of which tragedy developed (*Poetics* 1449a10f.) in which a chorus sings and dances in tribute to the god **Dionysius**.

Drama (*drama*) is derived from *dran* (to do or to act). See *Poetics* 3.1448b1.

Dramatic mode, the characters tell the story through their words and actions (*Poetics* 3.1448a1–7). It is contrasted with the **narrative** mode of storytelling.

Eikos (probable), that which seems believable.

Embellishments (*hēdusmata*), rhythm, melody, and song are the "seasonings" or embellishments of the language of tragedy (6.1449b28–31).

Empedocles (490–430 BCE) was a pre-Socratic philosopher-scientist from Sicily, who wrote about cosmology and cosmogony. He posited that the underlying reality of the universe consisted of four basic elements: Earth, Air, Water, and Fire. Change comes about when these basic elements combine in various ways.

Empiricism, the view that all knowledge derives from sense experience.

End (*telos*), the final cause or purpose for which a thing came into existence.

Epic poetry, a form of poetry with a serious subject matter that uses the narrative mode of storytelling (see **narrate**).

Epieikēs, a literal translation is "good" or "decent." This is the sort of person that tragedy (13.1452b34) and epic (13.1454b13) should imitate. Aristotle uses this term to describe the exceptionally virtuous person (see *Poetics* 13.1452b33) but this is an anomalous use.

Error, see **hamartia**.

Essence (*ousia, ti esti*) is what is revealed in an adequate definition of a thing (*Topics* 101b38) and it is a thing's basic nature. Essences are related to explanation. When we grasp a thing's essence, we understand *why* it has the properties that it has. So, for example, when we grasp that a human being is by nature a rational animal, we understand why it is capable of acquiring knowledge since a thing cannot obtain knowledge without having the ability to reason.

Eutrapelia, "ready-witted" or "good humored." This is said of the person who achieves a mean in making a joke. The "ready-witted" person avoids jests that are crude and explicit, but avoids the other extreme of not having a sense of humor at all. Instead she makes use of innuendo (see *Nicomachean Ethics* 4.8.1128a11–12).

First principle (*archē*), a thing's origin or beginning, an account that explains why that thing came to be.

Gorgias of Leontini (485–380 BCE) was a Sicilian orator, rhetorician, and philosopher.

Hamartia, error. In the best tragic plot according to *Poetics* 13, it is an error or *hamartia* that leads to the character's change of fortune (13.1453a7). *Hamartia* is distinguished from a morally vicious character and/or malice.

Hēdusmata, see **embellishments**.

Hegemon was an ancient Greek comic poet about whom not much is known except that he invented parodies.

Hexameter is the form of verse used by Homer. It consists of six "feet," each based on the alteration of one stressed and two unstressed syllables.

Inferior (*phaulos*), comedy imitates the actions of those who are inferior and laughable (*Poetics* 2.1448b25).

Komōidia, see **comedy**.

Language (*logos*) refers to the words spoken by characters during scenes with dialogue and not the words that are sung as part of a song.

Lyre, a large stringed instrument that was used to accompany performances of some kinds of poetry, such as the singing of epic poetry, as well as in solo, instrumental performances.

Manner is the way in which an imitation is produced, either by the use of narration, as in epic, or that of dramatization, as in tragedy. See *Poetics* 3.1448a18–23.

Manthanein, to learn or understand. See *Poetics* 4.1448b15 where Aristotle says that contemplating an image provides the pleasure of understanding.

Melody (*harmonia*) is, strictly speaking, the attunement of an instrument, and so the scale or set of notes available. When specific notes are selected and arranged they form a tune (*melos*).

Metaphor (*metaphora*, to transfer) involves a comparison of two distinct things in which there is transference of meaning from one term to the other, thereby facilitating recognition of a likeness. For Aristotle's main account of metaphor in the *Poetics* see 1457b7–32 and 1459a6f., and for the notion that metaphors involve the grasping of likenesses see *Rhetoric* 1405a8–10 and *Topics* 140a8–11.

Meter in poetry is the regular rhythmic pattern of stressed and unstressed syllables in a verse or individual line or unit of poetry. In the Mother Goose rhyme that begins, "Hey! Diddle, diddle," the syllables "hey" and "did" are stressed, while the syllable "dle" is unstressed.

Miaros, shocking. Plots that evoke this response are ones that show an exceptionally virtuous person going from good fortune to bad (13.1452b36).

Mimes (*mimos*) are a form of imitation in **prose** exemplified by the works of the fifth-century BCE Sicilian Sophron and his son, Xenarchus that featured farcical depictions of everyday life. Diogenes Laertius reported that Plato made use of them for the dramatic form of his dialogues (*Lives of the Philosophers* iii 13). See *Poetics* 1.1447b10.

Mimēsis, "imitation" or "representation." Aristotle uses the term in connection with forms of behavior (for example, children's make-believe) as well as objects. *Mimēsis* is the defining characteristic of all forms of poetry (1.144712–13).

Mousikē, music, especially instrumental music, but see 1462a16, where it is equivalent to **song**.

Narrate (*apangellein*), (narration (*apangelia*), exposition (*diēgēsis*) is a mode or manner of imitation in which the story is told through the words of a narrator. It is contrasted with the dramatic mode of imitation. See *Poetics* 3.

Necessary (*anankē*), the necessary, along with the probable, govern events that are related as cause and effect. Given that one event occurs, another follows, necessarily or probably (see *Poetics* 11.1452a20–22).

Nicochares was an Athenian comic poet, likely in the late fifth century BCE.

Nomes were a form of poetry that is similar to **dithyramb**. It involved lyrics that were set to music and sung by a chorus at a religious festival.

Paralogos, contrary to what is reasonable, so contrary to what is **necessary** or **possible**.

Pathos, suffering. It is part of the plot in tragedy and epic, and refers to the act of violence that one suffers (see 1452b10). Suffering is the basis of one of the four basic plot structures (18.1455b32f.).

Pauson was an ancient Greek painter about whom little is known, but from what Aristotle says we can infer that he either painted individuals who had a lower social and moral standing or he painted caricatures of individuals. See also Aristotle *Politics* 1340a36.

Phaulos, see **inferior**.

Philanthrōpia ("fellow-feeling"), a sympathetic response that justice has been served or a feeling for a fellow human being who is suffering.

Philia, relatives or close friends. According to *Poetics* 14, tragedy shows actions where great harm is inflicted between loved ones and family members.

Plot (*muthos*) is the composition or arrangement (*sustasis*) of the events (1450a4 and 15).

Poiēsis, from the Greek term "*poiein*," "to make." In one sense it refers to all activities that involve making something. At the time Aristotle was writing, it had a narrower sense, referring to **composition in verse**. Aristotle defines the term to mean composition that is a *mimēsis*.

Polygnotus was a mid-fifth-century BCE renowned painter whose is reported to have painted large wall paintings.

Possible (*dunatos*), the sort of thing that *might* occur in the sense that it is consistent with past human experience (*Poetics* 9.1451a38–b1).

Prohairesis, choice. The origin of human action is choice, which is a reasoned desire with a view to some end (*Nicomachean Ethics* 6.2.1139a30f.).

Proper pleasure (*oikeia hēdonē*), the characteristic pleasure of a genre of poetry is mentioned in several places throughout the *Poetics*. The proper pleasure of tragedy is the pleasure that comes from pity and fear and is produced through *mimēsis* (imitation).

Prose is written or spoken language without **meter**. Prose is the language of everyday discourse, as well as of other sorts of writing, such as that used in science, history, philosophy, and journalism.

Rationalism, the view that all knowledge comes from the exercise of the human faculty of reason.

Reasoning (*dianoia*, sometimes translated as "thought"), the parts of the tragedy in which a dramatic personality demonstrates or reasons about something and expresses their views (*Poetics* 6.14505–8).

Recognition (*anagnōrisis*), in which there is a change from ignorance to knowledge involving matters of good fortune and bad and leading to friendship or enmity (*Poetics* 1452a29–32).

Reversal (*peripeteia*), a change of fortune that is the opposite of what is expected, yet a turn of events that happens in accordance with probability and necessity (*Poetics* 1452a22–29). The change can go in either direction in tragedy, from good to bad fortune or the reverse.

Rhythm (*rhythmos*) is a continuous flow or a basic pattern of repetition or continuity that is established by the use of: (1) language (as in forms of poetry, through a use of short and long, and stressed and unstressed syllables); (2) sounds (music); or (3) bodily movement (dance).

Simile is a figure of speech in which two distinct terms are compared by the use of connecting phrases such as "like" or "as," as in, for example, the line from the famous Robert Burns poem, "My love is like a red, red rose." Aristotle thinks that because the simile only says that one thing is like or resembles another, it does not set in motion the same search for meaning as with a **metaphor**, and so there is less opportunity for learning something new. (See *Rhetoric* 3.101410ab15–35.)

Simple (*haplos*) **plot**, the plot imitates a sequence of actions that is a well-defined whole, with a beginning, middle, and end (1453b23–24), that moves according to probability or necessity invariably in one direction, either from good fortune to bad or from bad to good (11.1452a11–13).

Song (*melos, melopoiia*) tends to refer in the *Poetics* to the combination of rhythm, language, and melody (1449b28–30), but it can also refer to the melody of instrumental music (for example, in *Politics* 8.5.1340a where "*melos*" is used to refer to purely instrumental music.

Sophron (of Syracuse, fl. 430 BCE) wrote amusing but also sometimes serious **prose** dialogues, filled with everyday sayings and proverbs that imitated the lives of everyday Sicilian Greeks.

Spectacle (*opsis*) refers to the visual element in tragedy (1449b31). Because tragedy and comedy were performed on stage, spectacle relates to the dramatic mode of imitation. It can refer to costumes, performance, and perhaps also stage craft, and certain kinds of tragedy, ones that are inferior, use spectacle as the main way to inspire pity and fear in the audience (1456a2).

Spoudaios, good, admirable, serious. The people and actions that tragedy and epic imitate are called *spoudaioi* (4.1448b25–27).

Sullogismos, inference. This is a reasoning process that is used to reach a conclusion on the basis of accepted propositions or premises. When people look at images, they engage in an inference to the conclusion that the picture is an imitation of a certain subject (4.1448b15–17).

Teleology, see **End**.

Tragedy is defined at *Poetics* 6.1449b24–29. In *Poetics* 1 Aristotle says that tragedy imitates the action of humans that are better than the normal level. Tragedy has a changing **meter** (1449b9f.)

Verse is writing that is organized with stressed and unstressed syllables that make for rhythmic patterns.

Xenarchus was the son of **Sophron** and also a distinguished writer of mimes.

INDEX

Note: "n" has been used to denote note numbers and bold to denote Glossary terms.